Becoming Whole
the pychology of light

Tarajyoti Govinda

Becoming Whole: the psychology of Light

Govinda, Tarajyoti, 1958-1999

Copyright Govindamurti, G. A. 1999

First published 1998. 2nd. ed. 2015

Deva Wings Publications

www.devawings.com

Daylesford, Australia

Cover:

    Artwork by: Henning Klibo

    www.artalexander.com

National Library of Australia, Cataloguing-in-Publication

Govinda, Tarajyoti, 1958-1999

Becoming Whole: the psychology of Light

Bibliography.

ISBN: 978-0-9587202-4-3

1. Psychology. 2. Spiritual healing. 3. Mental healing.

4. Mind and body. I. Title

152

*This book is dedicated to
people everywhere who
seek to know themselves*

Contents

Towards a lightness of being

For many years I attended classes in psychology, sociology, media studies, astrology - anything to take me closer to understanding human nature. I wanted to understand and help others, I thought - little did I realise I was actually just trying to understand myself. The road was a hard one. The university halls, lecture theatres, tutorial rooms, queues in the library for the photocopier, the hours driving to and fro from campus seemed to do little to help me achieve my purpose. Yet all of this did give me time and space to think, and I met some lovely people along the way. However, the frustration that I felt was deep and from the heart, and finally, after a couple of deferred and terminated courses, interspersed with a few overseas trips, it came to me: The Wisdom was no longer being taught, at least not in the university I was attending, and I felt extreme grief. I kept feeling as though I'd lost something. Was it my keys, my parking ticket, my books, my pen? And then it dawned on me - I had lost my peace of mind amidst trying to meet all the requirements of the system and by trying to prove myself a worthy person in my own eyes, I had lost me!

Psychology is a science they said, a behavioural science. A science of how we think, feel and act. I thought it was about understanding human nature, discovering what gives us life, heart and enthusiasm, what makes us want to live, to rise each morning in anticipation of new discoveries within and without. As the assignments were presented, I would scan through the list trying to find one that would engage a part of me other than my mind. Occasionally we would get a lecturer with life and zest and a depth of wisdom. I would wait with bated breath for these lectures and try to breathe in all the life they would reveal. I was looking for a psychology of heart, something tangible and real that would help me come to know myself and help me communicate, relate, share and be with others. A psychology that would help me to work with my inner world, help me address my fears and my hurt, as well as reveal the incredible lightness of being which I had intermittently touched upon, but which I wanted to make my perennial experience.

I found great solace in the work of Carl G. Jung. What he wrote I could resonate with - and I found myself gathering his works and reading them whenever I had a chance, between doing all the other required assignments on human behaviour. Jung was not on the list in the curriculum. Even when we looked at all the different methods and psychotherapies, his name and works were notably absent. But I pursued reading avidly, and discovered the way of the dream, of paying attention to my own inner world of symbols; I had my own analyst, and I made my search for the "real" psychology into an active pursuit. I discovered the world of psychodrama, of role-play drama healing, of work with excellent psychologists using the methods of no name, and Inner Voice Dialogue work which found me as few others did. And I discovered that there was indeed a psychology of the heart. It was to be found in my own heart. I had looked everywhere, searched high and low; it came only when I looked within. There I found the map for my journey.

As I went within, following my map, I did not always like where it took me, or what I found inside. I discovered anger, fear, guilt, grief, ambition, pride, jealousy, doubt, resentment, arrogance and depression. All of these I was not so keen on. But they were there in my shadow and I strove to bring them, into the light, into consciousness, so that I would come to know myself in truth. I also found goodness in my shadow - skills, talents and abilities I had repressed as they did not suit my self-image. To acknowledge them required me to face that, a task too big to confront all at once.

Generally I would seek truth and respond to love and the notion of unconditional positive regard. I found that being confronted with truth brought revelation, insight and change to my life. It also brought me the choice of operating in illusion or in truth. I began to realise that if I was to become whole that would actually take time, and I would need to develop patience, compassion, determination, honesty and several other virtuous qualities. I realised that this process also brought with it its own share of pain that I would need to endure. I discovered my animus, my inner masculine, that for some time seemed as though it was my enemy, forcing me to work through all my issues with men, stemming from my childhood with my father, and finally to accept my own masculine self and purify it. Making my father complex more conscious helped me to separate issues within me which I had lumped all into one basket. Then more complexes emerged, one by one for me to deal with - inferiority, superiority, saviour, wounded healer - you name it, up it came. As the archetypes emerged I explored them, judged them and fought with them, until I could see and accept what they had to show me about myself. I also explored the feminine nature within me. Is there no end to what is stored in the unconscious?

I began to see that the unconscious was functioning somewhat like a computer. Once something was brought to consciousness - put on the screen, labelled and put on file - it could go back to the unconscious, yet would be ready to be brought up again when the need was there. Gradually, energies within us rise from the unconscious and "hit the screen." When they are on screen they are in the light; they have made it to our conscious awareness. The process of becoming whole is the process of coming to know more of what is committed to the computer memory, the process of developing awareness of not only what is "on the screen" (the ego or the conscious self), but also what else is held within us (the unconscious self). Becoming whole is the process of coming to know ourselves, and further, becoming whole is moving to a place of being where all of our inner bodies are in alignment with each other and are working together to achieve the purpose of our soul. We are more than our personality. We also consist of Spirit and soul. The existence of Light, to which many people are awakening, gives testimony to the existence of the soul and the Spirit. One can hardly imagine being separated from the soul, yet when we identify completely with the personality that is what in essence we become. A human being without a soul is like an ocean without water. Without it we do not have the same life force, and may be barren and empty. The Spirit moves in us, through the soul, and gives our personalities their life and vivaciousness.

In *The Healing Hands of Love* I have defined more fully the terms soul, Spirit and personality. Let it suffice here to say that Spirit is the principle of life - it is the spark of life - a pure, formless body of consciousness that is the essence of God. The soul is the basis of and source of awareness or consciousness which is produced through the union of Spirit and matter - it is the vehicle through which Spirit comes to us. The personality is made up of our emotions, our thoughts, our physical body expression and the interrelation of these aspects.

Let us look briefly at the nature of our soul. The soul possesses the quality of group consciousness, mediatorship, attraction and unification. Its nature is serene, calm, responsible, wise and the opposite of self-centred. It is love and the will-to-good. Its love is inclusive, gentle and unchanging, with detachment and indifference in the best sense. In the soul's realm, Light is the major characteristic. Light is Spirit in manifestation through soul. When Spirit manifests it can come to us as enthusiasm for life and as insight and inspiration towards goodness. It can be seen by some as we would see the Sun, a great body of Light. As this Light touches our heart it releases our divinity. It is through the Light that the soul intuitively understands and knows. The consciousness of the soul is one of unity, in eternal Light. It has

4

a great stillness and undisturbable peace. It knows the method of life. It is power, wisdom and knowledge, with a perpetual consciousness that is not limited by time or space. Perhaps the most notable qualities of the soul are spiritual will and spiritual love.

The soul provides us with the blueprint through which love may manifest. The soul possesses certain qualities and attributes which in our personality consciousness we are meant to cultivate, develop and learn, and it gives us Light which helps us to illuminate the nature of our personality. Throughout the ages, poetry, painting and music have all been inspired by the Light of the soul. It is the soul which gives our lives purpose and meaning.

The soul, which is in essence who we truly are, communicates to us through our higher mind. Our higher mind is a part of our soul. It is in contact with intuition and energies of our higher nature, such as compassion, loving kindness and will-to-good. It is an objective self that is aware of the life we live in relation to the whole. The higher mind is not to be confused with our lower mind. Our lower mind is the mind we generally refer to as the mind. It is our vehicle for thought connected with our everyday self. It has the ability to be intelligent, rational and irrational. We function at our best when our lower mind is subservient to our higher mind and acts as a tool for the higher mind to implement the higher qualities in our lives.

By opening to the inner language of the higher mind we can actualise and move into alignment with that higher part and allow ourselves to embody the higher qualities. Its language comes to us through symbol and metaphor, and it can come to us in our dreams, reflections, meditations or other experiences of heightened awareness or consciousness. This language is impressed upon our psyche. As we explore our inner symbols and our dreams, we can discover much about ourselves, and we can come to know ourselves as soul.

The Light of the soul, as it shines upon us, makes us aware that we contain both shadow and light within us. Our higher nature has great potential for good, incorporating the energies of compassion, love, justice, harmlessness, understanding, insight, joy and will, while our lower nature utilises self-sabotage and negative thought processes to steer us away from the truth in order to perpetuate beliefs, attitudes and values of a more destructive nature. It develops fear, guilt, rebellion, resentment, projection and anger. As the Light of our soul draws nearer, we discover that we have within us both a potential which works towards self-growth (evolution) and a potential that works towards self-destruction (entropy). We also begin to see that these potentials can be trained, shaped and nurtured, and that we choose where we want to be on the continuum between aspiration to our higher nature and our shadow nature.

It is these assumptions that form the basis of the psychology of Light. These are the concepts and principles of soul, Spirit, Light, evolution, the higher and lower mind, and the higher and lower nature of the psychology of Light.

As mentioned earlier, as well as our soul we have within us a combination of the mind, emotions and behaviours. We also have an energising drive that works towards the unfoldment and actualisation of the personality (reaching our true potential) and which strives towards wholeness. In this sense, wholeness is aligning of the mind, emotions and the actions of the individual. Alignment and realignment are constantly taking place and are made effective by the evaluation process that we choose to adopt. Alignment is also affected by the environment that we operate within or come into contact with. We strive for a sense of alignment or congruence, which we feel as balance and harmony. When we have it, we feel balanced and whole. When we do not have it, we may become mentally imbalanced, emotionally imbalanced, or even physically ill. Our emotions need to be expressed, experienced and managed. It is no use repressing them. They will just resurface later and gather momentum in a destructive way. Once expressed, the dysfunctional aspect of our emotions can be released and a sense of calm and peace can return. We will often feel much better after a good cry.

Our emotions are influenced by our thoughts and can influence our actions. When we become aware of this interrelationship between our thoughts, feelings and actions, we discover how we can be in control of ourselves in a new way and can become empowered, instead of remaining a victim to our mind and its thoughts, and to our emotions and how they "make us feel." We can consciously choose to do something about them - we can begin to take charge of our lives and steer our development towards where we would like to head. We can begin to overcome and release our emotional blockages that may stem from past experience or that have been created by our thoughts, and overcome the limitations that come from our narrow-mindedness. We see that we have the ability to make choices in our lives and furthermore we realise we can make reasoned, intelligent choices that are in accord with our higher good. This conscious choosing comes into effect when we develop our awareness of self and the world. Of course, this choice process will vary according to our upbringing and environment, the information available to us and the opportunity to practice it. However, if you are reading this book, then you also have the power and opportunity to do something to gain control over your mind and your emotions.

Our thoughts, feelings and behaviours become dysfunctional for us when we focus on the darker side of life, anticipate danger, perceive life events as threatening and minimise our ability to cope. We gather proof of the negative perceptions and assumptions we make. Our anxiety rises when we continue to make choices that expose us to events, people and patterns that reinforce our weaknesses. When we have these systemic biases we reinforce the negative view of the self, the world and the future, and can move to a state of depression. We are motivated to survive and maintain ourselves and so we perpetuate our weaknesses accordingly, acting within what is familiar.

When we have had certain experiences in life, we expect them to re-occur as we have previously experienced them. We often hold negative views that are out of alignment with the truth of the world. Instead of valuing and revaluing with every experience, we live within a mind-set that shapes our perceptions of the world. This can be functional or dysfunctional. We learn to judge experience as good or bad and develop energies such as guilt and fear accordingly. Often, a negative view is held of suffering or sacrifice, or anything which does not allow immediate needs to be gratified. Acceptance of negative life events and the ability to live in peace with them comes when we stop trying to judge the world as good or bad, but see the world as a reflection of the light and dark within us and attempt alignment with our higher nature. However, we need to be aware that aspiration towards developing particular qualities may not produce immediate gratification. It is an ongoing process which needs to be allowed to take the time it takes. Discrimination is required and choices need to be made based on where we would like to be in the continuum between aspiration and desire. We also need to have patience and perseverance in our process, which can be confronting and may not always feel nurturing and safe.

Compassion is needed in our process, and we must strive to develop it, along with forgiveness for our and others' imperfections. We have a need for a secure base and because of this, positive regard, being empathic, respectful and non-judgemental can become a motivational force. Where a positive regard is not felt from those around us, our evaluation process is affected negatively which results in the inability to discriminate and stay in alignment with the truth or reality. When this happens, weaknesses instead of strengths are acquired, and our self-esteem may be lowered. We need supportive relationships to help us get in touch with personal meaning. If we do not have them in our past experience, the presence of them in the helping process or just generally in our current life will help us begin to explore ourselves more fully and begin to do so in a loving, nurturing way. Strengths and weaknesses are picked up from parents and significant others. We need to look into our significant relationships and our past, especially with our parents, siblings and other important people who were around as we were growing up. Positive and negative experiences affect the development of self-esteem. Past experience shapes our behaviour. By coming to know our past we find great insight into coming to know ourselves.

To fully appreciate the process of becoming whole, or individuation as Jung would call it, it is useful to understand something of the nature and structure of our psyche. This background (or framework) will provide a basis for understanding explanations throughout the book. A glossary is also provided at the back of the book for reference to definitions of key terms.

Individuation is self-realisation. It is the path to self-knowledge, the path leading to inner wisdom. It is a *process* of differentiation between ourselves, others and the environment. Its goal is the development of our personality, whereby we let go of "false wrappings" (Jung, 1976, p. 123) and come to be who we really are.

Individuation involves consciously realising and integrating the possibilities that exist in us. It is the process of becoming whole, rather than the end of it that is pursued. The process brings with it a deepening of meaning in life. Through it we come to know ourselves and find our purpose in life. It is our way of accessing our true vocation, giving a sense of direction that feels right to us.

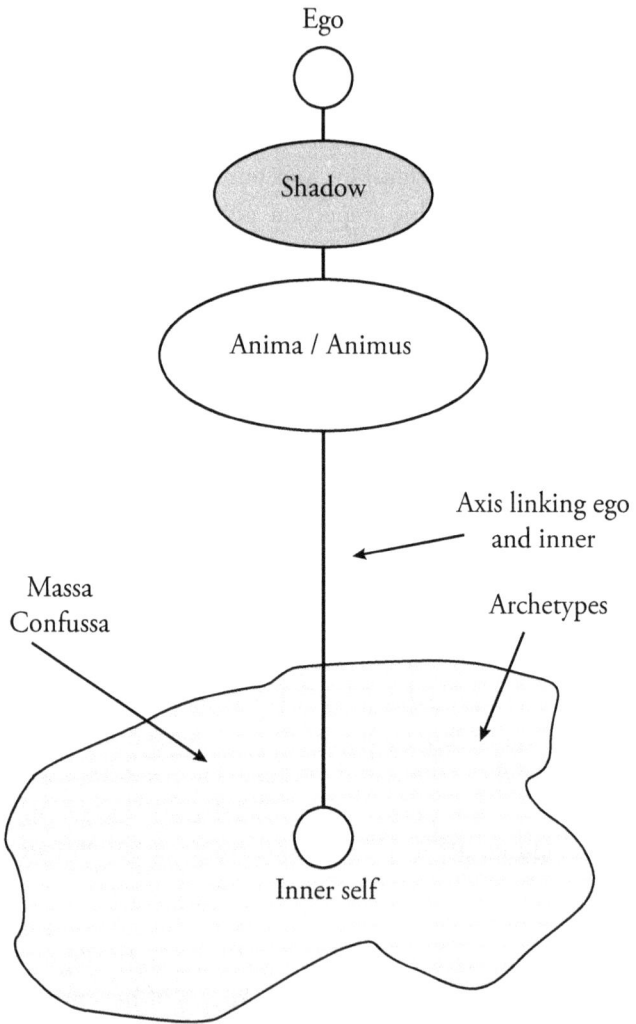

Figure 1. The Structure of the Psyche (Macris, 1994)

For many people, especially those who may not achieve success in terms of the outer world, the process of individuation brings validity and peace that cannot be shaken by the impermanence and transient nature of the outer world. An individuated person is not negatively influenced by what others may think, as he or she will not rely on outside approval for a sense of self worth. Rather, such a person will listen to his or her heart and strive to maintain all the inner bodies in a state of alignment. If balance is lost, which may happen to bring further learning, it will be quickly regained. For many years when I have tuned in to the inner, a very positive and functional voice will say, "Be yourself. Be at peace." This, to me, is the voice of individuation. It points in the direction we must walk if we are to become whole.

If we are prepared to delve into the psyche we can come to know ourselves. We must be prepared for the best and the worst, and take courage and heart in dealing with what we find. Our psyche contains many parts, yet it is one organism. Figure 1 gives a diagrammatic representation of the structure of the psyche. The ego is the conscious self; the shadow is the unconscious self; the anima is the female archetype found in a man; the animus is the male archetype found in a woman. Although it is not represented on the diagram, we also have a persona which mediates between our true self and our environment. To become whole we need to learn to dis-identify with the persona, and realise it is a mask, though it is a necessary mask. Self in Jungian terminology is not the same as self-realisation of ordinary psychology; rather, the self is seen as the inner centre, hence I have called it the inner self. This inner self is the pure unadulterated self, the true self.

In the process of individuation, of striving towards wholeness, the aim is to make this inner self our centre. Sometimes we over-identify with our roles or our ego, which causes us to become inflated. For example, if we are in a position of authority at work, giving orders to others, we may come home and revert to the same tactics with our partners or family. When we stay in this "boss" archetype we become engulfed by it and inflation occurs. Inflation is a state of the ego which occurs when the ego is "hypnotised by itself" and it becomes blinded to everything, including itself. It is unable to realise anything, will not be argued with and cannot see the world or others as they are. The ego becomes puffed up with knowledge like an inflated balloon which needs to be pricked to deflate. We are out of balance, and the pricking of the balloon helps us to find our balance again. If we do not do the pricking ourselves, inevitably someone else or a circumstance in our life will do it for us.

The massa confusa is the primary material of the unconscious that comes up for transformation. It contains the archetypes. An archetype is a form which pre-exists. The archetypes are the psychological themes that become activated and influence us. The archetypes have different roles and vary according to the different myths we choose to live by. They are an energy from the collective unconscious that have their own agenda and energy. They are like a sub-personality. They rise up within our psyche from the massa confusa and demand attention, as they enter into our personal lives. There are certain things that we as human beings want to do, that are inherent in us. We do them partly because our ancestors have. Things like birth and death, for example, are archetypes; marriage is an archetype. It is something that somewhere in us we feel we must do. If we are going to go against that overwhelming power, for example, if we choose to remain single, then we have to deal with that archetype in ourselves.

As we start to work with ourselves in our self-development, the confused mass of archetypes in our unconscious starts to surge up to our conscious mind, to the awareness of the ego. Our inner centre is within the confused mass. That is why it is sometimes quite difficult to reach. We can have things coming up that we don't quite understand and eventually when they come to the conscious mind, maybe through guided imagery or through dreams they will come in the form of symbols for us to understand. Symbolism is a language that our unconscious uses to try to make us conscious. For example, a common symbol found in the psyche is the inner child, which is readily talked about in many self-awareness circles; the inner child is an archetype. It is very useful to contact the inner child in the process of becoming whole. The inner child will challenge and correct us when we become too narrow in our way of being. As an archetype, the inner child expresses our wholeness. It can simultaneously express our vulnerability, our sense of abandonment, and our empowerment, joy and freedom.

Another archetype is what Jung (1976) refers to as the mana figure. The mana figure is the part of us that is in possession of higher knowledge and power - the inner magician. This part of us gives us a true sense of our individuality. This part can be accessed through processes such as guided imagery and in some circles is referred to as "the wise one." It is our own voice, not that of our mother or father. It has no 'shoulds' within it. Rather, it is perceptive and sees the whole. It often gives very valuable guidance that can direct us on our way to becoming whole. It can be the source of our empowerment if we own it and do not project it out onto another or see it as not part of us. We also need to be careful not to inflate it, because when we give it the power, we make ourselves - in contrast - worthless, stupid and inferior. In the chapter *Discovering our many selves*, other archetypes are explored.

When you look at figure 1, you will see an axis between the ego and the inner self. This represents the needed separation as well as the needed link that exists between the ego and the inner self in the structure of the psyche. If there is too much separation and the link to the unconscious is broken, we enter into a state of meaninglessness and despair, which often takes us into a state of depression. In the chapter *Looking for meaning*, this process is explored further. Also, if our ego is too identified with our unconscious, we can have a lot of trouble with day-to-day living. When our archetypes are activated out of balance, they bring forth the inflated ego. When we work through them, the integrated ego emerges. The integrated ego is the ego that has been reborn once the inflated ego reconnects with the inner self, making us whole and balanced once again. The integrated ego comes as a result of our hard work, in looking honestly at ourselves and dealing with the many aspects of the psyche that rise up to be considered. This process serves to make us integrated and whole. The nature of the inflated ego forces us to deal with the mass confusion of the archetypes that surround the inner self, until we again find connection with the inner self. If we do not deal with what comes up in us, we become disconnected from our inner self.

To reach wholeness, a woman must explore and integrate her animus (her unconscious masculine) and a man must explore and integrate his anima (his unconscious feminine). We must explore the inner masculine and feminine within us. The inner masculine and feminine come in the form of archetypes. As opposites within us, they demand that we grow. The anima and animus are often projected onto people of the other sex. Our relations with our fathers and mothers have a lot to do with the state of our anima and animus. Men have mother complexes, women have father complexes, where our experience and perception of our parents affects and colours our experience and perception of the other sex. A woman may, for example, project "the violent father" onto all men, and in her own self may suffer from a strong critical, abusive, tyrant-like aspect which appears as nasty men in her dreams. Her healing comes when she works through her father complex and is able to separate what is related to the father, what is related to other men on an individual basis, and what is her own animus which needs to be integrated and actualised. Much work must take place for this to occur as we are forever trying to create or recreate the warmth of the mother-son, father-daughter or child-parent relationship. This leads us many places, and often away from our centre. The concept of the anima and the animus is further explored in the chapters *Embodying the dream* and *Embracing the Grail.*

We cannot look at the structure of the psyche without understanding that both personal and collective aspects of the conscious and the unconscious exist in our psyche. The collective unconscious contains symbols that are universal in nature in that they are shared by others. The archetypes are part of the collective unconscious, while the complexes we have, such as our inferiority complexes, are part of our personal unconscious. The personal unconscious contains aspects that are unique and that relate specifically to us. The personal unconscious contains components that we may once have been conscious of, but which have become unconscious either through our forgetting or repression. These contents relate to us as individuals. Part of the process of individuation is to liberate ourselves from the power and influence of the collective unconscious and to make conscious the unique meaning of the symbols in our personal unconscious. In this way we come to know who we are, and understand something of our direction and journey.

To become whole, we also need to come to terms with our shadow. As the shadow is discussed in depth in the next chapter *Creating alchemy*, I will not go further into its exploration here.

In this book I have striven to provide an understanding of how our emotions and our mind function, as well as to give some practical guidelines which will help us work with them. The chapters are the steps upon which we must walk in our journey towards wholeness, towards a lightness of being. In *Creating alchemy* we get some understanding of the shadow and its role, and begin to see how we can bring unconscious material into the Light through the process of alchemy. In *Discovering our many selves* we explore the archetypes as sub-personalities or selves and consider examples of common selves which we can identify, as well as becoming aware of the uniqueness of our many selves. This takes us to *Empowering the higher mind* where we consider the role of the mind in our healing process and look at methods that can be used to help gain control of the mind in a way that empowers the higher mind and uses the lower mind to its best potential. Once we come to know what we are made of and how we function, we look for meaning in life. In *Looking for meaning* we discover the need to walk with one foot in the conscious and one foot in the unconscious in order to know ourselves and be balanced and whole. We see the need to be aware not only of our outer world, but also of the inner world, through which we find meaning. We also explore the reasons for depression and what we can do to overcome it. *Embodying the dream* awakens us to the forgotten language of dreams. This reveals the symbolic language of the unconscious, and helps us find ways to work with our dreams so that we may uncover the map of our psyche and so find our way to wholeness. We are taken into the world of the unconscious where we are often confronted with *Meeting the monster* and are challenged to deal with emotions such as anger, fear and guilt which we have frequently repressed. To do this, we find ourselves *Finding courage*, overcoming our fears and *Finding forgiveness*. Only then can we find ourselves taking the next steps of *Sharing from the heart*, *Trusting in immortality* and *Embracing the Grail*, which is our final step in the quest of *Becoming Whole*.

Creating alchemy

Life provides a constant array of challenges. If we are to open to it, we must, it seems, be open to change. Change comes to us often in an outer sense, for example, with changed appointments or changing structures of organisations of which we are a part. Change is also demanded of our personalities. If we are to grow and mature we must let go of our former selves like a flower releases its petals after it has reached its bloom. Like the flower we are cut back, and await regrowth. We are asked to die to ourselves, so that we may be reborn in Light. In the new season we will bloom again.

The ebb and flow of the tide echo this pattern in creation. Our openness to and acceptance of this process affects our experience of life; the more open, the more free we are to unfold and lift our vibration and consciousness from that of density to that of Light. This process of infusing the denseness of our personality with the Light of soul is called alchemy. It is the process whereby we become more divine, and radiate Light, come to know ourselves, and become whole. It is also the process through which negatively manifesting emotions such as anger, fear and greed are transformed to balanced assertion, love, and balanced generosity. Emotions such as anger have a heavy vibration within our emotional body (the body that houses our emotions). When Light is infused into the emotional body an alchemical effect takes place and the heavy emotion of anger is transformed by it to a more pure, lighter state, which may manifest itself as a healthy assertion. Through alchemy, change is total. We contact the heart which helps us to develop the necessary conditions to become whole and radiate love and Light in our lives.

The process of alchemy deals with our resistance to change. It moves us from separation to unity. It does this by dealing with, and helping us to integrate our shadow nature. In *Owning Your Own Shadow*, Robert Johnson (1993, p. 1) describes the shadow as "the part of us which we fail to see or know." By bringing the shadow to our awareness, and by putting it in the Light, we are able to discern what we will cultivate and what we will release to separate the wheat in us from the chaff.

The shadow

In *The Portable Jung*, Carl Jung (1976, p. 145) defines the shadow as:

> ... a moral problem that challenges the whole ego-personality, for no one can become conscious of the shadow without considerable moral effort. To become conscious of it involves recognising the dark aspects of the personality as present and real. This act is the essential condition for any kind of self knowledge, and it therefore, as a rule, meets with considerable resistance. Indeed self knowledge as a psycho-therapeutic measure frequently requires much painstaking work extending over a long period. Closer examination of the dark characteristics - that is, the inferiorities constituting the shadow - reveals that they have an emotional nature, a kind of autonomy, and accordingly an obsessive or, better, possessive quality.

He goes on to say that the shadow can be integrated into the conscious personality with insight and goodwill. The integration of the shadow is a necessary step toward self-realisation. However, he says, this happens with obstinate resistance. The resistance is usually bound up with projections (the tendency to attribute to another person, or the environment, that which is in oneself) the person will not recognise. The cause of the emotions is usually seen to lie in the other person. The projections make it almost impossible for the ego to see through its illusions.

> It is often tragic to see how blatantly a person bungles his or her own life and the lives of others and yet remains totally incapable of seeing how much the whole tragedy originates in him or herself, and how he or she continually feeds it and keeps it going. (Jung, 1976, p. 147)

So why do we have a shadow if it is such a potentially destructive thing? It isn't the shadow itself that is the problem as much as what we do with it and how we use or rather refuse to accept and integrate it. The shadow is necessary to contain all that is within our psyche. To survive in the world, to integrate within its culture, and to fit in to group life we put parts of ourselves into the shadow - we discard these so that we can survive and maintain the culture within which we live.

Returning to wholeness

According to Johnson (1993, pp. 9-10) the first half of life is generally devoted to the cultural process - skills, job, family - and learning discipline. The second half is devoted to restoring wholeness or making our lives holy. We do that through the integration of the shadow.

> We need to restore the wholeness of the personality that was lost in the cultural ideals or we will live in a state of dividedness that grows more and more painful throughout our evolution. (p. 9)

This need to restore the personality to its wholeness often leads to the mid-life crisis. This crisis is one of identity. We evaluate what has been so far in our lives as the second half is approaching, and we look to see what we feel must be changed so that we can live our lives according to our true values. This crisis can be very painful if we have not been doing the needed work on ourselves along the way. The shadow often rises as we need to deal with and integrate it. It may be experienced as conflict or depression. If we choose not to deal with it, we invite neurosis.

Neurosis

Neurosis, according to Jung, is being in a state of disunity with oneself. If we can recognise this, neurosis is not such a bad thing, as it provides a step or mechanism through which we can work to find balance again. The problem with neurosis comes when we are not conscious of it. Jung, in his *Letters*, says:

> The person with a neurosis who knows that he or she is neurotic is more individuated than the person without this consciousness. The person that is a damned nuisance to his surroundings and knows it is more individuated than the person who is blissfully unconscious of his or her nature. (Jung, cited in Sharp, 1988, p. 11)

Neurosis, being in a state of disunity with oneself, is nonetheless a problem. Neurosis can come through being in conflict with the mind or emotions which essentially disables one or the other of those inner bodies. We do not feel comfortable with the conflict we experience, and the world, due to our discomfort, becomes distorted in our view, as do we in our relation to it.

Neurosis comes from the experience of opposites within us. An example of such opposites may be "the perfectionist" and "the slob." It is precisely the presence of these opposites within us which helps to build our character and to expand our consciousness towards wholeness, even though the process may not be pleasant as we experience conflict. Jung (1976) believed that psychological development in mid-life is concerned with coming to terms with the problem of opposites, that is, the disparity between the conscious and the unconscious. For example, we may consciously want to conform and fit in with the society around us. The part that does not want to conform or fit in with anyone, which wants to be independant and perhaps even rebellious may lie in our unconscious. We may become conscious of it being there at times. While it remains unacknowledged it has the potential to create havoc in our lives. The presence of these opposites creates a certain tension through which balance is found and we grow.

Neurosis in our infant life is due partly to certain predispositions. As we continue on in life, we find the cause of neurosis to be the refusal to acknowledge and integrate the shadow. According to Jung (1976), consciously willed one-sidedness is one of the most important causes of the undesirable neurosis. The refusal to acknowledge and deal with our opposites results in neurosis, which can be dangerous when not seen or acknowledged. Many of us project our neurosis onto others via the shadow because we experience it as unpleasant. We project the neurosis and the shadow. To project is to perceive that what is actually happening within us is happening in others. This has been done throughout history between and within groups. This happens between the genders, between races and between religious groups. It also happens within organisations or groups of which we may be a part.

The shadow as disowned aspects

We often blame the organisation or our employers for acting as our own shadow. Johnson (1993) points out that if we are to produce a New Age and allow a true evolution of consciousness, we must learn to integrate the shadow, not only at an individual level but also at national and world-wide levels. Then we can elect governments that reflect our inner changes, governments that take responsibility for their shadows as we do. The current situation in Australian politics with the sudden rise of a political party with racist attitudes shows the emergence of the shadow of the Australian people. When the shadow is left unchecked, it grows, as does the power of the negative forces over us, which we feed by our refusal to own our shadow. M. Scott Peck, in *A World Waiting to Be Born* (1993), reminds us that when a challenge isn't faced it is like wearing another overcoat, and over a period of time if we don't face our challenges, we are weighed down by the overcoats and strike a lot of difficulty in our lives. It is better that the shadow emerges so that it can be dealt with, rather than remain repressed and grow in demonic power, which is what tends to happen to the parts of us that are repressed.

Our frustrations and desires often give rise to our projections. The projections then become the basic material of analytical and alchemical work. To withdraw the projections we must go through the process of alchemy. As we do that other aspects of the prima materia (the substance we are working to change), such as our frustrated expectations and desires, are also transformed. Let us look at the fairy tale of Little Red Riding Hood. Little Red Riding Hood is the archetype of the innocent naive fool, protected by innocence and youth, going forth into the world in trust on a mission to do good. Her shadow is lurking as the wolf. It is only when she confronts the wolf that she achieves wisdom, and is no longer the fool but is more aware of the world and its realities.

The shadow is often seen in a negative light as it contains those characteristics of our personality that we disown. However, some very good characteristics that we have disowned turn up in the shadow. Perhaps, for example, we have a low self-esteem and do not see that we are actually good fun-loving people; those good characteristics of ours that we cannot deal with are also put in the shadow - the skills, talents and abilities we have which we deny. It is this tendency to bury our goodness in the shadow which is responsible for hero worshipping. Perhaps we deny ourselves exercise or sport. We could become fanatical about sport as a result. If we can manage to locate the goodness we project and strive to come to a point of owning instead of disowning it in ourselves, we can develop our character. We project the positive onto others sometimes because we fear success, so we prefer to build it up in others around us. That way we can safely continue to live in our mundane existence. People resist showing their true inner "gold." According to Johnson (1993), ignoring the gold can be as damaging as ignoring the dark side of the psyche. Often this leads to severe shock or illness manifesting in our lives in an attempt to make us acknowledge that a large important part of us is lying dormant or unused.

The concept of disowning needed aspects of ourselves is not new. It has been acknowledged by many psychologists, including Jung (1976), Assagioli (1980), Moreno (1987), Johnson (1993), and Hal and Sidra Stone (1997), in their work with Inner Voice Dialogue. The latter work is looked at in detail in the next chapter, *Discovering our many selves*. In coming to find our disowned and unconscious parts, as well as exploring those we are conscious of, we can move towards becoming whole. In addressing our shadow, perhaps through the work of Inner Voice Dialogue, role-play, guided imagery, counselling or psychodrama, we come to discover that working with the shadow can sometimes be frightening, but most often it is incredibly fascinating to see what can be revealed. By exploring it, we sometimes come across the "gold" which awakens us to balance and gives our lives new meaning. Particularly in the work with Inner Voice Dialogue, the compensatory nature of our many parts becomes obvious. In this work we begin to discover a gratitude for the shadow as we see how it gives us balance as we explore our many parts and their opposites. Through it we discover the value and necessity of these opposites in helping us to become whole.

The shadow is simply the part of us that is unconscious. With some self-honesty, serious self-criticism and courage to look, the shadow can usually be discovered. I like the example by Johnson (1993) where he likens the shadow to an open tin of gasoline waiting ignition from another's shadow which acts as the match. He suggests the only way to avert being dumped on by another's shadow is to stand aside gracefully as a matador with a bull charging - simply move gracefully and let it pass by.

Psychologists and spiritualists have noted for a long time that when we project our shadow (making others at fault or the world generally because our desires and expectations aren't met) we can cause harm to others. We force upon them our darkness or our good qualities and it becomes a burden for the person who is supposed to play the hero or the ogre. We also "sterilise ourselves by casting off our shadow" (Johnson, 1993, p. 46) and deny ourselves the essential ingredient that will, if owned, reveal to us the way of change and the road to balance.

The process of alchemy

How can we stop projecting the shadow and inviting neurosis? It helps if we realise that we need to own our shadow for the sake of achieving our wholeness. Without owning it we cannot develop psychologically or spiritually. We instead create harm to ourselves and others. The way we can integrate it is through the process of alchemy where we infuse the shadow with Light and thereby work towards individuation, bringing to consciousness the unconscious aspects - coming to know the self. We face the dragon in ourselves. I have heard it said that the Tibetans suggest that the Bodhisattva has said that salvation does not come merely from sighting His Presence - which is the presence of Light. It takes effort, perseverance, diligence and one pointed effort to develop the quality of compassion and thus to live in loving kindness and harmlessness. So it is when we work with the shadow. It is not enough simply to make it conscious, though that does take us a long way to understanding ourselves. Rather we must work diligently to bring our shadow into the Light so that it may transform. To do this we need to acknowledge and accept the darkness in ourselves, dare to own it and be courageous enough to deal with it. We can look into what lies behind it, our programs and the reasons for its existence. We must then also decide whether we want to continue in this way or make change. The decision is ours. To change is to invite alchemy; to allow the Light of soul to reach down further into the denseness of our personality, so that essentially we become more soul-like.

To create alchemy we must find the prima materia (the substance we wish to change). Perhaps the substance we unearth is a negative ambition or drive for power. First we bring it into our consciousness, so that we can see it. We delve into the spirit of the unconscious and strive to bring the substance to consciousness. We look into what is driving that negative ambition and bring its essential fantasy content to consciousness. Instead of arguing with the ambition, we communicate with it and ask it what it wants and why. It comes to our awareness through the process we are working with, be it counselling, role-play, Inner Voice Dialogue, guided imagery, and so forth. For example, it may be that we dialogue with a symbol of the negative ambition. This allows us to find the deeper meaning and come to know what is behind the energy of negative ambition in us. We observe it objectively, look at it and dare to face it. The process of individuation (becoming whole) cannot be forced, but depends on time, balance and patience. The destructive emotions that we may uncover have to burn themselves out in a safe way, not, for example, by acting them out. We need to experience and/or suffer through aspects of them to attain the needed understanding for our transformation. This is the process of alchemy. We often feel an inner pressure as alchemy is taking place and we may even feel like we will explode. However, the fulfilment that we feel when we persevere and find the gold makes it all worthwhile as we move towards wholeness. We learn the value of true ethics and morals, and learn to live in truth and love.

Usually in working with the shadow there comes a time when the needed gold has been found and attention needs to move away from the shadow so that it may dissolve. If we begin to overanalyse or focus too long on these parts, we can spoil the transformative work. This act of turning our attention away from the shadow calls its bluff, and helps us to become empowered in Light. We move away from the shadow, taking from it what is needed to make us whole, yet without giving it our power or becoming caught in its games. The shadow self is clever. Sometimes it manifests through fear, guilt, anger, resentment or rebellion. These ways can be the most easily identifiable. At other times it can clothe itself in Light and appear to be loving, warm and kind when it is really manipulating a situation for its own end. However, if we are persistent in shining Light upon ourselves we will come to see the motives behind our supposed goodness and so uncover the shadow. By essentially accepting it, once we have acknowledged and dealt with it, it integrates and thereby loses its power and diminishes. As it gathers momentum in its darkness, the shadow can be an extremely negative force and we need to guard ourselves against it. We can do this by regularly checking it and dealing with it when needed, rather than letting it build and grow unchecked. We can also do this by adhering to the principles of harmlessness, justice, truth and love and by striving to redeem ourselves, atone for our errors, and embody the principles we adhere to. That is how Merlin battled the darkness and that is how we can. As we persevere and allow the alchemical process to proceed, Spirit rises up out of the transformative fire, creating our inspiration for new direction. We assimilate the gold - the activated, valuable unconscious contents - through Spirit. Having endured the process, we find the way of wisdom. The way of wisdom is not to go to the extreme of the shadow and yet not deny its existence either. We follow good principles as the way, as our ideal, and strive towards them, yet we have to acknowledge that the shadow exists or we lose balance. We acknowledge what we are, and we do not pretend that is all we are.

Alchemy is a unique process; even though there are aspects of it that are universal, we all experience the process of alchemy differently within ourselves. In the chapters that follow, I have striven to provide practical ideas and understanding that will help us to face our dragons and find the reward for having done so. For example, in the chapter *Meeting the monster* many practical ways to deal with the anger we so often find in our shadow, are suggested. In *Taking courage* ways of dealing with fear are suggested and in *Finding forgiveness* ways of dealing with guilt are suggested.

Alchemy is the key to change. It is like magic, yet it also takes effort on our part and the will to want to change. Through alchemy we can find our way out of conflict and depression. It also helps us to deal with emotions such as anger, rebellion, resentment, guilt, fear, pride, ambition and jealousy - all of which ultimately keep us in struggle. Alchemy helps us find truth and clarity, vanquishes our negative thoughts, illusions, and oppressive conditions. The choice is ours. If we wish to create alchemy and so invite change into our lives, we must dedicate ourselves to living a life where we seek to live in truth and live in love, and allow love to be in the centre of our existence. This will take effort, perseverance and determination. Sometimes it will mean that we will need to speak up when we would rather stay silent, and stay silent when we would rather speak up. It is a new way of being - that of living in harmlessness, truth and love. It may go against much of what we have been conditioned towards. But it brings its own rewards. As we allow love to enter, all that is not love is transformed by it and we no longer need to live in worry - rather, we can relax and enjoy life, the joy, the sorrow and the pain, knowing that all are needed for our growth and development. As we do this, our lives will become consumed by the power of love, and joy will begin to fill it - a deep soul joy.

Integrating the shadow

Dealing with the shadow is not an easy process, as the shadow often has us encircled and beaten, and we can move into a rut and become downhearted. Yet the shadow also contains a gift for us which becomes evident as transformation takes place through the process of alchemy. Our shadow can be our unrecognised ally which comes forward to be integrated. As we dare to open to assimilate it, we become aware of our limiting thoughts and rigid ideas, and we open to change, allowing the old ways to dissipate and make space for the new. Recognising, acknowledging and owning our shadow does not mean we should let it have control over us. If the shadow takes us over, it can devour the life force in us and we can become imbalanced and even dangerous, for example, if our shadow is full of aggression.

If we are to integrate the shadow, we must learn to accept and to love it, so that the gifts of dealing with it can be revealed. Johnson (1993, p. 40) tells us:

> We are advised to love our enemies, but this not possible when the inner enemy, our own shadow, is waiting to pounce and make the most of an incendiary situation. If we can learn to love the inner enemy, then there is a chance of loving - and redeeming - the outer one.

If we look at the fairy-tale of Beauty and the Beast, we see how Beauty's love for the Beast, in spite of its ugly appearance, enables the Beast to turn into a handsome prince. This serves as an analogy for what can happen with the shadow when we take the step of loving it unconditionally. The moral of this story touches the heart and teaches us to look beyond the mask, beyond appearances to the true essence of what lies within us. It reminds us to look for the good in all, instead of being critical and judgemental.

If we find darkness within us by shining the Light of truth upon our darkness, it can sometimes be quite a shock to see the stark reality of our shadow selves. However, this teaches us that we are made up of darkness and Light. It also lets us know that we are not perfect, helping us develop compassion for ourselves and others. If we wish to change, we need to deal with the shadow and allow our inner alchemist, the part of us that can shine the Light of soul on the shadow, to come forward. The Pied Piper is an archetype of the alchemist within us. He knows what to do to get the rats out of the town, and he does so by playing the flute and bringing in the fairies. He is the muse who knows how to create and work with light to cleanse the darkness. However, the Pied Piper has not yet learned to be selfless and master his pride. When his work is not recognised by the townspeople, he becomes vindictive by drawing the children out of the town. He is able to work with others' shadows, but, like many of us, has more difficulty when it comes to his own. Perhaps the more evolved version of the alchemist or magician archetype is represented by Merlin who is as wise as he is magical and uses his magic for the purposes of good. Even Merlin had his weak spots, though, which is something that we as humans must come to accept about ourselves, not with complacency and resignation but with grace and humility, as Merlin did. His aim was not to use his magical power for his own selfish ends. Rather, it was to use his inner power in the struggle against darkness, within and without, for the good of all. His aim was to radiate Light, not be consumed by darkness, and to lead a good, moral and ethical life - an ideal worth striving towards. The beauty of Merlin as the archetype of the White Magician is that he shows us the power of Light to create alchemy. It is the Light which is the main tool of the alchemists. Merlin also awakens us to the fact that we have Light within us, and this Light guides us to our wholeness. The Light helps us to become illuminated. It helps us to purify ourselves, transmute our shadow and enables our inner self to shine forth, radiant with Light and love. It is the Light which essentially enables alchemy to take place and enables us to become whole.

The value of the integration of the shadow is well summed up by Johnson (1993, p. 17):

> To own one's shadow is to reach a holy place - an inner centre - not attainable in any other way. To fail this is to fail one's own sainthood and to miss the purpose of life.

The process of alchemy helps us to actualise the highest qualities of the archetypes within us and to redeem the lowest aspect or their weaknesses. In the next chapter *Discovering our many selves*, we will explore the archetypes, or our many selves and consider how our many selves manifest. We will also consider ways in which we can learn to be more accepting of ourselves as well as create change where needed.

Discovering our many selves

We have many selves, some of which we identify with strongly. Others we disown and send off to the unconscious, deceiving ourselves about their non-existence. "Others are like that. Not us." Yet in fact we are. We have within us many and even opposing selves. These selves can be referred to as sub-personalities. A sub-personality is the embodiment of an archetype. A sub-personality has its own thoughts, feelings and way of behaving and once stimulated operates autonomously. They often operate in us, in an unconscious way. We are often not aware that they are in control of us yet they often determine our personality. These selves are inherently neither positive nor negative, however, sometimes they manifest in a negative way, and sometimes in a positive one. By looking at the various manifestations of the sub-personalities that are commonly experienced by many people, it is hoped that we will become more aware of our own versions of these sub-personalities. This awareness will expose our sub-personalities and help us see how they are working both positively and negatively in our lives. It will assist us in recognising that we do not have to be controlled by these sub-personalities and assist us in coming to a greater point of consciousness in relation to ourselves, realising that we have a choice about how we want our personalities to manifest.

Sub-personalities, complexes

Jung said that the human mind, or psyche, is made up of many complexes. Complexes are part of our personal unconscious. Marie Louise von Franz was a contemporary of Jung's and current authority in analytical psychology. In her book *The Way of the Dream*, von Franz (1990, p. 26) defines complexes as:

...motors of the psyche. They are like different motors which give the drive, the impulse and aliveness to the psyche. If we had no complexes we would be dead. You can experience a complex, for example, when you are terribly bored and suddenly something arouses your interest and you become engaged. That is a complex being touched. So the complexes are simply the energy centres of the psyche.

Complexes can be aroused in us in both positive and negative ways. Complexes, as energy centres, are neutral. However, much of the literature portrays complexes with a negative connotation. For example, a man has a mother complex, which all men have. How he reacts to his mother will determine how he acts towards women generally. This may be positive or negative. If we say someone has a sex complex, a mother complex, a father complex, an inferiority complex or a superiority complex, we are usually referring to a complex that arouses the person's energy in a negative way, in that it takes all the psychic energy and blurs the perspective of the personality as a whole.

By over-identifying with some complexes we sometimes reject or split-off others. For example, people who have creative talent may decide they are not good enough at creative pursuits, or find that it is too much work, and so stop doing it. With that decision they cut off their creativity. This gives them a split-off creative complex. Denying their own creativity, they are likely to become jealous of others who express theirs, or feel over-burdened with the responsibility of life and as though they never get a chance to express themselves. Hence they find that life loses meaning. By over-identifying with our workaholic selves we may split-off our ability to relax and enjoy pleasurable, leisure-time pursuits. A monk or nun may cut off the sexual nature and so create in themselves a sex complex. This is often the reason for closet sexual abuse in some of those who are supposedly "of the cloth."

By cutting off or denying certain aspects of our personality, and identifying too strongly with others, we develop complexes and we create sub-personalities that can become monsters, taking all our energy and rising up in inappropriate ways in our lives. For example, it is well known that when people drink alcohol they may become Mr. Hyde to the Dr. Jekyll of their sober self. Their usual control and defense mechanisms are weakened by the alcohol and a repressed sub-personality emerges in full force. In such circumstances women and men who are generally very controlled in speech and mannerisms suddenly blurt out all their hidden thoughts and agendas, which can bring forth anger, gossip and insecurities that they would usually not reveal. They may also become promiscuous, when if sober they would not dream of being so.

Archetypes and the dream

In Jungian analysis, it is stressed that we need to allow ourselves to become aware of our many different parts and to allow the inner symbology of the archetypes to reveal themselves to us through dream. Often what we stop ourselves from acknowledging in our waking life will reveal itself to us through the dream. We move towards wholeness when we accept the reality of being human, and acknowledge that we are composed of many selves, often, paradoxically, opposing selves. In the analysis of dreams we can witness the many parts of ourselves playing out in the drama of the dream. We become aware of the archetypes in us and come to know and accept these sub-personalities without judgement, allowing them to reveal the reality of the contents of our psyche. Only by first coming to know and accept ourselves as we are, can we begin to move towards change and transformation.

As more of the unconscious contents of our psyche rise to what Jung refers to as the conscious, the more we can come to know ourselves and the closer we move towards individuation, or becoming whole. When we deny that parts of us exist, we create split-off complexes that bring about neurotic conditions within us - that is, we are in a state of disunity with ourselves. When we do this for too long we enter a state of grief and depression, and lose the sense of meaning in our lives. For example, a man who throws himself into work, and cuts off his relationships with his family and friends in the process, who cuts off all his hobbies and interests, driven by ambition and the need for power, will at some point discover, though sometimes this may take ten or twenty years, that he is lonely and without the power to experience a sense of meaning and fulfilment in life. This may cause what many call "a breakdown." Jung would see this as transformational depression. The man is called to go within and recontact his split-off parts. If he can do this he moves out of the state of "breakdown" into a life of more meaning. These split-off parts can often be found through the analysis of dreams. For more on dreams see the chapter *Embodying the dream.*

Likewise, a woman who puts all her focus and attention into motherhood and "wife-hood," always putting others first, never thinking of herself, may go through an inner crisis when the children leave home and the husband retires. She has long ago split-off the sub-personalities she now needs to survive in the world. To go on in life, she will need to reactivate them. The self she needs to activate may well burst out rather aggressively and selfishly, and those around her will say, "Mum, that's not like you!" However, the selfishness and aggression are the repressed opposite of the caring martyr. At some point, if the woman is to find psychological balance in her life, it will need to come out.

It is natural, normal and crucial that we have a number of sub-personalities in the make-up of our personality. To get to know these sub-personalities or complexes is a helpful and healthy way of building self-understanding and ultimately directing our own inner change.

Let us now look at some universal sub-personalities of the psyche. I have given them names in an attempt to help crystallise their form and nature. You may wish to call them other names, and to attribute characteristics to them beyond what I do here. When we identify the energy of these sub-personalities within us we can begin to make choices about how we give them expression. An awareness of the different selves and their manifestations gives us the freedom not to be trapped in one or another sub-personality, but rather to choose how we wish to express our many selves. It enables us to learn to accept our different selves, to see how they help or hinder us, and ultimately to turn our weaknesses into strengths. We can even begin to communicate with them, help them to either have space for expression or to raise their awareness, and where needed, to heal them.

The various sub-personalities

This list is not meant to be exhaustive:

The martyr

A martyr is one who is able to sacrifice him- or herself for a principle, cause or project. In history, the acts of some who have martyred themselves in this way have done wonders for the victory of the human spirit and for the good of humanity. On the positive side, this energy shows the very valuable qualities of selflessness, devotion and dedication to something higher, a valuable quality attributed to certain saints.

On the negative side, this energy can manifest as a self-righteousness which seems to say "Look at me, look at all I am doing for you!" When manifesting in this way, the martyr is begging for attention and pity, and if gratitude is not shown, resentment builds and the martyr becomes bitter about the giving. In this case, the giving is not given freely from the heart; rather, the motive for giving is to gain something for the self. The martyr may also give to the detriment of his or her own balance and health.

The rescuer

The rescuer gives help to those in need; where rescuing is needed, this person becomes another's knight in shining armour. This sub-personality is prepared to help others when they are in need. Essentially this is a valuable quality.

It manifests negatively, however, when the rescuer does this for self-aggrandisement, so that it can feel good about itself. This rescuing can also take place to the detriment of oneself. An example is a woman who stays in an abusive relationship trying to rescue her partner from the addiction to alcohol. In doing so she may even put her own life at risk. This sub-personality needs to be needed, and thrives on that.

The perfectionist

The perfectionist likes to do things to perfection. It is a useful sub-personality to have when precision and attention to detail are needed, for example, in proof-reading for a book, or in achieving excellence in a chosen field.

When this energy manifests negatively, however, nothing is ever good enough. It may side with the critic and not rest until every aspect of someone is looked into and picked on. It can become extremely demanding, making one always feel unworthy or not yet good enough. It has one aim in mind - to make perfect, and it will not rest until this is achieved. When this sub-personality becomes activated in a person regarding her or his choice of partner, no one ever measures up to scratch. When it runs rampant, this sub-personality can help ruin our lives.

The inferior one

The inferior one feels inadequate. This sub-personality feels that it is lower in rank than others. In some cases we are inadequate and our skills are not what they could be. In these instances, the inferior one lets us keep a reality check on our ego. It reminds us that hierarchy exists and that we may be lower in position or not as advanced as others in certain skills.

This sub-personality becomes negative when the feelings around the inferiority become so intense that they move out of proportion to the reality of the situation and when they attach to a sense of inferiority that is illusory. This one feels that it is so inferior that it is of absolutely no worth; the energy becomes self-denigrating. When it takes hold we are rendered useless. It will then often link with the comparer and engage in comparison with others who will always be seen as better than it, and far more accomplished in both skills and value.

The superior one

The superior one feels more than adequate. In some way this one has reached the top of a chosen field and is excelling in achievement. For example, it may be that this one relates to a person's mathematical excellence or musical ability. It gives a sense of pride and makes a person feel worthwhile. Perhaps one has worked diligently in music for many years and begins to experience a superior status in this field. In this way a person can learn the value of effort and enjoy having a sense of mastery.

The superior one begins to manifest negatively when the pride experienced inflates the ego, giving a sense of "I'm better than anyone else will ever be." The superior nature is experienced to the detriment of others, and others are viewed as lesser in terms of their inherent value. Essentially, we are all as valuable as each other, no matter what our strengths and weaknesses are. This sub-personality delights in judgement of others and being "one-up." It feels good about making others feel inferior and weak. The superior one sometimes comes forward as a compensatory measure for the inferior one, perhaps to hide the real feelings of inferiority or as a means of balancing out these opposite aspects.

The comparer

The comparer helps us to gauge where we are in life and how we are developing. It can be useful to help us see our progress as we navigate our way through life. We can compare our progress with our prior progress, thus comparing ourselves with ourselves. This can help our self esteem, or help us see where we need to improve.

It becomes negative when it goes into overdrive and makes constant comparisons with everyone and everything; when it links with the negative critic, making us always come out on the losing edge; when it bolsters our egos to let us know how good we are. When it never lets up, it takes away our drive to achieve or do anything. We come to believe we will never be good enough so why bother (Stone and Stone, 1997).

The critic

The critic can dissect and analyse, giving appraisal of our merit and demerit. This can be useful to help us improve, or reflect on how we are going. We can employ the critic sub-personality to help us better ourselves in a chosen endeavour. When it is functioning at its optimum, it can point out the truth of how we are going, our weaknesses and our strengths, our achievements and our failures.

Often this sub-personality becomes one-sided, and instead of giving helpful criticisms or feedback, it begins to pull apart, analyse and criticise everything we do, and everything we are. It can become one-sided in that it only gives negative criticism. It can become relentless in its attack on ourselves, our family and friends. When it does this, it becomes a tyrant, dominating, authoritarian and never satisfied.

The wise one

This one has a great deal of wisdom and views life from a higher perspective. It can see the forest and the trees, viewing life from a broad perspective while still being able to see the needed details. This one gives helpful advice which enables us to see others, ourselves and the world more clearly. It can see beyond the limited perspective of many of the other sub-personalities and knows what is good for the person as a whole. It has vision of the many different selves and knows what is needed for balance and unity of these selves; what is needed for the betterment and growth of the person concerned.

This one can become negative when it loses touch with reality or if the person it is part of gives it all the power; that is, when the person hears the advice of the wise one, and follows it blindly, perhaps misinterpreting it or failing to take responsibility for the consequences of following the advice given. For example, in the New Age this one may be seen as someone's guide. The person may act abdicating responsibility for his or her actions by stating, "It's not me, it's my guide who said I should do it!"

The driver

This one motivates us; it drives us to "do," that is, do work, do tasks, do as opposed to "be." Without it we would get nothing done. It is responsible for activating us to achieve, or accomplish a given task. It challenges us to move ahead, complete tasks, and so be successful in attaining our ambitions. It remains positive, provided that which it pushes us towards is beneficial to the whole.

When it splits off from the whole and is concerned with ambition for ambition's sake, the driver manifests negatively. It becomes narrow-minded and does not consider the cost the person being driven will have to pay. It is often the energy responsible for turning people into workaholics. It does not consider the body's need for food or rest, or the person's need for leisure and fun. It will drive us to exhaustion and always find more things that need to be done.

In the news recently, a truck driver who had been driving for eight days straight had bad judgement and ran over a young boy. What the man concerned was driven by we can only guess - the need for money, an out-of-proportion devotion to the company who employed him, the inability to give himself the needed rest, or the desire to be seen as the winner of "the staying power" status with his work-mates. The reason cited was the fear of losing his job if he did not deliver the goods at a certain time. This is an example of being driven in a negative way: we are so driven that we lose judgement and balance.

The guardian and protector

This one looks out for our best interests and our safety. It steps in to protect other parts of us that are afraid or vulnerable. It has a comfort zone and monitors what comes close to us, and what is let in. It is aware of the state of other sub-personalities and will not allow us to be in danger of harm. For example, if someone is approaching our vulnerable child, it may step in and stop the person. This one helps us as we grow and develop from childhood to adulthood. It knows what we can cope with and what we can't. It creates a barrier that is sufficient for our protection and one that allows us the space to grow.

It manifests negatively when the barrier created by the guardian or protector becomes too solid, not allowing us space to grow. For example, the barrier may prevent the vulnerable child from getting the love it needs in order to feel safe. The guardian becomes detrimental to the whole when it guards in a way that is too rigid and does not discriminate about what it should guard us from.

In Inner Voice Dialogue work and work in psychodrama and role-play, this one is often found to be quite potent in helping to communicate with split-off parts. Stone and Stone (1997) suggest that often this one needs to be present when the aim is to contact parts which have been disowned such as the vulnerable child. I have found this to be a very useful technique in contacting parts which otherwise seem uncontactable. The presence of the guardian can make the vulnerable one feel safe enough to "come out." When the guardian or protector has become overbearing, which can happen, getting its permission and letting it be present while other parts are contacted helps to placate it so that the needed work may get done.

The obedient one

This one will do what it is told. It will await instructions and follow them to the letter. This sub-personality can be very helpful to have at certain times. For example, in our place of employment it can help get a job done without creating any unnecessary waves. It often aims to please, in a balanced way.

When this manifests negatively, it can become quite painstaking, as it has little ability to think for itself; rather, it goes into automatic and simply tries to please at any cost. When it gets into this mode it loses sight of common sense and becomes a stickler for rules and regulations, regardless of their appropriateness to the situation. This one can be overly concerned about what others may think.

The rebellious one

When this one is not happy with the way things are, it will say so and do what it thinks best, regardless of what others may think. It is capable of a degree of independence which, when balanced, is quite healthy.

When this one manifests negatively, it can be very stubborn and acts purely out of reaction, instead of balanced response. It is not in touch with even its own needs; rather, it will rebel for rebelling's sake. Say, for example, if an adolescent son or daughter is fed up with doing what his or her parents want and goes into the rebellious sub-personality. The parents may offer to take the adolescent to his or her favourite dance. Although the adolescent would love to go, he or she refuses to do so, simply because he or she wants to say "No!" to the parents.

The successful one

This one is extremely capable and diligent. It seeks mastery at whatever task it is working towards accomplishing. It has staying power, has courage and is determined and persevering. It is very helpful in relation to getting us where we want to go in life. It is confident, empowered and self-assured.

This one becomes negative when it becomes too focused on the self, when it looks to success as a means of experiencing glory for glory's sake, no matter what the cost. It will back-stab others, seeing them as opponents to its climbing the ladder. This one often sides with the negative driver, and will push a person to success in such a way that negative ambition and grabbing of power for power's sake are stimulated.

The failed one

This one is quite the opposite of the successful one. It is not competent and does not succeed in what it does. It is a fact of human existence and helps us to see our weaknesses and where we need to develop our skills or learn more. It enables us to discover the quality of humility.

It becomes negative when it links with self-pity and believes it is worthless, useless and stupid. It then renders us incapable of anything.

The controller

The controller likes to be in charge. It can offer assistance to keep things in order and helps us to reach places on time. It gives our lives structure and organisation in whatever areas we put it to use. It gives us a sense of being in control, and helps us to move through fear. It is basically rational, and generally concerned with keeping the other sub-personalities in a state of order, demanding from them appropriate behaviour. It has a sense of authority.

It becomes negative when it becomes too rigid and when it controls in a narrow-minded way. It may become overly concerned about controlling other sub-personalities to the point of fanatical control, not allowing them to have any freedom or even to have their own voice.

The knowing one

This one can look at things from a distance and gain proper perspective of any situation. It is somewhat like the wise one in that it is more in touch with a higher truth than some of the other sub-personalities. We can look to this sub-personality when we need help and guidance in a given situation.

This becomes negative when the "truth" this aspect contacts is actually illusion, causing it to give wrong guidance from its blinded perspective. It can also be negative when it becomes overly focused on the certainty of its own knowledge. It then becomes "a know-it-all."

The spiritual one

This sub-personality has its heart's desire in being in contact with the spiritual world. It has the potential for bringing meaning and purpose to our lives. It can also bring peace, a sense of harmony and beauty, and a connection to light and love. It has the capacity to be detached and not cling to matter. It is not interested in earthly needs such as power, ambition and success. It has transcended possession and desire for results. It is in a state of peace and constant surrender to what is. This sub-personality has united the polarities of existence and dances with Spirit. Its actions are based on the fullness of the moment. It brings life or Spirit into the earthly realm and transforms it as a result, helping all to become spiritualised, making us aware of the oneness of existence.

This one becomes negative when it simply splits off from life rather than strengthening the life-force. It also can link with aspects of the more negative sub-personalities. For example, it may become elitist and consider that it is more advanced or greater than the other aspects. This is not the spiritual energy per se but the negative sub-personality attaching itself to that energy.

The inner child

This one keeps us human, never grows up and is an important link to spirituality.

The playful one

The playful child is a lot of fun. It brings joy, humour and light-heartedness to any situation and generally lights up life. It can bring meaning and purpose to an otherwise dull and boring life. It brings freedom, spontaneity and a sense of adventure to any endeavour.

If manifesting in a more negative manner this one can become the trickster, the devious child, playing tricks or pranks on others simply to make its effect felt.

The creative one

This one is full of ideas and is in touch with active imagination. It sees endless possibilities of creation and expression and gives enthusiasm and inspiration. This one can be a wonderful vehicle for the Light of the Holy Spirit.

This one, when manifesting negatively can be unrealistic, and demand expression for expression's sake, without, for example, regard to others or cost.

The vulnerable one

This one wants to be needed, looked for and embraced. It has often been split-off by another sub-personality and so has been alone, in some cases, for many years. This one needs to be owned, not disowned, and protected, not shunned. It often has a lot of wisdom within it and knows what the adult needs to do to get more balance into life, to relax and become whole. This one can be very intimate with others, once it is found and listened to. It is capable of radiating love and warmth, that is, when it forgives the person for the long period of being abandoned. When we discover it within, there is usually an inner hug taking place to celebrate reconnection. If this one has been alone for a long time, it usually has a deal of anger to send to the person it is part of before it is ready to open to its vulnerability. It wants to make sure it can trust the person.

This one, when manifesting negatively, can be over-stubborn, unforgiving and indulge in self-pity.

The wounded one

This one feels wounded and has often been traumatised by real situations of abuse, perhaps from a parent or other adult, or an older child, perhaps a sibling. The world does not feel safe for this one, so it has gone inward. This one is similar to the vulnerable child but the wounding is more intense. It often does not have a voice of its own; rather, it has the guardian speak for it. It is in need of healing, which requires love, compassion, tolerance and patience. It has real needs that have never been met.

Its negative expression is as for the vulnerable one above.

The "tantrumming" one

This one is about the age of three and wants its own way no matter what. It pays no attention to rationality, it feels acutely that it has not got what it wants and it must have it. It cannot distinguish between need and want. It simply wants!

The opposites within us

By the time you have read through the list of various sub-personalities listed above you may get the feeling that we are very fragmented, and have many aspects of ourselves that are diametrically opposed. This is true, we are. However, we also function as a whole and our overall personality is a synthesis of our sub-personalities. Let us look at the paradox between the reality of the opposites within us, and the unification of these aspects in the synthesis of the whole.

In *Embracing Ourselves*, Hal and Sidra Stone (1997) give some wonderful examples of the opposites within. In their work, which is known as Inner Voice Dialogue, the therapist speaks to these different sub-personalities. For example, they call a sub-personality which is similar to what I have called the driver, a pusher. Its opposite is, in their terminology, a hippie, a bag lady or a sloth. This one is not interested in taking responsibility and would rather relax and be self-indulgent. When a person is identified with his or her achieving self, it is sometimes difficult for the person to accept that the non-achiever is also contained within. It is in such instances that we often attract someone else into our lives to embody the disowned self for us. In their work, Hal and Sidra Stone discuss primary and disowned selves. The primary selves are the ones we identify with, the disowned selves are the ones we split off from us. We generally accept the sub-personalities that fit in with our self-image. Those that do not, we reject. When we own our disowned selves again, begin to communicate with them and give them a space in our lives, we no longer need our family, friends or associates to play out those parts for us. Our relationships become easier and we become more balanced. If we deny that a sub-personality exists, it is sent to the unconscious and it can create havoc in our lives. We may want to achieve, for example, but find we have a strong unidentifiable resistance. If we dare to look and acknowledge the disowned opposite, we may be able to get on with our work again.

Most of our sub-personalities have an opposite. According to Jung, (cited in Sharp, 1988, p. 23), it is when we can successfully hold the tension between these opposites that we become whole:

> The repressed content must be made conscious so as to produce a tension of opposites, without which no forward movement is possible. The conscious mind is on top, the shadow underneath, and just as high always longs for low, and hot for cold, so all consciousness, perhaps without being aware of it, seeks its unconscious opposite, lacking which it is doomed to stagnation, congestion, and ossification. Life is born only of the spark of opposites.

The more each sub-personality is recognised and accepted, the more it can make its own unique contribution to the whole. Jean Hardy, in her book, *A Psychology with a Soul* (1987, p. 44), tells us that "in therapeutic work with the sub-personalities there are five stages - recognition, acceptance, coordination, integration and synthesis." These five stages give a good indication of the plan of action taken in most therapies that deal with sub-personalities. Firstly, the person must recognise the sub-personalities within; otherwise, it is impossible to bring them into awareness. Secondly, the person is helped to find acceptance of the fact that he or she has these parts and is then helped to find a place where it is possible to simply witness them, without judgement. Thirdly, coordination takes place between the person and the sub-personalities - a dialogue is entered into and any issues are negotiated. The dialogue takes place between central and peripheral sub-personalities, both among the sub-personalities and in their relationship to the "I" (the central self). Fourthly, integration of the new awareness occurs. This comes as a result of the dialogue in the former stage. The fifth stage is that of synthesis, that is, all the elements of the sub-personalities are combined into a complex whole. According to Jean Hardy (1987, p. 44) "the idea of synthesis is that both the whole and the parts retain their own integrity without rigidity."

Roberto Assagioli, in his article The balancing and synthesising of opposites (cited in Hardy, 1987, p. 44), tells us that:

> Synthesis is brought about by a higher element or principle which transforms, sublimates and reabsorbs the two poles into a higher reality.

In his work Assagioli looks at these phenomena as triangles. The two opposing points are at the base of the triangle and the midpoint is the place of the "I" where we find the common sense accommodation between the two. In figure 2 an example of these triangles is given. In the triangle on the top half of the page we see that pessimism and optimism are given as opposites. The commonsense accommodation between the two is practical realism. As consciousness rises and we move towards a higher awareness the quality of practical realism becomes clear vision. In the second triangle on the bottom half of the page, the opposing sub-personalities are expressed as self-depreciation (the inferiority complex) and arrogance (the superiority complex). The commonsense midpoint here is modesty. Assagioli suggests that in terms of higher awareness, modesty becomes spiritual dignity. Assagioli sees the "I" as being much closer to a place of higher awareness than the personality. Assagioli suggests that if a person could learn to live in a more centred way, the tensions between the unconscious material expressed by the sub-personalities could be resolved in a creative way. He believes that the pain and suffering experienced as a result of the conflict can lead the way to growth and awareness.

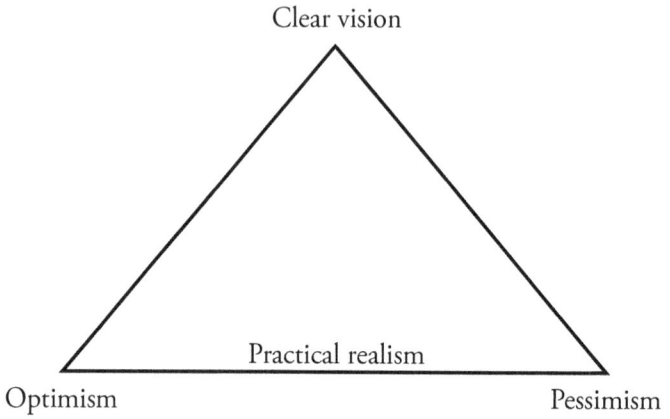

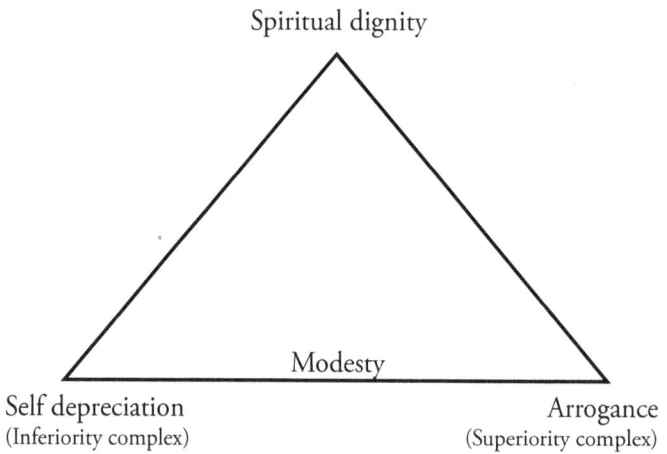

Figure 2. Assagioli's Triangles (cited in Hardy, 1987, p.45)

According to Jung, the integrated ego has awareness of the various sub-personalities and remains balanced between them. It is when we over-identify with a particular role or allow a particular sub-personality to take over the driver's seat for all our selves that we become imbalanced and neurotic.

In 1935, Jung (cited in Sharp, 1988, p. 16) gave a series of talks to a group of doctors in London, known as *The Tavistock Lectures*. In that conference he spoke about complexes:

> To have complexes is in itself normal; but if the complexes are incompatible, that part of the personality which is too contrary to the conscious part becomes split-off. As the split-off complexes are unconscious, they find only an indirect means of expression, that is, through neurotic symptoms.

Essentially it is through conflict that we find our wholeness.

> Daily psychological experience affords proof of this. The most intense conflicts, if overcome, leave behind a sense of security and calm which is not easily disturbed, or else a brokenness that can be hardly healed. Conversely it is just these intense conflicts and their conflagration which are needed in order to produce valuable and lasting results. (p. 22)

The power of the sub-personalities often lies in the fact that we are not conscious of them. By becoming conscious of them, exposing them and taking away their masks, we grow to understand them, and they cease to have so much power over us. When we expose these sub-personalities, we can work with any aspect of them that is harmful to us or is operating in an unhelpful way. We can also begin to control and use the energies in a positive way. This sets us free to enter into awareness of ourselves. We can become conscious, balanced individuals, functioning from our centre. It is this central self that is referred to by Jung as the "Self," by Assagioli as the "soul," and by Hal and Sidra Stone as "the aware ego." It is when we have a thorough knowledge of the sub-personalities, and an ego that is aware and operating from a higher place than the level of the opposites within us that we begin to be able to control the various elements of our personality, and begin to realise our true self, psychologically speaking. Once realised, we can reconstruct our personality around a more aware centre.

Finding a new centre to operate from

It was many years ago that I first realised that we have so many drivers in our psychological car. My psychodrama teacher introduced me to this concept. Throughout a series of psychodrama sessions I watched as many sub-personalities of those in the group took the stage to help work through and resolve specific life issues for people. Then it was my turn. One by one the sub-personalities emerged, like petals of a flower unfolding and revealing themselves. But not all the petals were in a healthy state. By dialoguing and role-playing with these parts I began to find out what they were, and how they had come to be in the state they were in. Some parts were manifestations of my parent's beliefs, some my peers', and some fewer, my own. Others were specific parts of me such as my mind, my sexuality, my anger, my fear - the array seemed endless. After meeting each part and exploring it in the role-play, I was taken out of the role-play to get an objective view. This gives the opportunity to be witness to oneself. In this way, I could view, without judgement, each sub-personality. In this way I could come to see the reality of my psychological state. I could see there was much work to do; the wounded child to be picked up and nurtured, many splits to be healed. That psychodrama session led to several others which continued in this exploration and became the theme of many healing and therapy sessions to come. I remember to this day, all the different roles looking at me as my psychodrama teacher got me to take a mental snapshot of the many selves. In that pycho-drama I simply met these selves. In the ones that followed transformational work was embarked upon. I found this to be revolutionary. It was wonderful, for example, to learn that my mind didn't have to be in the driver's seat when I was making decisions and realise there are some decisions the mind just can't make. Sometimes it's like a computer - it has all the facts, and it will just keep giving them to you without giving a positive decision. I was also able to reclaim my disowned heart and let that have more play in my life. There were many parts to be reclaimed, and others needed new lines to say - so boring, negating and useless were the old ones. Discovering the play within ourselves and coming to know the inner actors helps us to consider our growth as an evolutionary process.

Methods of contacting our many selves

Inner Voice Dialogue

Hal and Sidra Stone (1997, p. 21) suggest that to grow psychologically, we need to discover our many sub-personalities and spend time finding and creating an "aware ego" to sit in the driver's seat of our psychological car. The aware ego can move fluidly in and out of our sub-personalities. By allowing the aware ego to guide the way we do not get stuck in certain sub-personalities or clusters of them. The aware ego is an aware "... choice maker. ... As a more aware ego, it is in a better position to make real choices." "It is only when we become aware, that we realise we actually have a choice about how we choose to be." (p. 21)

Hal and Sidra Stone (1997) give many examples of how these sub-personalities work together. As well as the aware ego, the primary selves and the disowned selves, the Stones identify the voices of the sub-personalities - the protector/controller, the heavyweights, the disowned instinctual energies, the inner child and the parental selves. In the case of the disowned instinctual energies they show how energies that are disowned may come to haunt us in our dreams, as for example, the mafia running after us!

They show how even the aware ego may have let some of the sub-personalities take over the ego's executive function. Imagine the combination of the protector/controller, the pusher, the pleaser, the perfectionist and the inner critic. That combination gathers together a mighty power! To continually come to higher points of self-awareness we must be diligent in allowing these many selves to be uncovered. In the beginning we may see the powerful group listed above as all part of the one self. It is only with time and awareness that we begin to see that a number of selves are involved, and that we can begin to allow the aware ego to dis-identify with those selves and become a separate entity of our awareness. By identifying these sub-personalities we may still decide to act as they do, but at least - due to our new awareness - we do so with choice. When we have not developed an aware ego we do not have that choice. We think we are the sub-personality, and if the sub-personality is feeling hopeless, then so are we. If the sub-personality is feeling warm and playful, so are we. Imagine what it would be like to have more control of our feeling states. We must begin to become aware that we do have a choice.

In the Inner Voice Dialogue method the many selves are revealed through dialogue with an aware facilitator. Sometimes selves have been disowned for so long that people have difficulty accessing them - for example, the vulnerable child. In this method the facilitator can use a technique called "energetic induction," which brings in the facilitator's own energy of the vulnerable child, to help assist the person to contact it. In this process there may not be a voice; rather, we may experience the sub-personality energetically. Then when it feels comfortable a voice may come. If you are interested in knowing more about this method I suggest you look into the book, *Embracing Ourselves* (Stone and Stone, 1997).

Role-play drama healing

Role-play drama healing is a way in which we can come to know ourselves and our relation to the whole, and effect change where we know it is needed. It helps us to take responsibility for who we are, find where we are wounded and begin to heal that wound. In this process we become aware of the Light and the shadow within us all that becomes our outer manifestation. By coming to know and accept ourselves for who we are, we can then decide where and in what way we would like to implement change and set about that process.

Essentially, role-play drama healing is a para-psychological technique which combines spiritual healing with role-play and psychodynamic, Jungian and Gestalt methods. It looks at the psychology of the selves, and explores our inner archetypes through role-play and dialogue with the inner voices, helping us to come to know and understand our many parts. Once we know our parts we can begin to work towards harmony and unity within, and effectively bring about healing. Imperative in the process is the support of the group dynamic and the willingness of the participants to open to the process. As in psychodrama there is a protagonist (the one who is revealing his or her inner drama) and others in the group to play out the protagonist's many parts. Our various parts are given roles, and lines (some words) that represent those roles. In this process we get to meet our sub-personalities and can also work directly with energies such as anger, embarrassment, fear, and so forth. We can see where many of the sub-personalities have come from and how they are formed. We can also see how they are linked together with other sub-personalities and their interrelationships. Role-play drama healing is an incredibly enlightening process which can have us in fits of laughter and reduce us to tears as we work to heal and make whole our many parts and essentially bring those parts to a place which works for us, and not against us. It helps us to become whole.

Guided imagery

Guided imagery is a process through which our sub-personalities can be contacted. An image can be called in to represent each sub-personality and the person having the guided imagery can begin to dialogue with each sub-personality through the image. Aspects of ourselves that are revealed through dreams can also be worked with in this way. During guided imagery, people are guided into relaxation and then to a quiet place. It may be a place they already know, or an imaginary one. This helps them to further relax and to begin to explore the inner world. They describe their quiet place and spend some time there. When they are ready to work on the issue at hand, they leave the quiet place and allow an image to come to represent the issue (which may be a sub-personality) or they allow the dream image to return. They are then guided by the facilitator into dialogue with that part of themselves. They explore the image and its many facets, asking whatever questions they need, saying whatever needs to be said, and allowing to happen whatever needs to happen. For some people this process takes place in dialogue form. For others it may be a visual or feeling experience. It may also be a mixture of these. Role-plays can take place as they would in work such as Inner Voice Dialogue, role-play drama healing or psychodrama. It happens however on people's inner screens. For a detailed account of guided imagery and its method, see the chapter *Guided imagery* in my book *The Healing Hands of Love* (1997).

Dealing with our repressed selves

In working on accessing our lost sub-personalities we can access a sub-personality that we have consciously chosen to split-off from and for good reason. Perhaps it is extremely negative and even harmful. We must recognise that bringing a sub-personality to consciousness does not mean that we have to live it. It simply means that instead of denying it, we acknowledge that it is there. This way it will not run about affecting our lives from unknown directions and in unconscious ways. We make our conscious selves, our ego, more aware and give ourselves choice as to how we wish to be. I would not recommend exploring these extremely negative selves, unless it is done with a therapist who is a psychologist or a therapist well-versed in these matters. It is enough to acknowledge the existence of these parts and to choose from the aware ego to simply acknowledge them and move on.

A case study

Let us take the case study of Jane. Jane was in her early thirties, married, and had worked in an office for the last ten years. She came to therapy as she felt she was beginning to lose her enthusiasm for life. Her husband would have liked her to be more intimate. But she felt no energy for that or anything else. She knew she was beginning to get depressed as her house was becoming untidy, she was cleaning less and less often and there was a growing pile of clothes by her bed. She usually accepted social invitations but the weekend prior to her coming for therapy, even though she had the option to go out, she felt she couldn't bring herself to go. She had developed a habit which was starting to dismay her - she went shopping for clothes when she got her pay cheque each fortnight and her Mastercard was over the limit. She had another habit which took some time in therapy to be revealed. It was a growing compulsion to eat when others were not around, straight out of the packets in the cupboard. If it was biscuits, she would eat the whole packet; if it was raisins, she would eat the whole jar. In therapy, Jane described a dream:

> I was running from some aggressive men. I was worried that if I couldn't keep running they would catch me. I noticed a door off the hallway and went in the room. The room was very tiny but I went in there anyway. To my surprise I found a baby there which seemed as if it needed to be fed. I was worried that I didn't know how to feed it.

In the course of therapy certain sub-personalities emerged. Needless to say the critic, the driver, the perfectionist and the controller were all operating strongly. These sub-personalities quickly emerged as they had a lot to say. Most of their conversation entailed what they thought Jane should or should not do. Her inner child, her creative self were nowhere in sight. Jane worried a lot about what others thought of her. She went straight from home into marriage, and straight from university to her current job. But she was not happy there. When we began to talk to the part that wasn't happy, we discovered that this part had been repressed for some time, and initially it was very angry. Only a short time of allowing this anger to be expressed revealed that this unhappy part contained several sub-personalities that had been split-off and denied. These included her wounded child, playful child, rebellious one, the wise one and the spiritual one. We also talked to the parts that were engaging in the unwanted habits and discovered these were sub-personalities that were very unhappy, not only because she stayed at such a boring job but also because they could not come out in her home life or social life either. Her obedient one was busy trying to please the driver, the perfectionist, the critic and the controller. Around her, her parents, family and friends also seemed to play these roles for her. All her energy was going into being obedient, and into keeping at bay the parts that had ideas of their own about how they wanted to behave. It was only when Jane started to access these parts and give them a voice that she began to find enthusiasm for life again. By contacting her playful and vulnerable child she found she was able to be more relaxed and open to her husband in an intimate way. She discovered that she had been living an ideal that was actually not her own. Within twelve months of beginning therapy she had a new job and she had found a way to creatively make her life her own again.

Choosing to grow

The exploration of the sub-personalities of the psyche is a fascinating and endless arena. It is a major part of psychotherapy. It is a constructive way to approach the psychology of the complex nature of human beings and to help us access the denied parts of ourselves, which we need to do in order to grow.

The following story is from an experience in therapy as an adult. It illustrates how contact with the wise one helps the little girl within, and healing is the result. It is an excerpt from the chapter, *The Healing Tree* from my book, *The Language of the Heart: is spoken all over the world* (1991, pp. 93-99). I place it here by way of conclusion.

I was taken back to a time when I was a child, very small in the play pen and I could feel a real sense of safety in this play pen, grateful that I could be in this space and not further out in the world I saw beyond the bars. I stayed in the comfortable space for a short time and really let myself feel it. It felt beautiful. I could also feel a sense of curiosity about what lay outside the bars.

The scene changed and I was six years old. By this stage I was at the tennis courts with my mother. It was a happy phase in her life. She was quite self-actualised, content with her friends and lifestyle. She was playing tennis, an "A" Grade pennant player, dressed in her whites. It was a sunny day. I could hear the impact of the tennis ball hitting the racquet and the sounds of the umpire calling "Net!", "Fault!" and "Love!" The sounds were deep and rich and I could sense the fullness of concentration the adults had upon the game. I watched for some time. It seemed important this game, every hit counted, every hit mattered. There were smiles enough once the game had ended, a generally good feeling as the ladies came off the court. Thermos flasks of tea and an array of various cakes were presented. Mum had made lemon meringue pie which was my favourite. It was all I could do to stop myself sneaking some before we left home. Mum had a sense of knowing where she was in the world and how to go about being in the world. I felt safe with her. She loved life and all with which she was presented. Over in a corner I could see a baby in a play pen. I went over to it whilst the women were chatting. As I held the bars and stood before it I watched it chew upon a crust that its mother had given it. I could sense the feeling of dependency and safety it had. Standing there I could feel myself in dilemma. I was six years old, too young to be as dependent as the child in the play pen and not old enough to be as confident and assured as my mother. I began to wonder why I was seeing this image and I began not to like the feeling of confusion I felt, so I asked within. I was aware that I really didn't want to be with my mother at this place although I was happy that she was happy. I could not be like the child in the play pen. I could not be like my mother. There was nowhere for me to be, no place for me and this was the essence of my confusion. An inner voice explained:

"You have choice now. The baby is completely dependent on others. The mother is fully active and the girl is hesitating between the two. The mother is happy, the baby is happy, but the girl is torn by indecision. You are thwarted by indecision."

"Indecision about what? " I asked.

About being here. Make full commitment to being alive, there is no need to fear it."

I could sense that I wanted to be like my mother. The voice told me I could do it and let myself love life to the fullest.

"Be open in your relationship, fully. Everything is there to have a full life. All you have to do is have it. To have it all, all that you have to do is to decide to have it. Your parents' ways of doing things do not have to be yours anymore. You are growing up. It has to do with choosing the right structure. You see, the little girl in you feels as though she never gets what she wants. You can help her grow and change that. When children teethe, they change from having the world look after them to accepting the world as different and becoming more independent in it. As you are now becoming adult in a real sense, you also have to move in your perceptions of the world and take responsibility, initiative and action. Do not be frightened to move forward. There is not the same need to ask for permission. When you were young, you needed the boundaries, the limits around you like the child in the play pen. These are changing. For you are becoming self-actualised in life. Your life is quite well defined, if you choose to see it, and the roots run deep, the foundation is strong. It has strength. Open to this strength. You have pain because of moving beyond the play pen and your fear is not being able to find a space for yourself in life. Many have this fear. It takes decision and will. You must take these. It has to come from you, then the universe can empower you in it. The first decision is to decide to live and love, the rest takes care of itself, you will see."

I thought about what I had been told and wondered how I could help the girl within me grow up. I had found it difficult to contain her, for at times she got very angry. For even though I was an adult I could feel her within me, an explosion of childish emotion with no basis in rationality. She would appear when I would least expect her to and create havoc in my life. She seemed selfish and stubborn and I had taken to doing things that she wanted as it seemed to be the only way to deal with her.

"How can I help her grow?" I asked.

"Just recognise her and don't be controlled by her. She demands much and doesn't want things to change. Watch out for her, you will see her more clearly now that I have pointed her out, speak to her and comfort her but do not let her take control. She will not be able to manipulate you in the way that she has done for she has been exposed like the nerve of the tooth. It will not take long to heal, it will just take awareness, love and patience and these qualities are being developed within you. It takes time to change one's perceptions of the world, especially when one keeps anticipating failure, or the manifestation of one's fears and doubts. To look at the world from a positive viewpoint, to see that life might not be as bad as you think it is, or as bad as you have painted your past, all this takes time. Be patient with yourself. There are parts of you that need to be healed in order that you may become whole. These parts are showing themselves to you now. Trust this part of your process, for it will lead to wholeness, into a full and loving life."

From a very deep place I asked to be able to see, understand and release the pain that I needed to release. A scene presented itself to me from my childhood. I could see my father. He was in a psychiatric hospital and had been receiving shock treatment. This particular day I went with my mother to see him. The hospital had been painted white, but a long time ago. It was more cream now with the years of living imprinted on the walls. We came to a wall which had bars on it and a nurse came along. She had a set of keys and she unlocked the door. We began walking down the corridor. There were a number of people in this hospital. I was quite young, about eight. We passed cells of people. You could see them in the rooms in white strait-jackets. My father was in a ward at the end of the corridor. I could not understand the feelings I had here. I focused on waiting to see my father. Immediately I saw him I ran to him. It was his birthday. I had brought him some liquorice which was his favourite. He had been in hospital for some time. I hadn't yet understood that it would be some time longer before he would be home. We visited as usual for an hour and a half and my mother told me it was time to leave. From within I could feel an enormous burst of need and I ran to him and threw my arms around him and said,

"Daddy, why can't you come home? Why are they keeping you here?"

As I saw this vision within my mind, I felt enormous pain within my heart. I couldn't understand why my father, who had always been there for me, who had always put me to bed at night, whose love I'd always felt like a warm sunbeam, all of a sudden was not in my life. As I connected with him in this hug, I reconnected to the warmth of the bodily touch I needed. I could feel the fire in his blood, that feeling that I loved so much. He said, " It's okay love, it's the best thing."

Somewhere deep within me though, I didn't understand, I was too young, but I could sense that it must be right because he said so and I trusted him. I left with my mother.

The pain I felt was very deep. I cried and cried. I was beginning to face the deep pain I needed to see within me. I knew that if I began to listen more, and became aware, the way would become easier.

I knew within me that another healing process was beginning. These were some of the leaves that were growing on the plant that I was watering. They had come from the seeds of healing. I was giving it space and time and I had to give it more space and time. I could feel the process was well underway. I'd been fortunate my father was still alive and well. I am able to love him now and feel love from him. Still, there are pains from my childhood that need love and light in order to heal. I am aware that as the leaves unfold in this healing plant that grows within me, so too do the flowers and fruits of that tree. Everytime I get understanding from a leaf I know the fruit and the flowers are not far away. That is why the little girl inside thinks she can never get what *she wants because she wanted her father so much and wasn't allowed to have him. But she does have him now. He is within her and comes as an aspect of herself that she can develop. It is for me to teach her that and to show her that by bringing in those qualities of protection and caring. Although my father is still alive and well and loving I cannot expect him to heal the child within me now. I began to realise I have to be both my mother and father now as a grown up. I have to love myself, protect and care for myself and provide a space for myself in the world. I am no longer a child, my father is no longer ill and I must come forward into the now for that is all there is. I must let go of my past in order that it may heal and so allow myself to move into the present and future, in a full positive loving way. Being parent to my own child, I walk hand in hand with my Mother-Father God-Self.*

Empowering the higher mind

As we open to coming to know ourselves we discover the role the mind plays in creating who we are. We often become what we think and make others into what we perceive them to be. On the path to becoming whole the step of empowering the higher mind is a potent step. It helps us to acquire a greater awareness of ourselves. As well as empowering our higher mind we need to gain control over our lower mind and make it functional for us.

The mind as our own worst enemy

For many years I've been sitting in front of people on a one-to-one basis, people with problems of many different kinds, from losing a partner to trying to figure out what to buy at the supermarket, to simply trying to be themselves. One of the major factors causing problems for people is the lack of understanding of the role that the mind plays in our lives. Often a person's circumstances may not be so bad, but the mind makes it seem so. Sometimes traumatic circumstances are given to a person to facilitate some sort of growth or understanding or to push someone a little towards some wisdom. The way we often respond to such gifts from the heavenly worlds is to say "no, not now!" or "no, this is too much!" or "just go away!" The mind comes in and starts with its little churning thoughts. There is a very great need on the Earth now, amongst humanity, to bring the mind under control - that is, the mind that goes haywire, that makes everybody else into our enemies and ourselves into the worst type of person through its negative thoughts and energy. Our mind, when left unchecked, can become our own worst enemy. We all have a mind which we have to deal with, and we can either let it work for us or work against us. It helps if we look at the mind objectively, as a part of us that we are responsible for.

The mind as a valuable tool

The mind is not always used negatively and can be a very valuable tool. Within it we find common sense. It tells us to think before we act. It can work in a very good way and prevent us from getting into some messy situations, if we choose to hear it and listen. When we hear it, it can change our reality. The mind has the capacity to change our reality through the thoughts that we have. When we understand this we begin to see that we have a choice of either going down in consciousness with the mind into the negative thoughts or we can choose to go up in consciousness with the mind, and then, transcending it, go into a higher consciousness. The mind acts as a tool for that choice. Will we start to create negative thoughts and therefore attract to ourselves and our lives negative situations, by attracting energies of the same low vibrating matter? Or will we choose instead, to think positive thoughts, or to look at them if they are negative, stop them, change them into something positive, and lift in consciousness to a positive state of being? The mind is a very powerful part of the healing process.

Thoughtforms

Theosophy (the study of Divine Wisdom) teaches us about thoughtforms. Thoughtforms are the forms or matter created by our thoughts. They have a life unto themselves. We will not go into detail about thoughtforms and how they are created scientifically. A detailed account of how thoughtforms function, their life span, and an understanding of the inner bodies they come from [that is, the emotional (astral) and thinking (mental) body] is given in Charles Leadbeater's book, *Thoughtforms* (1986). We will, however, acknowledge the reality of thoughtforms and consider the impact that they have, in being created by and in affecting the mind. For example, if we get in the car and begin to drive to work and start to think about something that is bothering us, we will find that the more we focus over and over again on that particular thought or issue, the stronger it will become. We create its strength by giving energy to it. The energy given creates a cemented or concrete thoughtform. The more attention we give to it, the more difficult it is to let it simply disperse or just let it go. By our thoughts, we often make issues bigger than they need to be. What we then battle with is not so much the issue, but where we have taken the issue to in our mind. Sometimes we simply start with a hypothetical thought, such as

"What if she doesn't like me?"

The "what if" is the clue to the thought being a hypothesis. We don't know whether she likes me or not. Yet before long, especially when the negative sense of self comes in on the scene, we become convinced that

"She doesn't like me!"

The thought process may go something like

"What if she doesn't like me? She doesn't smile at me, she must hate me. She hates me. How dare she hate me, I'll show her!"

The initial question, perhaps coming from a poor self-esteem, goes through a scientific process of gathering information to prove the worst. In this case the proof needed is simply that she doesn't smile. If we were to conduct a thorough scientific process we might look further. Perhaps there are other reasons for her not smiling. Perhaps she is preoccupied. Perhaps she hasn't even seen me. Perhaps smiling isn't something she generally does to anyone, even those she likes. This more thorough scientific enquiry is rarely employed, however, when we are trying to gather evidence to support our low self-esteem. Instead we suggest:

"See, told you so, nobody likes me, she doesn't like me, why should she?"

How can we create positive thoughts?

The example above gives us a few keys for studying the mind and for seeing how it works. It also gives some keys as to how to create positive thoughts instead of negative thoughts and in so doing to help heal the mind. What are the keys? Let us look first of all at the mind's thoughts in the quotation marks. The thoughts of the mind are commonly referred to in psychology as "self-talk." It is the chatter that goes on in our minds, the things we tell ourselves, the positive and negative thoughts about situations, issues, ourselves and others. Positive self-talk has to do with thoughts that are positive, and negative self-talk has to do with thoughts we have that are negative. Our negative self-talk is often characterised by quite a pessimistic outlook. Often it is absolute, employing language within it such as "she doesn't," "she must"- that is, there is no room for doubt, everything is black or white, there are no in-betweens. When we recognise this about negative self-talk, it becomes easier to be aware of when we are running negative self-talk in our minds. When we become aware of it, the first step to change it to positive self-talk is to question its relation to reality. In the case above we did this by finding possible options for other reasons why she might not smile, rather than taking it as a total proof that "she doesn't like me." We question the absolutist thoughts and think of other possibilities, other options, and are not so quick to simply grab whatever evidence we can to prove our negative beliefs which underlie the general theme of the self-talk. By taking our self-talk into check, that is, seeing how it fits in with reality, we find ourselves creating another reality. It can provide us with a way to remain balanced and realistic about who we are and what is happening to us. We can, through this process, start to root out what is behind our low self-esteem. We are also using the mind, the intellect, in a positive way, using the logic of the mind to prove to the mind that a part of it has gotten out of touch with reality. We meet the mind and stop it from playing unhealthy games. In essence, we wake it up and have it begin working for our good. In the example above we would tell it that, in the light of the fact that we cannot be sure why "she doesn't smile at me," we cannot reasonably assume that "she doesn't like me" and therefore, realistically, we need to reserve our judgement.

The power of thought

When we think about a fear we may have, perhaps a fear of being seen, or a fear of having some part of us that we like to keep private exposed, we can create a strong thoughtform which will, if we leave it unchecked for too long, attract the very thing that we are trying to avoid. As a human being, we have a soul, we have our mind, our emotions, and our physical body. The mind, the emotions and the physical body make up our personality. It is in the personality that our mind, emotions and physical body interrelate. When we start to think, our emotions can attach to our thoughts, especially if we are thinking about something we desire. Maybe we desire a chocolate, or to have a relationship with someone, or to leave our job and so we start to think about and put energy into that. The matter of the thoughtform related to our desire exists on a particular vibration of energy which will attract to itself other matter of the same vibration. This may then attract other people to us who will play out part of our drama because of their own thoughts and desires which link into ours. We may attract a situation then, if we put too much energy into a particular thoughtform and associated desires, where we will leave our job. We may eventually become convinced by our mind and by the increasing weight of energy for those thoughts that it is the right thing. Suddenly another job comes along, just the job we've been waiting for, and we have our excuse to leave. Is it the job we've been waiting for, or is it that we've put in so much energy and created the thoughtform which attracts it?

It may not be what we really want to do at all. It may simply be that we cannot control our mind and emotions in a balanced way and so they get out of control and we act accordingly, leaving ourselves then to deal with a situation we are not really happy with. In this way we can become victims to our own thoughts and feelings. We need, therefore, to begin to be careful what we spend time thinking about. If we think it for too long, and it is not something we particularly want to have happen, we may well cause it to happen.

The mind needs to be watched. It can become a vehicle for negativity as well as positivity. When we focus on negativity and simply let the mind run with it, we do not work for our good or the good of others.

The role of our self-talk

Our thoughts really influence our actions. Say, for example, I see an acquaintance called Genevieve and I think about saying hello. I saw her last week and I don't think she likes me. When I go to say hello, my self-talk, which I hear as a little voice in the background, says, "she doesn't like me." I listen to it and I believe it, and instead of saying hello I stay quiet and walk by, because I've listened and given power to this thought. My sense, my feeling, my heart-felt thought was to go towards her and say hello, but the negative self-talk of my mind actually makes me do otherwise.

Let us take another example. Say you have a fear of authorities and you have to go and hand in your exam paper which is a week late and you have forgotten to ask for an extension. To do that you have to go and meet the very lecturer who you fear the most. What would you be telling yourself?

"He won't accept it" or
"Go ahead and do it."

Here we have one example of negative self-talk and one of a more positive self-talk that gives you encouragement. However, if you were to continue in the negative mode of self-talk, what could you tell yourself?

"No one has ever liked me. I'm always late. Everyone will know that I'm hopeless."

The fear of being rejected and ridiculed starts to rise up. Imagine how you feel when you walk up to that lecturer. Can you imagine it? The stomach region feels as if it is tied into a knot - gurgle, gurgle, gurgle - and all around becomes blurred as you begin to sweat and become more and more tense. Your lecturer is sitting there, feeling calm, serene, and not particularly perturbed by anything, very peaceful in fact. But to you he looks like a monster, and you feel totally stupid. The thoughts and feelings are so stirred up within you that the reality is distorted. You are so caught up in your self-centred thoughts that you don't see beyond yourself. The thoughts are self-centred because in the process of thinking that your lecturer doesn't like you, you do not consider that your lecturer might have a very busy schedule, lots of other students, a life outside of this relationship, and that you handing in your assignment late might not have the same meaning for him that it has for you. If you could see beyond yourself and really thought about these things, you might be a bit more relaxed and might just say something like, "Here's my assignment, it's a week late but I've done it." It is these day-to-day seemingly small things that can perturb us a great deal. If we learn to work with our self-talk we can reduce our stress quite considerably.

You may be able to think of your own example or situation where you become unnecessarily stressed by your own mind. Just allow yourself to think about it now. What was the situation? What was your self-talk, that is, what were you telling yourself before the situation, during the situation, after the situation? Did your self-talk help the situation? Did your self-talk make it worse? Think about how you would change your self-talk to stop that situation from occurring. What could you tell yourself instead, before, during and after that event? If you start to work with your self-talk on a daily basis it is amazing how much you can transform your experience of your day to day life.

In Cognitive Behaviour Therapy Meichenbaum (1977), suggests that our self-talk affects our state of well-being, and that we can be aided by exposing our self-talk and by self regulating or controlling our actions and speech. It was Meichenbaum who devised the method whereby our self-talk is looked at before, during and after a situation we may generally find stressful, and work to use our self-talk to help us cope. We can change our thoughts *before* we come to an event that we would consider to be stress provoking; work on changing our thoughts *during* the event; and *afterwards* tell ourselves something positive about that event. In the example earlier of the student handing in a late assignment to a lecturer he or she fears, the self-talk of the student could be looked at by considering "What were you telling yourself as you prepared to go to meet the lecturer? What were you telling yourself while you were with the lecturer? What did you tell yourself afterwards about that event? How did that make you feel? What could you have told yourself before that would help you? What could you tell yourself during that would help you remain calm? What could you tell yourself afterwards that would help you? How would that make you feel?"

The focus is not on getting rid of the anxiety. It is on re-training ourselves to use self-talk that assists us rather than self-talk that works against us. We can look at our negative self-talk and irrational beliefs and learn to talk ourselves through situations. "This may upset me but I know how to deal with it." The steps are:

1. Preparing
2. Confronting
3. Handling (coping with overwhelming feelings)
4. Reinforcing positive self statements (even if you don't get the desired reaction).

Let's take an example of a time when you've been angry, you've said nothing and in your state of passivity you've let a feeling of resentment build. After a while you begin to experience a sense of shame because you know that you are not expressing your true self. A form of self-pity, "poor me," creeps in. The energy of self-pity attracts to it other lower thoughtforms, such as a sense of guilt and fear. The negative self-talk - "I'm no good!" starts. In your mind you begin to get aggressive, and start projecting upon the other person. Projection is when you have something going on in yourself and instead of owning it and taking responsibility for it you see it in (project it onto) others. It may lead to blame and anger and stimulate other negative self-talk, for example, "you're no good!" Either you beat up yourself or you beat up another person in your mind. Both are just as detrimental to your state of health. It doesn't help to beat up other people, either in your mind or in action, because you will suffer the karmic consequences. Like attracts like, and you will attract back what you give out. So even if you are really tight-lipped and you never actually tell the person your negative thoughts towards him or her, but continue to think them all the time, you are causing that person harm.

We need to listen to our self-talk and think about the effects we are creating by it. By constantly telling ourselves we are no good, or that we won't get things right, we effectively undermine ourselves and sabotage our possibilities for success. By constantly affirming negative things about others we sabotage any potential for a genuine relationship with them and we totally distort our perception of the truth of who they are.

Personal rules

In *Rational Emotive Therapy: a skills based approach*, Albert Ellis (1980) developed an approach to help challenge the negative mind. He claims that people have unrealistic personal rules which need to be challenged if the mind is to re-establish itself in balance. An example of such a personal rule would be "I must never be late for anything." Richard Nelson-Jones (1990, p. 51) in his book, *Thinking Skills*, describes these personal rules as

> ... the do's and don'ts by which you lead your life. Each of you has an inner rule book that guides your living. You may be aware of some of your rules, but there are others of which you are unaware. Some of the latter may be fairly easy to bring to the surface; however, others are more threatening and anxiety provoking. Consequently you may have more difficulty acknowledging them.

Personal rules can form part of our unconscious, from which they strongly affect our feeling, thoughts and actions. As they are personal rules, we demand that they be followed; otherwise, we get angry and upset. It is only by awareness, choice and action that we can hope to change them. First, though, we need to identify them, and that is not always easy. Here are some clues. Sometimes we can find them lurking beneath persistent inappropriate feelings, for example, excessive anger or harmful actions that are not appropriate to the situation (Nelson-Jones, 1990). Ellis (1980) suggests they are characterised by "musts," "oughts" and "shoulds."

The following are examples of personal rules that are, as Ellis suggests, "mustabatory:" "I must get what I want," "Others must be kind and considerate to me," "The place in which I work must revolve around my needs." Through our personal rules we make demands on ourselves, others and our environment. If they are not followed, our ego gets disturbed and we experience emotional discomfort, often in the form of frustration, which may become acute annoyance towards those whom we see as not adhering to them. We often "catastrophise" if they are not adhered to; we demand perfection, have no flexibility, and have a high degree of frustration if we see them not being followed as a result of ours or another's imperfection. Unrealistic personal rules are based on irrational beliefs. To change them to more realistic rules we need to challenge the beliefs, or as it is classically referred to, dispute the false assumptions that we hold about ourselves, others and the world. Having done that, we then need to reformulate beliefs and subsequently, the rules.

Our personal rules are deeply internalised. We need to look at our inner talk to find them. Often accompanying them we have things we tell ourselves to make sure they are followed, for example, "be liked," "be in control," "achieve at all costs," "be kind," "always get what you can," "always give to others before yourself." Nelson-Jones (1990) sees them as internalised directives which create pressure. They may also take the form of "don'ts". For example, "don't think," "don't trust," "don't feel," "don't take risks." We generally have a lot of rules we try to live by, our own and what we perceive as rules others enforce. We must always remember that the way we choose to live, the rules we choose to live by, are our own, and we are responsible for them. If we are too pressured by them, and living under the stress of them, we need to look at them and reformulate them to better suit our needs.

Speaking your mind

Sometimes to actually speak your mind, to give it expression, is one of the best ways to heal it. The mind, like muscles, begins to atrophy if it is not used. We need to use it in good ways. One way to help is to start to speak your mind, to express your mind, say what's on it. All the things you've been driving around thinking about or sitting at home thinking about, you start to say to someone else who's there to hear you, for example, a friend, or a counsellor in a counselling situation. The simple act of speaking it out can bring a lot of release of built-up pressure. The counsellor or friend can help just by listening to what has been stored up. As it is released, balance is slowly found again. Sometimes, we immediately see that what was on our mind and disturbing us is actually not even true. Other times it may be true. Talking to another allows us to bring our thoughts into the Light, air them and discover their truth. Working in such a way, where a person expresses his or her "stuff," enables the person to see what the "stuff" is made of. When working this way with anger, for example, the person, after expressing the anger with particular people, usually comes to see his or her own part in creating the situation, and often finds the anger held towards him- or herself. The exposure of this anger is usually enough to help the person decide to take responsibility again, instead of just blaming the other or others involved. There is release of anger through expression, through being heard, which enables the person to get a better grip, find rationality and the heart again, and go on.

In this process of expression and healing we get a more objective view and find out what is really going on beneath the surface. If a person has some congestion in the aura from an old emotional experience, a healer will work with that and "smooth it out." In counselling the same is done with the mind; the counsellor listens for where there is congestion in the thoughts or the emotions of a person, and may just reflect that to the person and help the person to realise or feel it is there. Together they may work out what the underlying congestion might be, for example, guilt, fear, anger or resentment. Another person's help is invaluable in seeing where our mind gets stuck, where the rut of the overload is. "There's that thought again, I can't seem to get out of it, how do I get out of this thought, it's there all the time, whenever I'm alone it seems to come back again and it is always the same, it never seems to change, how can I change it? I pray, I try all the time, I try to think positively, but it's still there!" To speak it out is like getting a knot in hair that's completely tangled and undoing it hair by hair until the knot is released. Sometimes we have to do that with our mind because of the energy we've put into building the thoughtforms in the first place. In our ignorance we create thoughtforms and then we become victim to them. We put in all our energy and make them very strong until they don't need much from us anymore, just a little thought now and then is enough to feed and sustain it. Counselling, healing and meditation all help. When we start with these processes we begin to see, "well, hang on a minute, what is that knot?" and we start to look at it.

"Oh, I've created it, I've created it from all my thoughts, my thoughts about this, my thoughts about him, my thoughts about her, my thoughts about me. I have created this and it's a monster and now I'm its victim!"

Taking responsibility

The negative thoughtforms we create cause negativity between people and conflict within ourselves. We create a low vibration of matter and affect everything around us. We make it difficult for ourselves to find peace and harmony, and we are the ones who are responsible. The degree to which we are prepared to take responsibility for what we create in our life through our thoughts, feelings and actions marks the degree to which we will be able to grow and develop. If we choose to blame others constantly for our lot in life, we will not grow, but stagnate in the illusion we create. In relationship conflicts people often blame the other rather than looking at their own behaviour. We will also stagnate, often through stress and depression, if we constantly blame ourselves for all our problems and so take too much responsibility and blame ourselves. If we wish to live life in truth and cease to be harmful to ourselves and others, we must own responsibility for our own lives.

Nelson-Jones (1990, p. 26), gives us the following personal responsibility credo:

> I am personally responsible for my choices regarding how I think, feel, and act in relation to myself, others and the environment.
> Within the realistic limitations of my existence, I make my life through my choices.
> I am always a chooser.
> My choices always have consequences for good or ill.
> My choices always have costs.
> The sum of my life is the sum of the consequences of my choices.

We can free ourselves from the trappings of our mind by thinking about how we think and by taking responsibility for what we are thinking, by realising we have a choice about what and how we think. Choosing to take control of our mind helps us to learn how we can influence how we feel and act. We can develop a capacity for thinking about thinking which will in turn help us to remove blocks in our emotions and our abilities to act.

The relationship between thoughts, feelings and actions

There is a direct relationship between our thoughts, our feelings and our actions. We very quickly put our thoughts to action, and to feeling. In psychology there are many schools of thought about the relationship between our thoughts, feelings and actions. Cognitive Behaviour Therapy (Meichenbaum, 1977) points to a direct relationship between what we think (cognitive) and how we act (behavioural). Psychologists have not figured out which comes first. Is it the thought, the feeling, the act? Which do you think? Is it one or the other or does it vary? I guess it doesn't really matter whether it is the chicken or the egg which comes first; both have their purposes and there certainly is a direct relationship between them. Simply by acknowledging the relationship we can do a lot to find ways of working to better our thoughts, feelings and actions.

In *Reason and Emotion in Psychotherapy* (1963) and *A New Guide to Rational Living* (1975), Ellis suggests that it is not our emotions which create disturbances in us, but our thoughts, or at least the beliefs we hold about certain events. He suggests that it is our thoughts which affect our state of being. In challenging these thoughts or beliefs, that is, by making them rational and alignming them with reality, our behaviours and perceptions of ourselves and our world become more balanced. We hold beliefs that are both rational and irrational. These beliefs determine our worldview and how we see ourselves. By dealing with our irrational beliefs we move towards wholeness.

While it is helpful to hold a person in unconditional positive regard and acceptance, the person's behaviours and irrational beliefs do not need to be held in such regard and can be disputed in a direct and active way. If we become aware of our irrational beliefs and dispute them, we can change them (Ellis, 1962).

Ellis (1962) outlined eleven commonly held irrational beliefs that provide the basis for this theory. He suggests that these irrational ideas cause and sustain emotional disturbances. For the purposes of brevity they are presented in my own words:

1. I must be loved and approved of by everyone.
2. I must be perfect in all respects to be okay.
3. Some people are evil and must be punished.
4. It is awful if things aren't as I would like.
5. If I am unhappy it is other people's fault and I can't help it.
6. I must worry about dangerous possibilities.
7. I must avoid difficulties in life.
8. I am dependent on others. I need strong people around.
9. I am this way because of my past. I will always be affected by it.
10. I am upset by the problems of others.
11. There is a right and perfect solution to all problems and it is a catastrophe if that solution is not found.

Ellis claims that these are distorted perceptions people commonly have about the world and that, as we let them go, we move towards a happier existence. By challenging our irrationality we discover "an anti-awfulising, anti-demanding, anti-indulgent, and anti-whining outlook" (Ellis, 1980, p. 14). In later years the eleven irrational ideas were reduced to three:

1. "I must do well and win approval for my performances, or else I rate as a rotten person" (Ellis, 1980, p. 5).

2. "Others must treat me considerately and kindly, in precisely the way I want them to treat me; if they don't, society and the universe should severely blame, damn, and punish them for their inconsiderateness" (Ellis, 1980, p. 6).

3. "Conditions under which I live must be arranged so that I get practically everything I want, comfortably, quickly and easily, and get virtually nothing I don't want" (Ellis, 1980, p. 7).

What is common in the irrational beliefs are the underlying statements in each. In *A Practitioners Guide to Rational Emotive Therapy*, Walen, DiGiuseppe and Wessler (1980, p. 115) outline the underlying statements as "should statements, awfulizing statements and need statements." The therapist challenges the accuracy of the person's perception.

In *Cognitive Behaviour Modification*, Meichenbaum (1977) suggests that there are a number of things to look for when reviewing our inner self-talk. They are:

- when we have two different ways of thinking, either it is black or it is white, there is no in between;
- when we personalise something which need not be personalised and use subjective reasoning instead of objective reasoning;
- when we over-generalise (to infer a general principle from specific facts in a way that takes things too far);
- when we magnify or minimise a situation or ourselves with our mind (exaggeration and under-estimation);
- when we have a fuzzy line between something that is fact and what we are inferring about it.

Meichenbaum also suggests we consider the role of our negative view of self and the impact of seeing ourselves as inadequate, worthless and hopeless.

Considering our self-talk - what does it reveal?

When we look at our negative self-talk, we begin to see how damaging it is and how strong the negative patterning is in us. Is it any wonder things are not going as well in our lives as we would like? At times in my own work with people, when we look at the underlying self-talk of stressful situations, patterns from the past reveal themselves to be healed. Sometimes traumas from our past or negative patterns of contorted beliefs appear which are obviously outmoded and need updating. The negative self-talk has a huge array of associated feelings which can seriously affect even our physical health. A number of people I counsel suffer from acute anxiety in group situations. Their self-talk is invariably very negative when the group situations occur. On looking at a person's self-talk, underlying issues of low self-esteem become evident. In some cases the source of the low self-esteem can come from the past, for example, from guilt for actions taken that have not ever been really understood or forgiven. We need to learn to discriminate about what we remember from the past and about what we do with that memory when we have it. It is of no value in terms of our healing to remember the past and to use it to continue to hold grievances towards another, merely using it as a source for finding yet more ammunition of times when we have been wronged. Nor is it of value to find yet more instances of things we can feel guilty about. This behaviour simply perpetuates a negative cycle and no development is made. Development comes when we, through right use of our memory, put Light into our past and come to learn the lessons we need to learn through it - when we begin to develop the qualities of love, forgiveness and compassion for others and ourselves and acknowledge that we are all human beings with strengths and weaknesses.

Acknowledging the role of the past

In looking at our past we become aware of the strong impact it has had on us. Our childhood, for example, helps us to formulate our own inner parents that are part of our psyche. Here again we do not need to remain victim to our childhood. Whether we have had a rough childhood or whether we have had a more settled one (which can sometimes give all the problems of a really rough one) we are influenced by it, but we are not without power to effectively change and heal that within us. We carry the family dynamic with us in our psyche. We have an inner mother, father, brother, sister - the dynamics of which we project out onto organisations, onto groups of friends and to work colleagues. Other people become like an empty coat hanger onto whom we put the coat of our unresolved issues. With qualified help in therapy, we can become aware of this phenomenon and actively work to change it.

We all have our own inner child who needs help and healing. Healing comes when we acknowledge this and begin to take responsibility for it. To take responsibility we need to put in the time and effort required to know ourselves. We need to revisit our past and heal the wounds we find, with compassion and love. Such has been the focus of psychology for many centuries. It requires effort, diligence, perseverance and courage to face the truth of who we are. Only when we do that can we begin to think and work on what we might become.

We can learn from our past experiences; sometimes instead we choose to trip up again and again. If you wish to choose the path of learning from your experiences, the following tasks provide some ways to review the past and "re-view" their meaning for you.

Think about a time in the past, recent or distant, where you felt you dealt with a situation quite well. Describe the situation and write down what you did to successfully deal with the situation. What were your strengths? List them.

Think about a time in your past which was not successfully dealt with. Describe the situation and write down what you did that caused the situation. What were your weaknesses? List them.

Think of a more current situation which you need to deal with. Try to visualise how you could utilise the strengths learned in the situation where you dealt with the situation successfully. Try to think what you could do to make sure you do not create the same mistakes due to the weaknesses of the unsuccessful situation. What can you do to ensure that you do this?

Allowing room for weaknesses

When we begin to see that, as humans, we are made up of strengths and weaknesses; when we get to a point of not judging ourselves and others about this, and let go of the need to be perfect, we begin to learn the lessons of tolerance, humility, and acceptance. We all have strengths and we all have weaknesses. To have them doesn't make us good or bad, it is simply part of being human. Unfortunately, many see weaknesses as a fault or a negative thing. A weakness is something that perhaps we haven't yet developed, or around which we have some struggle or issue, for whatever reason. If we can learn to accept others, ourselves and our lives, we could rest our mind from the constant battle around "not being good enough." To do this does not mean that we would not try to better ourselves or our lives, learn new skills and develop better qualities. It does mean that we would overcome our negative perfectionist and judgemental qualities, become more realistic and honest in our lives and may even surrender more to life and learn to trust. We could learn to relax.

Deciding to change and not blame

If we are not happy with something in our life, instead of simply being negative about it in our minds, we can use the mind to think about what we can do to change it. We can:

1. Be honest when we don't agree instead of keeping silent.
2. Accept what we are feeling.
3. Act if we see something unfair, do something about it.
4. Tell people honestly what we think and feel.
5. Give others and ourselves time and be patient.
6. Write a letter.
7. Let the matter go and not say anything, provided we can truly let it go.
8. Acknowledge and accept our strengths and weaknesses, know our abilities and our limitations.
9. Be prepared to face our emotions and inner patterns, explore ourselves and make the unconscious conscious.
10. Write down things we are learning, keep a journal (we often learn simply from writing things down).

Making space for the joy of life

People spend a lot of time in negative thought processes. Can you imagine what we could do with our minds if the negative thought processes stopped and space became available for other more positive activities of the mind? Can you imagine having space to dream, imagine and create with the mind? In 1990 I had an experience of depression for a number of months. My thoughts were quite negative and spiralling downwards. They were very self-centred and paranoid. I was often thinking that others were having negative thoughts about me and I would spend a lot of time in my mind in self-defence. I would have running dialogues with people based on my hypotheses which would quickly turn into absolute negatives. I would run a whole court scene with my own inner lawyers and jury. I was convinced no one liked me, that I could never do things right, that others were far superior in their intelligence. All they had to do to have me totally convinced of this was to be silent or arrogant and they would immediately, by me, be given all the power in the relationship. If, on the other hand, they displayed a similar lack of confidence to mine, I would seize the opportunity to bolster my ego and raise myself up in power over them, just so I could keep some sense of self-esteem. Then one day this obvious imbalance began to become obvious to me. I had developed an observer-self who had been noticing that for a very long time I was telling myself, far too often, just how worthless I really was. I became desperate within the low self-esteem, and I prayed for help to stop this destructive cycle. The words came:

"When in self-doubt ... remember.... You must realise that you are nothing and you are Everything because I Am in you and I Am Everything. When you doubt yourself, you doubt Me. The energy of doubt will go away when you realise this."

I had a lot of doubt about myself which I had projected onto others and onto God. I thought that God had no confidence in me either, but I was wrong. I had allowed my mind to take over my vehicle and sit in the driver's seat. I had lost my power, not to God or to others, but to my own negative, imbalanced mind. To allow inner balance to return to my life I had to let Spirit take the driver's seat, to realise that without Spirit I am nothing and with Spirit I am Everything. With Spirit I can co-create a balanced, loving, healthy and whole life. Soon after this realisation began to sink in, I found that my mind, which before had been clogged by self-centred and negative self-damning thoughts, became quite empty for a time. It was very strange. Soon thereafter a creative mind seemed to fill the space, one that was positive, that thought constructively, that employed imagination, that had ideas and enthusiasm to carry them out. This new creative mind I came to know as Spirit. What a relief it was to have that in the driver's seat! What a difference to life! I couldn't believe it! I wanted to tell the world, "Hey, just stop your negative mind and see what happens, it's amazing!" The energy, the enthusiasm, the capacities it had were a revelation to me, and with this energy I proceeded to write my first book, *The Language of the Heart: is spoken all over the world* (1991). In a way this title represented the new language that I found when finally I began to slay the dragon of the lower mind. There is another language in us besides the negative lower mind, one that is governed by heart. With persistence and will it can be uncovered and placed in the driver's seat where it belongs.

The two aspects of mind - the higher and the lower

Spirit helps to lift our thoughts, feelings and actions to a higher place, and our consciousness changes. We begin to become aware of a higher reality. We also begin to be able to distinguish between the higher mind and the lower mind. As mentioned earlier, the lower mind embodies the intellect. It is where our thoughts come from. The higher mind is one with the Divine Mind. It is a higher intelligence, which relates to higher aspects of our being, functioning where there is no form. The ability to differentiate between the two minds assists us to bring the personality into check, as we also recognise that the lower mind is a part of us that - rather than being in control of us - is best utilised as a servant to the higher mind.

In order to start to heal ourselves from the effects of the mind we can do two things. First, we can become alert to the power of our thoughts and be aware of the reality our thoughts can create. Second, we can become alert to the higher mind and open to discovering the power of the higher mind in helping us lift out of mundane thoughts into a higher consciousness. We can often get trapped by the illusion and limitations of the lower mind.

By recognising and controlling our tendency to be caught by the limitations of our thoughts, and by cultivating awareness, concentration and meditation, we can break through the illusions of the lower mind and enter into the higher mind. We allow Spirit to take over. When we become one with the higher mind, we find the Light within, and truth can be experienced.

Through our intellect, truth is made intelligible to others; it is the instrument through which the inner vision can be interpreted. It is also the instrument we use to decide what aspects of our experience we have to communicate. The intellect serves a valuable function. Even the processes of the lower mind such as daydreaming and scientific thought, when used appropriately, are of value. The intellect is the instrument, the higher mind is the living power within. Through concentration and meditation we can quieten the intellectual instrument so it can appropriately serve the higher mind.

Buddha's teachings and the mind

Buddhism is in part a study of the mind. It recognises and acknowledges the wisdom of the mind and also the power of emptiness of the mind - that we can empty the mind of our thoughts and thereby raise our consciousness to the higher mind. The higher mind can give us beautiful insights that lift us out of our problems and take them away. The higher mind can function during meditation, healing, guided imagery, and role-play as well as at other times, revealing to us the language of Spirit and the language of the heart.

In the Noble Eightfold Path which consists of guidelines for balanced living, Lord Buddha gives the step of Right Mindfulness. He suggests we cultivate mindfulness for our own and others' protection. Mindfulness is a state of awareness of or attention to the moment. Right Mindfulness is to become detached from thoughts of self. It involves paying systematic attention and not drifting into ignorance or a thirst for becoming. It is about remaining aware and staying present. The Buddhists say, "when you walk, walk. Don't wobble." Through mindfulness we can cultivate harmlessness, loving kindness and compassion and become conscious of our thoughts, words and acts. Mindfulness guards against deviation from goodness and encourages us to do good. It involves training our mind to examine things in such a way as to recognise what is important and not be led astray. We must be mindful with our body, our feelings, and the ideas that arise in our mind. When we pay proper regard to these fundamentals of mindfulness, we can move towards enlightenment.We need to apply mindfulness to everything we do, in all our movements, whether we stand, sit, speak, stay silent, eat or drink. Right Mindfulness helps us to understand and clearly comprehend.

Right Memory is an aspect of Right Mindfulness. Buddha suggests that we apply Right Memory to the world within and without, always, everywhere during our waking life - remembering the good, putting out of our mind the bad, always remaining mindful to cultivate the goodness. For example, if someone speaks unkindly to us and we keep it in our mind for weeks, months, even years it will not do us any good, it will only annoy us. There are some things we must forget. Right Memory consists not only of remembering the good things, but also in putting aside the negative things, for example, to let go of a grievance held, and find forgiveness.

We sometimes forget to have compassion. The Buddhists talk about the meditation of compassion where the focus is on bringing compassion into our lives. To do this effectively, compassion needs to enter into all aspects of life. It does not only mean that we develop compassion for the starving people in India or those who have had a hard life, it also means that we develop compassion for parts of our personality that aren't functioning as we would like. It means we cultivate compassion for the mind also. When we treat the mind with love and compassion, it has much more of a chance of healing. We must always remember that we create the thoughtforms that we allow ourselves to become victim to. Getting angry with them, trying to banish them will not help them to go away. We need to unravel them, have compassion for them, and dissolve them with love.

Ways of opening to the help of the higher mind

Guided imagery

Guided imagery helps a person to be more in touch with his or her inner nature. As mentioned earlier, guided imagery is a process in which we form a symbol to represent something that is going on for us, and then we talk to that symbol because it can tell us what we need to know about it. Symbols are the language of the higher mind. By communicating with and exploring its symbols, we open to the ideas of the higher mind. A symbol, may come in the form of an image, or a sense or a feeling. We talk to it, dialogue with it, and treat it like a friend. The person is asked to create a symbol which represents the wisest, kindest, most compassionate part of him- or herself, called the inner adviser. As this takes place, communication is developed between them. For example, the healer/therapist might ask, "Now that your inner adviser is here, is there anything it would like to say to you?" According to

Nimrod Sheinman (1987), in his handout *Medicine of the Mind*, union with this aspect of the self can be facilitated by the person "becoming" that aspect of him- or herself and looking back at him- or herself (through imagery), thus becoming aware of the discrepancies between the different selves and what needs to be done to integrate them.

Meditation

Meditation and yoga also facilitate our moving to a state of harmony and deepening the connection with the higher nature. It is a practice that we can undertake on our own. Meditation purifies our inner bodies, and it is a way in which we can start to enhance our alignment to our soul. It is a state of being in which we can invoke, visualise, affirm, and contemplate. The aim, according to Bailey in her book, *Letters on Occult Meditation* (1979, p. 145),

> should be the development of the habit of meditation all day long, and the living in the higher consciousness until that consciousness is so stable that the lower mind, desire and physical elementals become so atrophied and starved through lack of nourishment that the three-fold lower nature becomes simply the means whereby the Ego (the soul), contacts the world for the purposes of helping the race.

Bailey (1979) goes on to explain that meditation provides a vehicle whereby we can step out of the lower consciousness into the higher.

When we free ourselves from the self-centredness of the lower mind we access much greater energy. Imagine freeing up the amount of time and energy spent in these negative states. Suddenly you have a mind free to create - you could write books, you could create symphonies, you could build new houses with beautiful architecture. So much could be done with the space, the energy and the time that generally is used negatively. You could send prayers, heal every day, and set aside time to meditate, a time where you can learn to think positively and to slowly let these new-found thoughts take over each day. When you eat your lunch, you could actually start to notice the orange you are peeling and smell it, maybe even eat it section by section and notice the parts that are a bit dry, or a bit moist and taste it when you eat it. You will notice the world around and change it into a wondrous world that is yours to live in. You can begin to help others because you go beyond yourself; your self-pity and your anger fall away in that higher world and you become the being that you really are; the Lightbeing, ruled by your heart, with your mind a tool for your use, to help you understand things, comprehend and communicate your thoughts.

As a guideline to meditation, the Lord Djwhal Khul, one of the Masters known in Theosophy, suggests that we come to "know thy self." In the process of meditating we become truly acquainted with the self, come to know all the parts, the strengths, the weaknesses, the nice parts, the not-so-nice-parts, the healed parts, the not-so-healed parts. He also suggests we "study the effects, aim at regularity, proceed slowly and with caution, and cultivate the realisation that eternity is long and that which is slowly built up, endures forever" (Bailey, 1979, p. 95). Just as we have spent so many years cultivating our negativity, we can slowly turn it around and spend time cultivating positivity and gradually, something that endures, a peace, an ability to cope in life, trust, a faith starts to develop, and our nature changes.

Role-play

Use of role-play can help to make people aware of the different aspects of themselves and their relationship to others. It can also facilitate them becoming aware of where these different aspects of themselves have come from. As they become the different parts, for example, while they are in role, the therapist may stop midstream and ask the role, "who are you, what is your purpose, why are you here, where do you come from?" This has the effect of awakening the people to whether or not the role being played is how they actually feel or something they have learned from someone else. In seeing clearly the source, they can then choose whether they want that role to continue functioning in such a manner, or change it into alignment with their current needs.

Regression

Another approach to opening to the help of the higher mind is guiding the person to the period of time when his or her personal rules were established. This is done by consciously going back to that time in the person's memory (this may arise from the unconscious). The helper facilitates whatever changes are necessary to move the person into a state of healthy and whole functioning. In this way unrealistic personal rules may be released. For example, if the person in regression began to feel strong emotions, the helper would give him or her space to feel it, ask the person what is happening and keep the person in contact with the safety and security of the present environment while the desensitisation and release of the remembered event is taking place. The helper would ask questions such as "what's happening now?," "what decisions are you making?," thus bringing awareness of the decisions made and assisting the person to decide if that is still the decision he or she would like to live by. The person can both be in and observe the process in order to facilitate his or her own change.

Music, healing and mantra

Music and healing can lift us to the higher worlds, as can the use of mantras. Mantras are sentences that have higher meaning and may be repeated to create positive effects as well as positive vibrations. They may be affirmations of a higher energy, perhaps the name of a higher being, or an expression of devotion, or just an expression of the higher world. By chanting the names of "the Gods" we help create an energy whereby we can become like them, in that we lift to a higher vibration. Many in spiritual organisations take advantage of the calming effect of mantras. Music has a soothing effect. It can also calm our lower mind and take us to another state of consciousness.

Developing positive energies within us

We can work to change energies that perpetuate dysfunction by developing the opposite. For example, we can develop assertion and release anger; develop the ability to take personal responsibility and release blame and projection; develop a sense of justice and release defensiveness and develop good conscience and release guilt.

Our thoughts play an enormous role in the state of our well-being. There are many methods that can assist us in bringing the mind back into harmony. The role of the lower and higher mind is becoming increasingly noted in both spiritual and psychological fields of enquiry. Awareness of this and the decision to implement some of the methods designed to help heal the mind make positive change not only possible, but immanent. Let us open to the help available and transform our lives through healing the mind.

Looking for meaning

As we start to access the gifts of the higher mind and empower it, we begin to discover a consciousness which gives life meaning and purpose. In this day and age it seems that while many are making this connection to the higher mind, there are still many who are not. Many who, if only they knew it, could be greatly helped by doing so. As we approach the second millennium and go through a rapid introduction to the technological age, we find an increase in depression among people extending from those who have entered old age, those approaching and enduring the mid-life crisis, to youth depression and a large increase in youth suicide. The whiskers of depression enter into many suburban homes, affecting households world-wide - business people, drug-oriented people, home-makers, old, young and in-between. It is a sign that something is wrong and we are being asked to stop and look at what that is.

The whiskers are our barometer for when we run into something foreign. They are our protection. Just as humanity is depleting the Earth of its resources, so are we depleting ourselves of resources needed to maintain meaning in our lives. The rapid advancement of technology and its consequences have meant, for many, movement away from the Earth and the enthusiasm of life lived close to nature and connected to Spirit. If we wish to tune in with God, it is often through high rise floors filled with noxious radiation, and the sought-after spirit comes through the bottles of alcohol consumed on weekends, whereby we can forget our woes until the next working week. Everything is sped up, and it seems there really is not enough time - no time for catching up with friends, for experiencing a daily contact with nature and for stopping to see the sunrise or sunset, if one can catch it amidst the smoking exhaust pipes of peak hour traffic. Occasionally a moment is spent making conscious contact with nature or with the sense of meaning in life, and that moment must last through the weeks and months that follow until the next moment comes along. Some are finding that it is possible to maintain contact with Spirit amidst the city hustle and bustle. Some, burnt out by many years of meaningless existence, drop out exhausted and spend the last years as zombies, in lament of life and purpose lost. When will we wake up and see that balance is needed and meaning must be not only sought after but found?

We must learn to give life its due and live it with a sense of peace, justice, goodwill and harmlessness, living our lives in love and truth. What is the state of our relationships? Do we in fact relate to each other? Do we give, without counting the cost? Where are we focused? Are we doing with our lives what we have come to do? Is there love around us and flowing from us? How do we create a better life? Will it all be better when we have more money one day, when we can pay off our car or our mortgage, or is that just a pipe dream? How do we find meaning in our lives now? As we merge with the materialistic way of life and forget our values of heart, we become like the machines around us, in need of repair after many years of use, and dispensable. Technology is a marvelous facility which can help us in so many ways; with communication alone we can see an enormous growth and benefit. Computers can create great possibilities for the common person. So where are we going wrong? Why, instead of being excited at the new possibilities, are we instead depressed? Many are becoming too identified with material existence. If we do not have a job, something is wrong with us. We feel we are no good. We measure our worth by what we own, what we possess, by our success in the outer world. But is that success?

When I visited Iceland, I went to a rather glamourous place for a cup of coffee and a sundae. I made a comment about the surroundings which suggested that people there must be wealthy. "Why wealthy?" replied my Icelandic friend, "they just have a lot of money." For my Icelandic friend, wealth and richness have no relation to the amount of money someone has. What a revelation that is! We have lost contact with the needed values of the heart. To find meaning in life we must re-connect to them, and do it in a world of technological advancement. When we do this, technology will work for us and not against us, and we will once again find the liberation of Spirit for which we yearn.

The pit of depression (a case study)

Let us consider the case of Jason. Jason is depressed; he is sitting in the pit of depression. He is not quite sure how he got there, but he is aware that he is not really interested in the outer world any more, at least he can't find any interest. When he was functioning in the world, he was working on overdrive. He had always tried hard to achieve well in whatever he put his mind to and focused on looking after his wife and family. It was very important to him what she thought of him. He was attending night classes to qualify for a promotion that was coming up at work. It was difficult to keep up with everything, with his family and his full-time job which often needed attention out of the normal working hours. Sabrina, his youngest, was having behaviour problems at school. His mother recently had a heart attack, and as she was a widow, he was concerned about finding time to be with her and support her as he felt she needed it. His brother and two sisters were living interstate. His stress had been great for some months now and not even his drive for perfection was enough to stop him from starting to make errors in judgement. His boss at work was noticing that he could not be relied upon as he had been in the past. His wife could not rely on him to remember what was needed with the children, and she was also suffering from feelings of lack of intimacy. Jason's task of handling the household tax and finances was way behind, the accountant giving him deadlines for needed information. He had lost a stone in weight over the last month and seemed to have lost a sense of time. He was clearly unable to make decisions and had lost the ability to do even small tasks. Jason has entered the pit of depression (see figure 3).

Jason can stay in the pit and be apathetic; weep; scream for help; moan and blame others; take drugs to numb himself; or try to climb out, which, when in depression, seems impossible. What Jason most needs to do is to dig more deeply into the unconscious to find out what has led him into depression. In this way the unconscious matter is made conscious, and each part of that matter can be used to create steps to help Jason walk out of the pit to a more balanced and integrated existence. (see figure 4).

Transformational depression

Jason needs to go within to compensate for the imbalance in his psyche. He needs to detach from the external world and go through the death of his old ego (conscious self). The death and loss of his old ego is experienced as depression. His energy is attracted into the psychic content of the unconscious to further his individuation (process of becoming whole). Seen this way, the transformational qualities of his depression are evident. Jason needs to look into his unconscious to discover what attracted him there. He can do this through creative work involving fantasy, images and dreams. In the pit of depression the rules of the external world no longer apply. He finds it difficult to feel the pain inside him. He is in a process. He is a highly creative and motivated being who is quite sensitive to the demands of all around him. His self-concept needs to change. For this to take place, a flow of energy from his existing ego to the unconscious contents is necessary. Jason must bring up what he has repressed that is causing the depression, throw out what is not needed and keep what is valuable. He can only do this by making a voyage into the unconscious, with "one foot in the unconscious and one in the conscious and dialogue between the two" (Jung, 1987).

What is depression?

Depression is a term commonly used to explain a state of being that occurs when we are lower in spirits than usual. When this happens we may say we are a bit depressed. Depression is a term we use to describe our mood. It also is a term used clinically to describe a specific mental state related to a personality disorder. What the person attributes as the cause of depression may vary from major life traumas to dropping a carton of milk and spilling it over the floor, which may be the last straw of stress before we turn inwards and give up. Depression varies in intensity, sometimes according to the situation or our mood of the day, and our personality disposition. Some are more prone to depression than others, and that may vary according to the stage of life, the life circumstances, the daily circumstances.

> A major depressive episode is defined as a depressed mood and loss of interest or pleasure in all, or almost all, activities, and is associated with symptoms such as appetite and sleep disturbance, change in weight, psychomotor agitation or retardation (slowed speech, body movements, increased pauses before answering, markedly decreased amount of speech or muteness), decreased energy, feelings of worthlessness (may vary from feelings of inadequacy to completely unrealistic evaluations of one's worth) or excessive or inappropriate guilt (exaggerated sense of responsibility for a tragic event - reaching delusional proportions), difficulty thinking or concentrating and recurrent thoughts of death, or suicide attempts or ideas. It is seen as a major depressive episode only if an organic factor has not initiated or maintained the disturbance, and the disturbance is not the normal reaction to the loss of a loved one. Symptoms would occur relatively persistently during at least a two week period. (American Psychiatric Association, 1987)

The conscious world

Stress
Exams
Worry
Mind out of control
Child struggling at
school
Working long hours
Parent ill

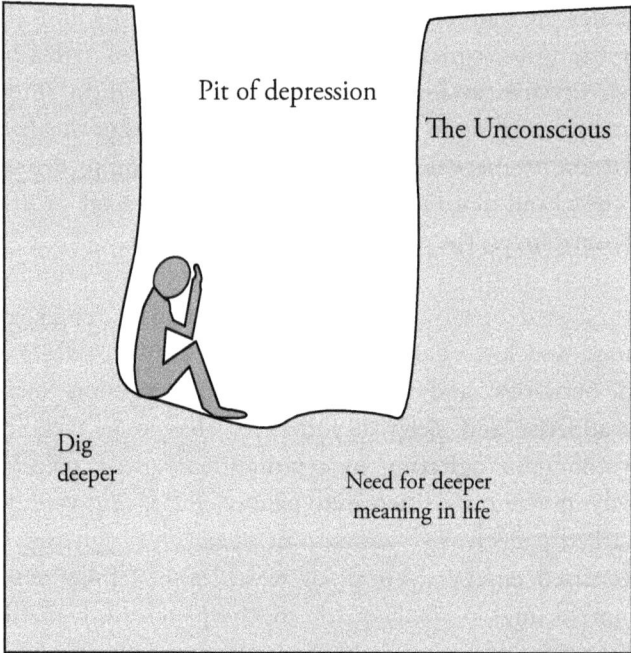

Pit of depression

The Unconscious

Dig
deeper

Need for deeper
meaning in life

Figure 3. The Pit of Depression (Macris, 1994)

Depression is the draining of ego energy into unconscious life. We experience the depleted energy from the old ego as depression. This is what Jason feels as depression. Jason's ego starts to introvert (go within) and explore unconscious material. His depression can be alleviated once the unconscious material is integrated and he

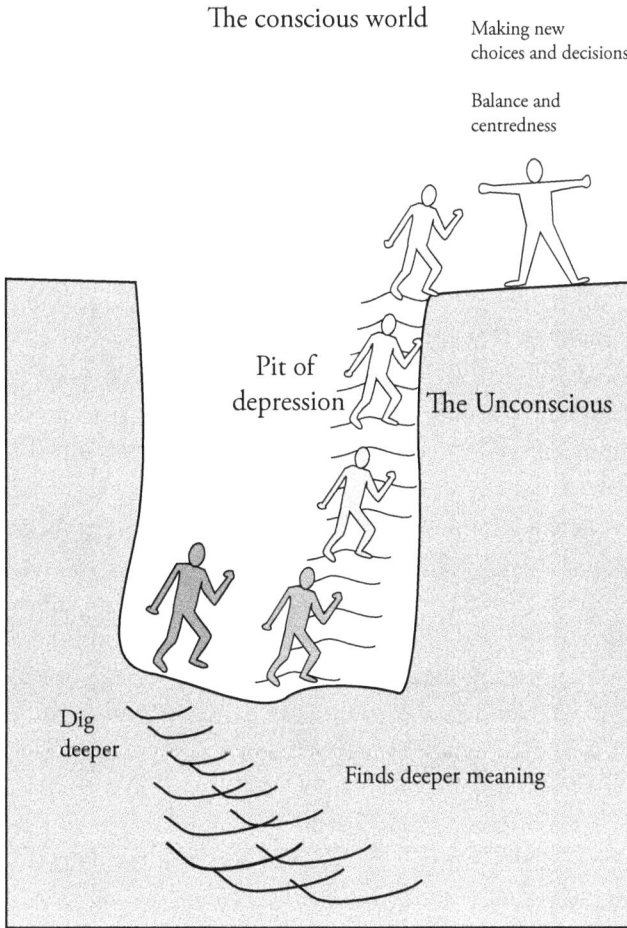

The conscious world

Making new
choices and decisions

Balance and
centredness

Pit of
depression

The Unconscious

Dig
deeper

Finds deeper meaning

Figure 4. The Way Out (Macris, 1994)

experiences the birth of a new ego. In order to re-establish the
connection with the inner self in a balanced and clear way where
there is transformation and integration, the old ego must die and
then the new ego is reborn, bringing with it a new understanding
and new consciousness - a new conscious self.

The stages of life

At certain stages in our lives the psyche goes through a lot of changes. These changes can be seen when we consider Jung's (1976, pp. 3-22) proposed stages of life, which he illustrates with the emergence of a day. Depression can be seen to be a part of the process of coming to terms with some of these changes, or an indication that these changes are not taking place well. The stages Jung talks about move through from the morning of life to the evening. They are: the development of the individual in childhood (from birth to puberty), where we are governed by impulse; youth, or puberty to middle life, which is seen as a time of clinging to the level of childhood consciousness; thirty-five to forty, where there is a dramatic change in the psyche; the death of parents, which is a very significant time for changes in the psyche; during middle life, when achievement and usefulness come into question; the fifties, where there is the danger of intolerance and fanaticism; and old age, where we become submerged in unconscious psychic happenings. In this latter stage, we become aware of our dualistic nature, have stronger awareness of the inner life, and come to the end of conscious problems. The inner wisdom of symbols returns. Jung (1987) suggests that there is danger to the balance of the psyche if older people do not cease to compete with the young, and let go of attachment to the material by going more within during old age. In the second half of life there is the threat of sacrifice and loss. During this time, life is valued and precious. At this time there is a change in the psyche of men where it becomes necessary to put to use their leftover feminine substance, and for women to put to use their leftover masculine substance. After their fortieth year many women wake to social responsibility and social consciousness, which can be a time of great transformation.

From the morning of life to the evening, if we are to individuate (become whole), we need to go through a change whereby the ego

102

moves from the central position of our psyche and the Self (the inner self) takes its place, as illustrated in figure 5. The inner self comes to play a more prominent role as we mature, and it becomes a more centralised part of our being. There is also a greater appreciation of the unconscious. The circle on the left-hand side of figure 5 represents the prominence of the ego in earlier life and the separation from the inner self. The circle on the right-hand side of figure 5 represents movement due to the maturing process whereby the Self takes a central position and the ego is less prominent. The movement of the ego from ● to • causes pain. This pain brings with it legitimate suffering.

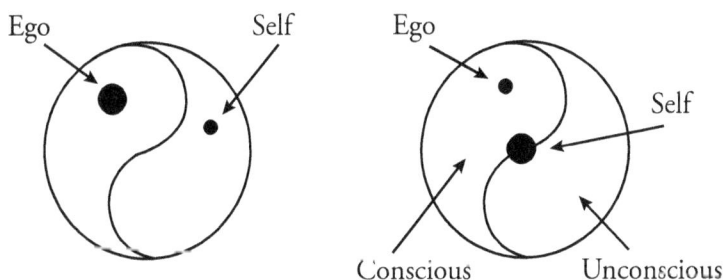

Figure 5. The Way Out (Macris, 1994)

Legitimate suffering, disillusionment and depression

Jung's notion of legitimate suffering helps to give some insight into how we can discriminate and accept the suffering that is needed for us to become whole. Legitimate suffering is necessary suffering given for the purpose of soul growth, growth which requires from us acceptance of our crisis and willingness to evolve.

The process of enduring suffering helps us to open our hearts and develop compassion and tolerance. When we speak of legitimacy we are referring to the suffering that is given to us according to the spiritual Laws. It is genuine, proper and justified. We have earned it karmically, and it helps us to grow: that suffering is legitimate suffering. Yet the presence of even legitimate suffering is often found to be disturbing, and we will do whatever we can to stop it, sometimes stopping growth, leading to spiritual stagnation.

There is also a kind of suffering which is manufactured by the ego. We need to take responsibility for our part in creating this suffering in order to let it go and get on with life. *In Psychology and Religion: West and East*, Jung (1973) tells us that "neurosis is always a substitute for legitimate suffering." It is our attitude to our crises and traumas in life, our acceptance of life as it is, the joys as well as the sorrows, that determines whether or not we manufacture unnecessary suffering, or whether we grow through the experience of legitimate suffering.

An understanding of karma (to every action there is a reaction) can help us to accept the suffering that we go through on this planet. Understanding karma helps us to understand the responsibility we have in creating our lives through our every thought and deed. Such understanding can sometimes be enough to alleviate the suffering we create by not accepting the lessons and life events that come our way. It can help us to let go of the blame, anger, shame, fear and guilt that so often lead to depression. When we understand karma, we take responsibility for who and what we are, and can let go of our victim or oppressor consciousness. Then we may find balance within, aware that our joys and sorrows are equally essential in our development and occur as a necessary part of the unfoldment of life. In *The Healing Hands of Love* (1997) I have given a detailed understanding of karma.

When we see around us so much pain and suffering, and when things in our own lives do not go as we would like, it is sometimes difficult for us to keep faith and hope. This is especially so if we do not understand that the pain and the suffering are necessary for our growth, to help us open our hearts and to develop compassion for ourselves and those around us. It is through our acceptance of the karma we have created for ourselves that we are less likely to be upset if things do not go as we had planned, and less likely to wallow in disappointment which will ultimately take us into depression. If we could open to trust in love and its influence on us and the events in our lives, we would spend a lot less time being worried or angry that events do not go as we have planned them. We would come to see that the universe is unfolding according to its universal plan which we can open to one step at a time, in trust and love. To live in hope and faith of a better life, a better world, is to open to love.

If we have expectations that are unrealistic, we become disappointed when we are met with reality. In many ways the media has a lot to answer for here. Our desire for material goods is exploited and false expectations are created. We have also lost the awareness that what is worthwhile takes time to manifest. Instead we want things instantly and become frustrated when our desire for instant gratification is not met. This can lead to disillusionment and depression. This state of disillusionment can take away our faith. The very existence of disillusionment shows the level of attachment that needs to be let go of if we are to accept the flow of life. In this sense, disillusionment can be seen as a selfish state, centred around the wants of the ego. Its value is that it can make us aware of where our glamours and illusions are. In letting go of disillusionment, we are exposed to ourselves and can connect with truth and reality once again. We again find acceptance of life, acknowledge that we have been caught in glamour and illusion, and find humility once again.

Why do we get depressed?

Depression comes essentially because we have failed to contact the inner life and we therefore live our life out of balance. The resulting chaos and disorganisation caused by long bouts of depression force us to go within and find the true meaning of life, or live a meaningless one, or to join the long list of people in hospitals and out, receiving drugs, electro-convulsive therapy and psychotherapy, in an attempt to return again to life. In the process of such treatment we may be risking brain damage and the stigma of being a mentally ill person, and face changes in life that may or may not be for the better. It is good to stop depression before it goes too far and try to find meaning while our brain cells are still able to help us find it.

Sometimes when a person goes through a spiritual awakening they may exhibit symptoms which mimic those of someone who is mentally ill. They seem not to make sense and to have another sense of reality for a time, often lasting only a few days. Such people have been affected by the rising of kundalini which is pure Spirit rising up the spine. This creates altered states of awareness that may alarm those others even though the person concerned may feel quite happy. Such people often end up in psychiatric hospitals and are placed on drugs. This could be avoided by proper education about the kundalini and by psychology embracing more of the spiritual life of human beings. With the right care, psychotherapy and spiritual healing can prevent the need for such treatment and bring the person back into balance. See *The Healing Hands of Love* (1997), if you wish to know more about the kundalini.

Besant and Leadbeater (1991), when speaking of control of the mind, suggested that we should never allow ourselves to feel sad or depressed, because it affects others and makes their lives harder, which we have no right to do. They suggest that if depression comes, we should throw it off at once. To many this will seem easier said than done. Let us look at some ways in which we can throw off depression.

Ways to overcome depression

It is useful to look at creating space in our lives where we can meditate and contemplate regularly, so that we will be less likely to be met with an unwelcome bout of depression that may take some months or years to overcome. Depression also can be overcome when we use our will to step out of ourselves and give. Sometimes in this act we find connection with our heart once again and the depression is, or begins to be, dissolved.

Music that is uplifting in vibration and songs that have positive lyrics can help us to move out of depression. Some songs may help us get in touch with needed emotions. For example, there may be grief in us that becomes like a frozen substance, creating a sense of stagnation within, which can be felt like depression. The healing energy created by the music helps to thaw out the grief so it can be experienced. The sense of depression we had shifts, and we have the experience of feeling emotions that lead to our healing. About music, Ananda Tara Shan, in her book *The Living Word of the Hierarchy* (1993, p. 78), writes:

> Good music is the voice of God, which tries to purify the heart and illumine the mind. Music is one of the best healers of disease, grief, unhappiness, mental disorders, and general depression. Listen to the music which helps you come to terms with life. Make music your daily companion into worlds unseen, unknown.

> Music opens the doors to the inner worlds. Good music opens the door to Christ's worlds; bad music, to worlds of

darkness. Whereas good music has only positive effects of numerous kinds, bad music has vibrations which lead to madness and suicide. Discriminate with the music that you listen to a lot, and use music to feel God within. Music that makes holy is, of course, unique.

Depression can also be alleviated by attempting to find its inner message. Why has it come? Is there something we need to see in our selves, our lives? Is there something we need to accept? Is there something we need to change? Are we open to the flow of the universe? Are we taking the needed responsibility for our actions, thoughts and feelings? We can move far in attempting to answer these questions and begin to address the core of the issue.

How is depression treated?

Psychotherapy is seen to be necessary and effective in the treatment of depression (Beck, et al., 1979; Berke, 1979; Fennell, 1991; Robinson et al., 1990; Stafford-Clark and Smith, 1978). Until the late 1960's major depressive episodes were treated almost exclusively with electro-convulsive therapy (shock treatment), medication, hospitalisation and traditional insight-oriented therapy, or a combination of these. The 1970's saw the development of behavioural approaches to treat depression by increasing reinforcement or by building assertion skills (Barrow, 1990; Sanchez, Lewinsohn and Larson, 1980). The late 1970's saw the introduction of cognitive-behavioural therapy in the treatment of depression (Beck, Rush, Shaw and Emery, 1979). Beck's cognitive model of depression is illustrated in figure 6. The cognitive therapist breaks into the vicious circle of depression by teaching people to question negative automatic thoughts and to challenge the assumptions on which these are based. The biases are systematically looked at, considering: the negative view of self, which is usually seen as inadequate and worthless; the

(Early) experience
↓
Formation of dysfunctional assumptions
↓
Critical incident(s)
↓
Assumptions activated
↓
Negative automatic thoughts

Symptoms of depression

Behavioural
(lowered activity)

Motivational
(loss of interest)

Affective
(sadness, anxiety,
guilt and shame)

Cognitive
(indecisiveness,
criticism, suicidal
thoughts)

Somatic
(loss of sleep-appetite)

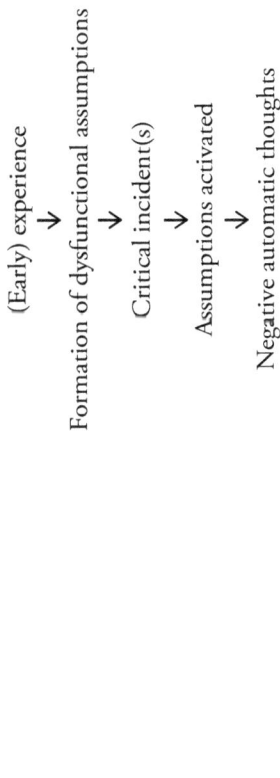

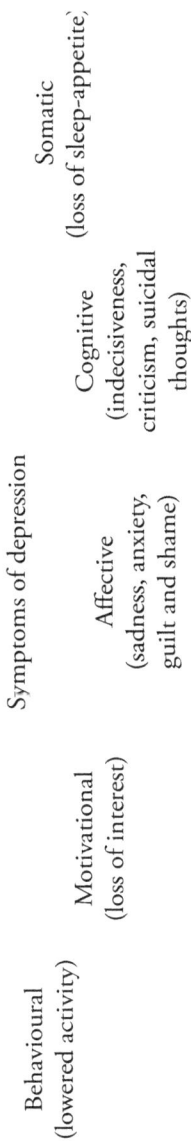

Figure 6. The cognitive model of depression (Beck, cited in Fennel, 1991, p.171)

negative view of the world, which is usually seen as devoid of pleasure; and the negative view of the future, which is generally seen as hopeless. The therapist and person concerned become co-investigators, making and testing hypotheses, with a good working alliance. The method of questioning examines meaning for the person and assesses the consequences for him or her if the negative thoughts and behaviours are maintained. The method helps to clarify, define and assist the person in identifying his or her thoughts and images, for example, by asking "What is the meaning for you?" Methods of guided discovery are used to help modify the beliefs and assumptions the client may have.

Serious depression has been characterised as "bipolar" or "non-bipolar," referring to whether the depressed low state alternates with an unrealistically high, or manic, state. Bipolar disorder has been labeled over the decades as "manic illness;" "manic depressive insanity;" "manic depressive psychosis;" "mania;" "manic psychosis" and "bipolar disorder - mixed, manic or depressed" (American Psychiatric Association, 1987; Carpenter and Stephens, 1980; Crowcroft, 1975; Kraeplin, 1913; Stafford-Clark and Smith, 1978). The evidence for the effectiveness of Beck's model of depression was initially confined to treatment of non-bipolar depressed clients (De Rubeis et al., 1990). Research in the last decade has indicated the model's effectiveness in bipolar disorder as well (Cochran, 1984; Fennell, 1991).

Depressive people may need hospitalisation as they are at risk of death by suicide. They may also withdraw so much that they do not eat or sleep at all, taking no care of their health, which may need constant monitoring. The degree of support, supervision and treatment available to them outside the hospital must influence the decision about whether they stay in hospital or not. In severe depressive states, electro-convulsive therapy has been used to bring an end to these episodes which would be barely controlled by large doses of drugs (Carpenter and Stephens,

1980; Stafford-Clark and Smith, 1978). The long-term effects of electro-convulsive therapy may result in irreversible brain damage (Goldman, Gomar and Templar, 1972). A number of theorists and psychotherapists present evidence to seriously question the use of electro-convulsive therapy (Berke, 1979). Pharmacological treatments that may be used include anti-depressants, hypnotics, sedatives, tranquillisers and lithium. The application of lithium therapy has proved effective for clients who have not responded to anti-depressants. Lithium is shown to have therapeutic and preventative effectiveness in treating depression as well as mania, which is the opposite pole to depression (Murray, 1989; Shaw et al., 1987; Shopsin, 1979; Stafford-Clark and Smith, 1978). However, despite the large amount of evidence in favour of lithium therapy, a study of people with affective disorders in remission who were receiving lithium therapy showed that lithium has a significant detrimental effect on memory and motor speed (Shaw et al., 1987).

Another problem concerning pharmacological treatment is that it greatly hampers effective treatment of affective illness (Cochran, 1984). Some people in their depression may lose the ability to be objective about themselves and are often convinced there is nothing wrong with them. They are not ill, why should they take drugs as treatment? Why should they look into what may be causing their depression? Frequently they do not recognise that they are ill and resist all efforts to be treated (American Psychiatric Association, 1987). Further to this, Simons et al. (1985) show that cognitive-behaviour therapy may be more effective in preventing relapse than antidepressant drugs. Further research is needed. The severity of effects that are possible with electro-convulsive therapy and drug treatments, as well as the research that shows psychotherapy is of benefit and the new headway in cognitive therapy, suggest that effort should be made to find psychologically based alternatives to the more physiologically based treatments. At the very least, combinations of these treatments should be applied. Emphasis needs to centre on factors responsible for improvement so that appropriate interventions can be applied.

If we look at M. Scott Peck's work *The Road Less Travelled* (1986, p. 175), we see that love is an important factor in the healing of those who are mentally ill. Peck tells us:

> For the most part, mental illness is caused by an absence of or defect in the love that a particular child required from its particular parents for successful maturation and spiritual growth. It is obvious then that in order to be healed though psychotherapy the patient must receive from the psychotherapist at least a portion of the genuine love of which the patient was deprived. If the psychotherapist cannot genuinely love a patient genuine healing will not occur.

Love is the needed ingredient which, when linked with psychotherapy, creates a powerful tool for healing one who is depressed. Often people are depressed because they have not given themselves time and sometimes because others never give them time. There is a stigma attached to depression, and "madness" is often associated with it, as the person concerned may have stopped responding normally because of other people's difficulty with dealing with the ill person's withdrawal or difficulty relating. Others around the depressed person may respond with judgement, which works against the depressed person's healing. When depressed people take time out of their lives, either on their own or with a therapist, they can begin to reclaim some of the needed unconscious matter to help get them out of the pit of depression. In my own work, I have found that people respond to genuine caring, love and compassion, and that love is indeed the most crucial factor for successful therapy.

Role-play drama healing and Inner Voice Dialogue also are effective in lifting people out of normal depressions. They create the opportunity for people to separate from that depression and see their depressive self as only one of their many parts. This brings freedom to look objectively at that self and explore it. Why is it like that? What is distressing it? Why has it gone numb? They also are able to become conscious that they have other parts which are not depressed and which can help them get out of the depression. They may also see what is behind the depression - perhaps wrong assumptions about life, perfectionism, or even decisions made in childhood which are negatively affecting them because they have not reconsidered them from their new adult perspective.

When a person is depressed, the etheric energy (vital energy) becomes depleted. Because of this, depressed people can be draining on those around who are more abundant in etheric matter, making depression infectious, bringing down the mood of all in the vicinity. The negative viewpoint of those depressed also serves to bring a heaviness to the energy field around such people. The negative thoughtforms reside in matter around the area where the depressed person lives. For this reason, regular cleansing of the environment is one way to help guard against depression and can make life more bearable for those around. It is helpful for a person to get out of the heavy environment he or she may have created and visit nature - the beach or the forest - where etheric energy is abundant, and then to clean up upon returning home. Spiritual healing (the transmitting of Light and energy into the aura of a person) can have the effect of lifting the dense matter of depression in the aura, making the person lighter and more able to lift in mood.

Before using any approach, the nature and severity of the depression, and the willingness and condition of the client must be considered so that the appropriate methods of treatment can be found. The aim is to assist people to find balance and function as well as possible in their daily lives.

Normal depression, as opposed to psychotic depression which is not normal, can be seen to be a needed state in the changing process of our lives. It can be creative, purposeful, compensatory, cyclical and transitory. The understanding of depression in the transformational approach, clearly illustrated through the case of Jason, gives us a framework in which we can come to grips with the nature of depression.

The notion of legitimate suffering gives us faith and helps us come to terms with suffering as a necessary part of our process of evolution. When depression occurs, it must certainly be a hint to look more deeply into the unconscious for the needed help and understanding, there to see where our life has gone out of balance. It is also time to search for meaning, and to drop unrealistic expectations. Whatever the reason for depression, we must not give way to it but rather open to its higher meaning. We must not give up, and open to reassessment and reorganisation of our true values. We can begin this process by opening to our higher mind for the guidance and direction we need.

Embodying the dream

As we travel on our journey towards wholeness we often look for signposts to point out the way. Dreams, and the symbols within them, are one way of finding the signposts we need. Dream symbols provide us with a map of who and where we are, and help us to ascertain the direction in which we might also wish to go.

For many, dreams are the forgotten language. Each night we dream, and our dreams can often provide great insight as to what is needed for us to heal and become whole. If we are to find meaning in our lives and come to understand the nature of our psyche and its contents, we must awaken to this forgotten language and pay attention to our dreams. Dreams are a way in which we can chart the unconscious. The path of dreams is sometimes called "the royal road to the unconscious." Jung travelled down that road and brought back a map of the human psyche. Dreams and dreaming offer proof of the existence of the unconscious mind.

In the case of Jason, for example, whose depression we discussed in the last chapter, great benefit would be derived from recording and analysing his dreams. This would help give him the unconscious material required to help him know the way to heal. In *Looking for meaning* we discussed the need for him to "dig deeper" in order to uncover the unconscious matter which would help him become whole again and thus provide the steps out of the pit of depression. The exploration of our dreams is one way in which we can dig more deeply in the search for meaning in our lives. As Peter O'Connor (1986) in his book *Dreams and the Search for Meaning*, tells us, dreaming is a psychic phenomenon which offers easy access to the contents of the unconscious mind.

Carl Jung devoted much of his life to the exploration of the psyche, dreams and symbols. I have placed below a number of quotes from Jung for you to ponder on. They give us a lot of insight into dreams and their meaning for us. These quotes have been cited in O'Connor's (1988, pp. 172 - 189) book, *Understanding Jung*:

> Dreams are impartial, spontaneous products of the unconscious psyche, outside the control of will. They are pure nature, they show us the unvarnished, natural fruit and are therefore fitted, as nothing else is, to give us back an attitude that accords with our basic human nature when our consciousness has strayed too far from its foundations and has run into an impasse. (Jung, 1945)

> The dream is specifically the utterance of the unconscious mind. Just as the psyche has a diurnal side which we call consciousness, so also it has a nocturnal side, the unconscious psychic activity, which we apprehend as dream like fantasy. (Jung, 1933)

> I took great care to understand every single image, every item of my psychic inventory to classify them scientifically and to realise them in actual life. That is what we usually neglect to do. (Jung, 1963)

> The dream shows the inner truth and the reality of the patient as it really is; not as I conjecture it to be, and not as he would like it to be, but as it is. (Jung, 1934)

> There is no rule, let alone a law of dream interpretation, although it does look as if the general purpose of a dream is compensation. (Jung, 1934)

To concern ourselves with dreams is a way of reflecting on ourselves - a way of self reflection. It is not our ego-consciousness reflecting on itself; rather, it turns its attention to the objective actuality of the dream as a communication or message from the unconscious, unitary Soul of humanity. It reflects not the ego, but on the Self. (Jung, 1945)

Why do we dream?

The act of dreaming gives expression to the unconscious. It helps us to find balance. Sometimes we deny aspects of ourselves in our daily lives. These aspects turn up in our dreams. Dreaming helps us to compensate. If, for example, we have fear or guilt that we find difficult to face in our waking life, it may find expression and even release through our dreams. Dreams are also a way we can get messages from the inner self and the soul, or the inner spirit. Dreams point to our blind spots. They rarely tell us what we already know. It is beneficial and healing if we engage in dialogue with them, or the symbols within them, while we, at the same time remain in our conscious life. We can get lost in dreaming, and can be afraid of dreams because of what they may reveal. We might not want to know our blind spots, yet it is coming to know them that helps us achieve our wholeness. If we can tap into our dreams, a lot of healing and helping work can take place. We can learn a lot about ourselves. In Jungian terms we have a centre, and that centre is the inner or Divine Self, where we are balanced. When events in life occur we move from that centre. Our dreams bring us back to our centre and help us to see where we have moved away from it.

How do we get in touch with our dreams?

We begin to get in touch with our dream symbolism through a process of writing down dreams each night. It is sometimes difficult if you are not a structured person. You can do it by having a tape recorder beside your bed and recording them as you wake. If you can start to write down your dreams regularly, you will find it a very valuable tool to use. Sometimes access to our dreams can be found by setting the alarm a little earlier, or allowing ourselves more space in the morning before getting up, allowing space for contemplation and solitude. Certain crystals, such as rose quartz and feminine or cloudy quartz crystals are said to facilitate dreaming and to help us remember dreams. The crystal should be placed near the bed, perhaps on the bed-side table, or, if small enough, under the pillow. In my own work with dreams, with myself and others, I have found that just setting the intent that you want to remember your dreams can be enough to help retain their memory.

Keeping a journal

To do dream analysis it is good if you have a book - like a loose leaf folder - and you write your dream on one page and on the page opposite, write what is happening in your life at that time, what is going on, and what the issues involved are. When you go back perhaps a week or three weeks later, you will see more in your dreams. Sometimes you can see that aspects of the dream were quite prophetic or visionary, they were telling you something that was about to happen. Sometimes dreams are visionary.

It can also be useful as you write the dream to divide the page in half with a line vertically down the centre. You write the dream from start to end in one column and when you've finished write in on the opposite side of the column what the symbols mean to you, and the feeling of them.

Over time, as you become sensitive to your dreams and start to record them, you will find your own symbolic language. You may see there's a person in your dream one week and then three months later the person might be there again. When you look back to the dream in which he or she appeared before, you can often find parallels of development from one dream to the other. It is often surprising which people appear and why. As you become more familiar with your unconscious through dreams, you can work out your own symbols and what they mean.

Dream symbols as a key to interpretation

Dream language isn't very rational. It is the unconscious. It is expressed in metaphor, image and symbols. The key to understanding the dream is the knowledge of the symbol. A symbol possesses specific connotations in addition to its conventional and obvious meanings. For example, falling could mean some part of you needs to come closer to earth. Being killed may indicate a radical change. There are many different ways in which images can be interpreted. Consequently there are dangers in trying to analyse too quickly or telling others what you see in their dreams. There could be many interpretations for someone walking downstairs, for example, one could say, "You had better be careful ... you are heading for a crash ... ," or, "You are going into a special place." These interpretations have a very different energy and meaning. Rather, in helping someone analyse a dream, you would say to the person: "What does that mean to you?" The person would tell you what he or she felt. When we jump in with our own interpretation, which is what we tend to do even with lots of practice of dream analysis, we can see that the mind wants to concretise it, give it form, box it and analyse it quickly, to give meaning. We also tend to do the same with our own dreams.

There are many possibilities for interpreting symbols. As a therapist it is better not to give your interpretation, as the client often won't look further. It is important to change the dialogue and ask things like... "What does this mean for you?" And then, "What else could it mean?" Look at the overall context, not just what comes - what else could it be? The meaning might not be sitting very close to the consciousness, particularly when the dream arises from a blind spot in the unconscious. We have to remember that it is not necessarily easy to grab and get a hold of its meaning. Giving fast and easy interpretations is especially inviting when the client reports a so-called "collective symbol." However, we all have our own unique interpretations of collective symbols which depend very much on the context in which the collective symbol appears. Some collective symbols, or collective archetypes, are: falling, flying, floating, running, going up stairs, animals, water, churches, bedrooms, being chased. Often if people have a dream in which they are falling, there may be some sense of danger. Sometimes people have dreams in which they are floating and it may be that they are not grounded and may need to come back into reality more. Running... are they running away from something or are they running to something? These are possibilities, several of many possibilities of how to interpret the collective symbol. We can only try to work out what it is.

Interpreting our dreams

Because of the unconscious nature of dreams it is very difficult to interpret our own dreams without help. Our ego will often try to come in and assume knowledge of what they may mean by providing us with an analysis that makes sense to the conscious self. However, just because it makes sense is no reason to believe that the interpretation is accurate. When looking at our dreams we need to be attentive to what unconscious attitude might be being compensated for in the dream. We must also remember not to be too quick to define this. When dealing with the unconscious we need to allow time and space for its contents to emerge and to find their place in the conscious. It is best not to jump in too quickly and try and tell what our dream is about. Rather, it is best to just let ideas come, let them be there, and let them take their own form. We might think we know immediately, as we have a tendency to want to know what is going on and we like to be in control. This makes us interpret dreams too quickly. If we don't interpret dreams quickly, we have much more chance of finding the truth of them. Sometimes we might have a dream and we might not know the actual understanding of it for twelve months.

Because we are dealing with the unconscious, getting qualified help with dream interpretation can be invaluable. Dream therapists are alert to the structure of the psyche and the role of dreams in helping us to find our wholeness. They can help reflect back to us significant aspects we might otherwise overlook. This help assists us in finding the whole view, whilst still maintaining a subjective enough approach to have the dream retain its personal meaning. Dream dictionaries are often not very helpful because we often don't find our own symbolism or meanings in them. As the dreamer, we need to ask ourselves "what does this mean to me?" If we look at the dream without prejudice, we can reserve judgement and place our trust in our psyche to make its own judgements. Our qualified help can then prompt us when needed, to help us explore other possibilities and move towards a more accurate view.

In my own dream analysis I have found dreams to be an invaluable source of direction for my personal growth. They bring aspects of my personality, and life generally, to my attention so that I know what needs to be dealt with. Often it is not the interpretation which provides the inherent value of the dreams, it is the process of exploring them which provides rich material that can be used for the purpose of my growth.

The Jungian approach is one of amplification, by exploring and defining the context of each of the main symbols and grasping the meaning for that particular person. Questions which succeed in finding this are ones such as, "What does this or that mean to you?" "What is the atmosphere of the dream?" "How did you feel when you woke up?" "What strikes you as significant about that?" We let the dream speak for itself rather than pursuing it with intellectual analysis.

When we dream, we can see all the symbols represented as aspects of our own psyche. If they are things like a door or a house or a road we need to ask, "what is that road representing?" Our dream symbols give us a portrait of the state of the unconscious mind. Jung said that dreams are the letters the Self (our inner centre) writes to us every night.

When we have an image of someone in our dreams, does it refer to a person or is it a projection of the masculine and feminine side of ourselves? According to Marie Louise von Franz (1987), in her book *The Way of the Dream*, it can be both, but it is generally relating to an aspect of ourselves at least 85 per cent of the time. A good question to ask ourselves when someone we know enters our dreams is, "what aspect of me may it be referring to which is like that person?" This helps us not to project the dream and its contents on to others.

Does the unconscious have a solution?

Please bear in mind, while we look at a possible approach to exploring dreams, that there are no rules for interpreting dreams. However, in looking into dreams certain structures become evident. There is usually an introduction, the ups and downs of the story and the end solution.

In the introduction, the characters and the setting are introduced. Usually in the first sentence of our dream we say, I was with such and such and I was at so and so. It is important to look where we are and why we are there. We consider what significance that place has for us. We also consider who is with us and what they represent. We ask, "what do these people mean to me?" As we explore our meanings for the characters and setting we come to know a lot about what the dream may be telling us. For example, if it is a friend we had from high school, why has she come now? Am I psychologically working with a part of my psyche that is still in my high school years? Am I with parts of myself that are represented by that girlfriend in high school? By inserting the meaning of the setting and the characters into the text, for example, I am psychologically in (the setting) and I am with parts of myself that are (the characters) we come to discover a lot about what the dream is telling us. The setting may be the childhood house, suggesting the psyche is working through aspects of itself that are linked with childhood attitudes or values. The characters may be aggressive, critical aspects of the self represented by aggressive men. Once we have established this we can begin to ask and explore how these discoveries apply, in a tangible way, to the dreamer's life in the moment of the dream. Why are we having that dream that night? What events are happening at the present time? By exploring what is happening we can often name the problem.

By exploring the ups and downs of the story and what is happening throughout the dream we may discover points of change or danger in the dream. Do the characters stay in danger or is there a change? This tells us what is actually going on in the psyche, and whether healing and growing is occurring through the dream. By exploring the changes, the ups and downs, we can become aware of where and how we have moved away from our centre. When we come to know this, we know where to work in ourselves and can begin helping ourselves to return to a more balanced and peaceful life. The dream reveals where the work is needed. It will tell us when we are getting out of touch and it will also let us know when our life is going well. Some dreams are very beautiful and we wake with a good feeling; sometimes we wake with a dreadful feeling that stays. Acknowledging these feelings provides us with positive insights.

By exploring the end of the dream we assess the solution or the catastrophe and can begin to explore what the dream is driving at.

A case study

Josie's dream:

My partner was sitting at a table in a very expensive restaurant, he was looking at me very directly and seriously. He was wearing a suit. He was sitting there and his hair was curling up. He had dark hair. He said "I don't want to conform for anybody, I don't want to follow anybody's rules and I don't want anybody patting down my curl of hair. If it wants to sit up, then I want it to sit up. I don't want to have anyone interfering with me." He was very arrogant in some way, but also sure of himself. A spiritual teacher appeared in the dream and said to that character, "Come over here, I've got someone for you to meet." My partner went over and there was another man sitting there. This man was quite calm and self-assured, but in a much more positive way than my partner. My partner just couldn't take meeting this much more refined, self-assured, much more confident, much more natural, fatherly male. He sent him up with a terrible laugh. My spiritual teacher pointed straight at my partner and said, "there is something wrong with you and it is not good." Then I woke up.

As mentioned earlier, it is important to own all the characters in the dream as being aspects of ourself. What does this setting have to tell Josie about herself? In this case the dream took place in an expensive restaurant, and when Josie looked at what an expensive restaurant meant to her, she found that it was very much concerned with the stereotypical roles of the masculine and feminine. Seeing this gave valuable insights into many areas of her life, and made her look at the masculine and feminine balance.

As Josie traced it back, she found a lot of links to her experience of maleness as dominant and self-concerned; when she talked to males, it was as though they knew all the answers. She knew that if this was her model of maleness, that was not the model she wanted to continue with and she would rather change it. She had been noticing her behaviour at certain times, such as at business meetings, when her inner male seemed to come out more. She had noticed that her "know-it-all" aspect would linger in the shadowy background. Even though it did not always actually come forth, she didn't like having it in her. She wanted to transform it as it had come to her consciousness through her dream. In the dream she also has the clue as to how she is able to transform this aspect, with the introduction of another type of male. Josie could also see through the compensatory nature of the dream that often she was not speaking assertively when she could have and that she needed to bring out her assertive self more.

Josie had another dream where her animus exhibited quite a shift from this more stubborn male figure:

A red-headed man with a lot of energy was seated in a car ready to take me places. He looked confident, seemed to have a clarity of purpose, was self-assured, and was seated in the driver's seat. I was looking forward to moving on. So I jumped into the car with him - but instead of sitting in the passenger seat I sat right on top of him so he couldn't move!

In this dream Josie was introduced to the aspect of her feminine shadow that had resistance to her masculine self taking part in her life. Sitting on the red-headed man meant that she was unable to access his confidence, his clarity of purpose and self-assuredness.

Working with a dream

In this section we will look at how a dream can be worked with. Not all of the dream appears here. I have simply used sections of it to show how the psyche of the dreamer is stimulated by the questions of the therapist, and how aspects of the dream reveal aspects of the psyche.

I'm in a house and it was my childhood house. I notice that there are still the old fashioned lampshades and they have lots of missing bulbs, with only a few lights shining.

When you are doing this with yourself or someone else write the actual words used so you keep all the valuable information. It is important to get the exact words that the person says.

Therapist: Do you want to go on a little bit more?

I go into my parent's bedroom and my boyfriend is on the side of the bed where my father sleeps and he is crying.

As the setting is the childhood house, we know that there is some part of this dreamer's psyche which is still in her childhood. We begin to see also that a father complex is operating which colours how she sees her boyfriend, as her boyfriend is lying in her childhood house on her father's side of the bed. Some aspect of her masculine self needs resolution as it is still very much affected by her childhood experience and her experience of her father.

There is also part of the psyche that is dim, that is leaving a lot out. In essence, some light needs to be shone upon this aspect of the psyche, and upon her past to help her update her psyche. In the dream, light is missing. It is very specific, there are only a few shining bulbs and the sense is that more light needs to be shining. So in order to move into a balanced state, the dreamer needs to bring aspects of her past with her parents - her home life as a child - into the light. It is affecting her now, with her current boyfriend. Her inner male, and perhaps her boyfriend also, is being perceived in relation to her understanding and conception of her father.

Therapist: How did the dream end?

Not with much resolution and it stuck with me, it was quite a short dream. My boyfriend told me to go away and I told him it really hurt and he rejected me anyway. He was expressing that I was taking advantage of him being unhappy, in order to go and be with him. I told him that it was hurting me a lot when he said that. It was as if he was scraping the skin off my arm.

Something needs to be resolved in relation to the dreamer's relationship to the masculine. The dynamics need to be looked at and hurt needs to be healed, as it is quite damaging to her and her boundaries.

Therapist: Can you tell me about your childhood house?

I found it oppressive, I found my parents oppressive.

Therapist: And you go into your parent's bedroom ... is there anything more that you would like to say about that?

My mother was more oppressive, my father was quite passive.

This reveals the aspects of the oppressive mother and of the passive father - the male self not standing up for itself and the female self being a bit overbearing. That could be worked with further in therapy.

Therapist: What about the old-fashioned lamp shades?

Actually I went and had a look at the house in recent years and it had been updated a lot. But in this dream I go inside and it still has the old lampshades, of the sixties, and they are sort of a cream colour and there is some kind of association with not having made any updates.

Therapist: You said only a few shining bulbs and lots missing.

Yes, I look at my relationship with my childhood and my parents and it is quite dim. It is dim and there is lots missing.

Therapist: Your boyfriend is crying. How did you feel about that?

I did take advantage of that, I thought I could go and talk to him.

Therapist: You sound happy about that?

Yes.

A part of the dreamer's psyche is aware that she is taking advantage of her boyfriend's tears, perhaps even the pain of her father. To explore this further would be beneficial. This could be done by having a dialogue with or working with an image of the male part that is crying. Doing this would bring more to the dreamer's awareness, and help reconcile this masculine self that is somehow crying for help.

There is also the sense that the dreamer would find pleasure and joy about opening up communication with her inner male. The lack of communication does not help her sense of self and her sense of rejection. More needs to be brought into the light. These are all possibilities which need to be explored further with the dreamer, using a method that enables the dreamer to amplify the symbols and find the inner self-portrait.

Perhaps you may like to consider what other questions would be worth asking, and what areas may be worth further exploration.

Working with the masculine and feminine

Peter O'Connor (1986), who also uses the Jung approach, talks about the shadow side. He suggests that in the first half of our life when we are dreaming, we're really working out the material ability to adjust to the outer world. In the second part of our life, we start to link more to the inner world and our inner self. He shows that women don't really have men in their dreams until they hit a mid-point in their lives where they start to go into that inner self and similarly men don't dream about women until they've hit that point of moving towards, or trying to understand, the inner female in themselves. It is part of our process of becoming whole to explore the other side of ourselves, but often this doesn't happen until the second part of life. Until that point we are dealing more with other aspects of our shadow side, women dream mainly with female characters and men dream mainly with male characters. Of course, we will still keep having dreams about both sexes. It is not the case that as soon as you reach a particular point in life all of your dreams will be about men if you are a women and vice versa; however, integrating the masculine and the feminine will become a stronger theme once the mid-point of life is reached.

The following is an exercise for you to get into touch with your inner male and female.

Close your eyes and go within. Let yourself go into a dreamlike state, a quiet place, somewhere personal to you. Go there and relax completely. We are going to call on the feminine part of yourself to come forward in whatever form it chooses. Know it to be the intuitive feminine part of your being. You may experience it as a feeling or colour. You may have an image. Just allow it to come. It may be someone you know. A relative.

Just let it be there and explore it. If you have feelings, let them come into your whole being. If you have an image, let yourself see every aspect. It may have human form, it may be another symbol. Just be aware of what it is for you and explore that. Open to that feminine aspect.

Start to talk to that part. Is there anything you want to understand about the feminine part of yourself? Ask it. Is there anything that part wants to tell you? Open your inner ear, and listen. Be aware if there is anything you would like to change about that part. If there is, you can ask that part "what can be done to bring about that change?" Let the feminine take you wherever it wants to take you.

We call now upon the masculine to come forward. Allow the masculine to come forward in whatever way it choses. It may choose to come and unite with the female. It might come on its own. Be aware of the form it takes or the lack of form, for instance, it may be a feeling.

As it comes forward, allow yourself to explore it in the same way as you did the feminine self. Ask if there is anything it has come to tell you. Be aware if there is anything you want to change about it.

Ask if there is any way you can do that. Begin your dialogue and image process.

Allow the male and the female within to come together. Be aware of what happens when you do this. Become aware of that union within, between the male and female parts of yourself. If you don't at this time have the awareness of what you need to do to create that within yourself, let yourself return to the quiet place where you began. If you do, continue to develop images or have dialogue with these united aspects.

Come back to consciousness slowly and gently.

You may wish to do a drawing of what you have discovered.

This chapter provides you with a brief introduction to the world of dreams and its language. Dreams are one way in which we are able to make conscious some of what lies in our unconscious.

When we delve into the unconscious we become conscious of much about ourselves. In the chapter *Meeting the monster* which follows, we will look at some other ways to deal with what we may find, especially in relation to dealing with the anger we may hold in our unconscious.

Meeting the monster

When we begin to dig in our unconscious we often meet the monster of anger. Many of us look upon anger as an energy that we would rather not deal with. Yet anger can sometimes give us the impetus needed to move forward and bring action to our lives. It can motivate us to speak up when we have been silent for too long. It is also an energy which, if left unchecked, can escalate beyond reason and cause harm. Through clear communication and the development of skills of assertion, we can dissipate anger and move out of the negative patterns associated with anger escalation.

What is anger?

According to the Macquarie Dictionary (1982, p. 107) anger is defined as "a strongly felt displeasure aroused by real or supposed wrongs, which is often accompanied by wrath or the need to retaliate." It can be conscious or suppressed; when suppressed, it becomes unconscious. Anger can also take many forms, ranging from rage to a general disgruntlement. In the aura, intense anger appears to those with clairvoyant ability as black and red spikey swirls. Irritation is seen as a series of red spots that can give the sense of prickles.

What is the cycle of anger?

The common cycle prevalent in the psychology of dysfunctional anger is the cycle from passivity to aggression. People usually either suppress their anger and say nothing, or let it all out at once. The same person can do both of these things. It is very rare that a person is only doing one or the other. An aggressive approach is one where the anger comes out in an uncontrolled manner, either verbally, physically, emotionally or mentally. A passive approach is one where the anger is kept in the form of depression or apathy. There is no expression.

This cycle of anger is shown diagramatically in figure 7. The central "egg" in the diagram is divided into functional and dysfunctional areas, referring to our behaviour patterns. The top part of the diagram represents functional behaviour patterns that we can choose to engage in. When we remain engaged in the energies associated with anger in the lower half of the diagram such as shame, self-pity, guilt, negative self-talk and apathy, we trap ourselves into dysfunctional behaviour patterns and stay locked into the negative cycle between passivity and aggression. The arrows in the lower section, at the base of the "egg," suggest that there is a dysfunctional swing from passivity to aggression and vice versa.

Negative self-talk is putting oneself down by using a negative inner voice. These energies are self-blame oriented - "I'm no good." The energy of apathy is on the left side because it is a very withheld energy. On the right side of figure 7 are energies of negative other talk where the energies are oriented towards blaming others - "You're no good." Negative "other-talk" is putting others down by thinking negatively about them. Rebellion for example, moves outward in its manifestation. It lives on blaming others. On the lower right side is the blame and the projection, where everything is wrong with everybody else, the system, people at the top, the partner, the kids, the dogs. The lower left side has the sense of self-denigration. The whip is out and the person beats him or herself up. None of these states is very comfortable. We can't live in any of them for very long, so we flip between them. It is uncomfortable to stay in the self-pity, the shame and the guilt. We realise that something is out of balance. We may not know how to get out of that imbalance, except to go to the other side of the scale, which seems to give us some freedom from it for a time. We go from "It's not me, it's them," to "Oh, I've been blaming them," etc. We return to the shame, self-pity and the guilt for thinking nasty things about our partners, the system, and our friends. The cycle is a constant swinging back and forth, which is the negative dysfunctional cycle of anger. We can flip between the two in ten minutes or in an hour's space, or over a day. Sometimes we can be in the grip of the pendulum swing for months.

In the top section of figure 7 we see more positive qualities being implemented in life - truth, love, integrity, right confidence, respect, harmlessness and acceptance. In functional behaviour there is no swinging from passivity to aggression, as the qualities here make our behaviour patterns positive. There is balance and assertion, which enable us to maintain, in a psychologically healthy way, our right to be as we are. We also expect and acknowledge that others have the same right. We act with harmlessness and learn not to place unrealistic or our own expectations onto others.

When we learn to communicate assertively, we can express our feelings, thoughts and wishes without violating the rights of others. We can also stand up for our own rights and limits. The key is to be direct, clear and non-attacking. We can do this by making "I" statements: "I think," "I feel," "I want." It is also assertive just to state facts as you perceive them without judging or blaming. This is not always easy to do, as you may have to separate facts from feelings. Doing this helps reduce anger. For example, you might say "The car ran out of petrol," rather than, "I was stuck because you didn't fill the tank!" Sometimes when we are assertive, others will still feel attacked. You can't do much about that, except to persevere with compassion and communicate your intentions as best you can.

You will see also in figure 7 the words "I am." These words are placed here as they provide the key to our moving out of our dysfunctional patterns into functional ones. The concept of "I am" is used in both psychology and the spiritual world. In the spiritual world, using the phrase "I Am," helps us get in touch with our Spirit and make space for our spiritual Self to manifest. A common phrase or mantram is "I Am that I Am." In the psychological world, "I am" helps us to define who we are, and to find our boundaries and the essence of our personality. This helps us to separate from others, to see what belongs to us and what belongs to them. In taking responsibility for how "I am" feeling we can move out of the energy of blame. As we start bringing "I am" into our speech, we begin to develop the skills of assertion. We start saying, "I am hurt." "I am annoyed by this." It might be that another is doing something which seems aggravating. The annoyance is ours, not his or hers. Saying "I am" helps us to take responsibility for what is going on inside us. It is a key for moving away from negative self-language and negative other-language into an acceptance of the self and others (it is also a key for being assertive). For example, Jim didn't come home when he usually does. He was half an hour late. Joan was upset about it. If Joan says to Jim "You're always late!" Jim will most probably just close down. If she says, "I am upset. I find it difficult without you here," he is much more likely to hear her and acknowledge both her upsetness and his lateness.

In order to live in functional patterns of behaviour we need a balanced sense of self-worth. This suggests that we allow ourselves and others to have imperfections whilst maintaining respect for ourselves and others. It suggests a balanced confidence, one that is not out of proportion to reality. We also need to employ the use of our will and decide to work at cultivating finer qualities, such as compassion, acceptance, trust, truth and love. When we do this we move out of the dysfunctional patterns outlined in figure 7. We no longer get caught in the negative patterns. We begin to know the way out. We work with our language and thoughts, and start to develop our skills of assertion. When we truly learn to be assertive, the negative cycles of passivity and aggression are no longer needed. We don't need to get frustrated because we didn't

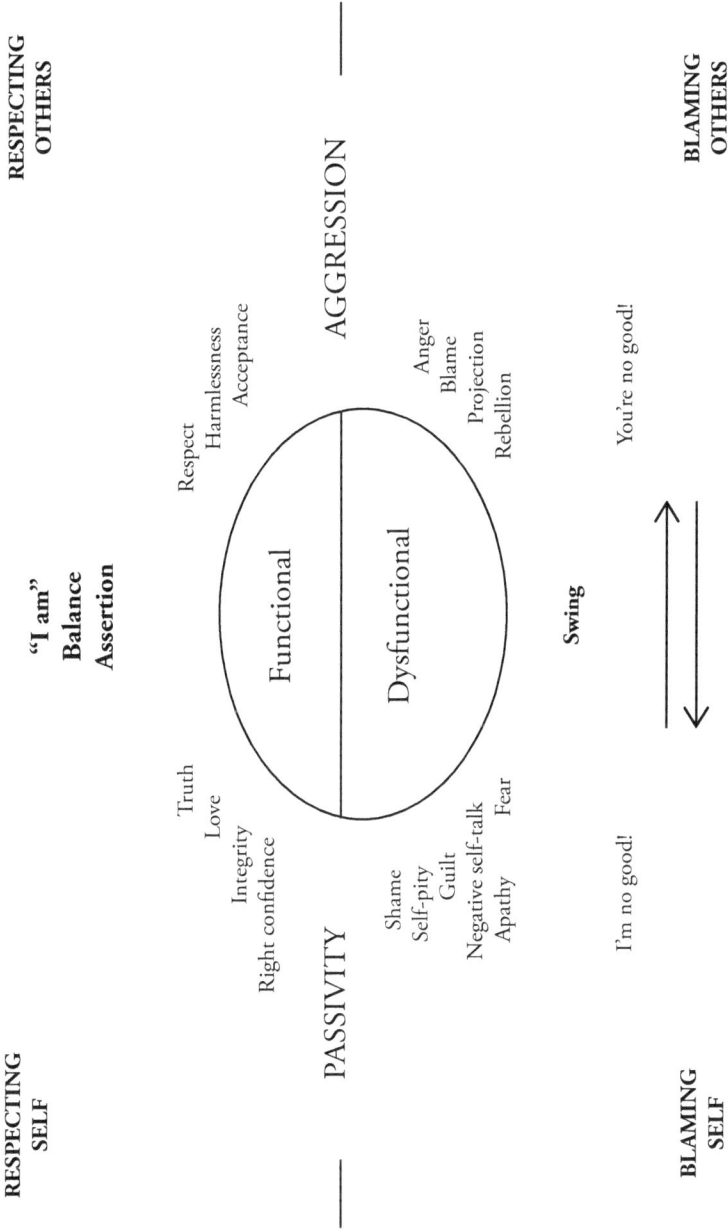

Figure 7. The anger cycle

speak our mind, or angry at another because they hold another opinion. We have found right respect.

Learning to live in Right Human Relations according to the Noble Eightfold Path, acting with goodwill and harmlessness and acting according to a higher sense of justice, provide further keys to living in a functional way. To live in Right Human Relations means choosing to live according to good, and exercising our ability to truly love, seeking truth, harmlessness, justice and liberation of Spirit. When we think of the consequences before we act, give to others in need without counting the cost, speak our truth in the energy of love, bring forth the energy of forgiveness to our lives and relationships with ourselves and others, work towards the purification of all our inner bodies, work to better our thoughts, feelings and actions and give our energy, time and effort for the benefit of all, doing our best to live our dharma (fulfilling the purpose of our soul), and manifesting our God-given talents, skills and abilities for the betterment of all around us, we are beginning to embody the seeds of Right Human Relations. When we bring these qualities to our community or group life we begin to sprout the needed roots that will make a solid foundation for humanity's future.

The Noble Eightfold Path is the way of integrity and balanced living given by the Lord Buddha as a means of attaining enlightenment. The steps of the Eightfold Path are: Right Belief; Right Effort; Right Meditation; Right Action; Right Thought; Right Speech; Right Mode of Living and Right Memory. To understand these steps it may help to substitute the word "balanced" for "Right." It is balance in all things toward which we must strive. For example, the step of Right Speech suggests that we stop and think before we speak, and that we do not speak ill of others, or gossip, rather we cultivate harmlessness in our speech. Harmlessness is a quality that is cultivated in all the steps of the Eightfold Path. The Lord Buddha suggested in His Teachings that the key to overcoming suffering is to accept that it exists and do not try to cling to that which is impermanent or temporary, as it only creates further suffering that is unnecessary. He suggests the way out of suffering is to let go of desire and attachment. If we remain unattached to having our desires fulfilled we are much less likely to get angry. When we actively strive to incorporate the fundamental steps of the Eightfold Path into our lives, and use them as a tool to help us when situations arise that are difficult for us, we go a long way to reducing anger. Divine principles such as these give us the way out if we start to live by them. We can use the Eightfold Path as a way of moving out of anger, because it shows us balanced ways of refraining from living in the extremes of energies such as anger.

Why do we get angry?

Anger can be a defence. Anger is sometimes used to stop us feeling hurt, fear, guilt or pain. It actively prevents us from dealing with fear and examining ourselves. Sometimes we use it so that we do not have to face loss or to deceive ourselves about our hurt. It also keeps us from feeling our sense of low worth, shame or embarrassment. It can give a sense of empowerment and takes away self-doubt. It mobilises us into action. When in anger, others' needs or pain are nothing to our own. We are convinced of our own rightness. The sense of power anger gives can be addictive, and this sense supports us when we use it to justify not having to look more deeply at ourselves.

How does anger grow?

Escalation

When we are convinced by our own personal rules or the "shoulds" and "musts" of our inner self-talk and remain attached to having our rules followed, blaming commences and anger is triggered. Our thoughts fuel the fire of the anger and it escalates. Our expectations of self and others have impact on increasing our stress and anger. It helps to look at our expectations and the expectations of others involved in the situation of the anger. Are there differences in what is expected? Often there are and sometimes understanding this, and the reasons for the differences in expectations, can help diffuse anger. For example, Bruce has an expectation that he will achieve at least the equivalent to what his father has achieved in life. He also holds that expectation of other men, and relies on them to perform their tasks at a standard he has set for himself. Billy, on the other hand, is choosing not to push himself as hard as he saw his father doing, but rather lets things take time, and is focused on the means, rather than on the end. He has no desire to achieve in the sense that Bruce does. Billy and Bruce get a job with the same company, working as project managers. Bruce often works late and, as Billy always leaves at 5.00 p.m., Bruce begins to think of him as lazy. His attitude and manner towards Billy becomes aggressive and unpleasant. Bruce is projecting his own desire for achievement onto Billy and cannot see that Billy has the right to choose differently. If he could let go of his expectations of Billy, which are a projection of his expectations of himself, he would also release his anger toward Billy. As we start to release expectations of others, we begin to be free from the disappointment which leads to the anger.

Perpetuation

Anger is often re-perpetuated. Anger can be re-perpetuated if we don't know how to deal with it and choose to continue expressing it. Say, for example, that Janine has been in the situation of the victim for most of her life, has been the doormat, the one walked upon. She discovers that and thinks "I've never expressed my anger. I've got to start expressing it!" So Janine goes into a pattern of expressing that anger for years. She remembers the injustice of having not done so when she was little, and she decides therefore to express it. The anger becomes damaging as it is perpetually expressed. It gains momentum, like a huge gigantic snowball. The snowball has to be stopped or, as it moves down the mountain, it can do a lot of damage. If we allow the anger to continue, it gets worse and becomes out of control.

To stop this dysfunctional process it may be that what is needed is forgiveness. It may be necessary to go back to that time in Janine's memory when she didn't express anger when she was little, and to express it to her mum and dad by imagining her parents present and communicating what she needed to say or do, but didn't, thereby helping to heal that situation. Janine doesn't have to bring the injustice forward into this part of her life and continually replay it with her partner and everyone else that she meets or works with. In order to go into our past and heal it, we may take it to our healer or counsellor, or do our own guided process, or simply write it down in our journal. Some people continually and inappropriately keep expressing that anger because they think they have to. This does not deal with the anger. It merely perpetuates it.

Response versus reaction

Anger also grows when we are in an automatic reactive state rather than in a balanced state from which we can intentionally respond. A reactive state is when we have a stimulus of some kind that we react to. We are not in control when this is happening as we are simply reacting. When in reaction we are caught in energies such as shame, self-pity, guilt, blame, apathy and rebellion. We enter into negative self-talk and negative other-talk, either verbally or in our inner thoughts. We swing between passivity and aggression.

A responsive state is one where we stop and think and choose how to respond. We become aware of the stimulus instead of being merged with it. We are able to separate what is me, what is others, what is the situation, and to choose. When we respond we acknowledge the potential for choice. For example, we can decide, "There are two ways I can do it. I can respond by being angry and I can choose to respond differently. Rather, I will stop and listen to what my friend is really trying to say, and I will accept that this is happening because I have something to learn. I can make a choice." This makes a total change to our state of being. Responsive and responsible are what we are aiming to become.

Criticism

One of the main occasions from which anger arises (or may arise) is when we are criticised by someone. We don't like to think of ourselves as being wrong. For example, think of an area in your life where you feel that you are really functioning well. It is not an area where you are concerned because you are doing well. Say someone in authority decides that she or he would like you to do things differently. It is not quite as it should be. How would she or he go about telling you? It is likely that because you feel that you are doing well it would be difficult for you to hear or accept this from the authority figure.

We find the idea of criticism difficult. If we are in the business of trying to be better people and we think that we are pretty good at something, how do we refine ourselves if we can't hear criticism? If we simply look at criticism as an opportunity for valuable feedback we may not then fall over and not be able to work for a month, or two years, or however long it takes, before the ego gets over the shock of what we have perceived as criticism. We think someone has hit us with a mighty boulder. The authority may think twice next time about giving that bit of finetuning because we might not work for the next couple of weeks or the next month. We cannot develop if we can't accept feedback. To grow we must open to it. To open to it would mean that we could work with the feedback given instead of getting angry about it.

Trusting in this flow means trusting the universe when it is asking us to refine ourselves. If we want to change and grow and if we want to move into love, compassion and acceptance, we need to be open to feedback. We may be shown an area where we could improve. This does not mean that we have failed. It means that we are learning, that we are growing. We don't have to take it so much to heart that we collapse and become incapable of doing anything else for too long a time or get angry and give up. There are areas we need to work on and areas that we are strong in. We can still do better because we are imperfect. To become better people we can nurture ourselves to goodness rather than whip ourselves to it.

Authority - rebellion pattern and criticism

An authority-rebellion pattern may be at work when people can't hear criticism. The rebellious type won't listen to any sort of criticism. Those whose self-esteem is dependant upon seeking approval may be totally floored by it, and may not surface again for months.

Some examples of authority figures are people such as a general manager, parents, teachers, partners, nurses, doctors, and God. Our need for love makes us very vulnerable so we often don't acknowledge the need. However, if we acknowledge that need, it means that we open to our vulnerability. If we haven't worked through our anger with our teachers, parents and partners, we project it onto systems or bosses at work, our partners, even God. We need to work at transmuting the anger in all of these relationships. To do this we need to surrender and open up to the Light and to be prepared to face ourselves and others we have given power to in our past. If we let the Light shine upon the situation, and dare to deal with what we see, we get all the help we need in dealing with our past angers.

Often, in relationships with people, especially those we see as authorities, we are not really seeing the person at all because we are stuck behind the veils of our own projections. We have to take up the veils so that we can truly see the people who are around us. Think of some of your thoughts about other people. Do you think you are seeing the truth of who they are? Think about how you think about people. What parts of them are you seeing? Is it their truth, or is it a projection of one of these unresolved aspects of yours? Some people wear these projections very well, they seem to suit them - but that doesn't make the projections true or healthy for either party.

How do we move out of anger?

When we make a decision to change and that decision is one which is to become more loving in life, we invoke the will to love. This will is strong and will help us if we really wish to overcome our negative habits and ways. If at the same time we strive to accept what life brings, develop a trust in life itself and cultivate compassion for ourselves and others, we will find less reason to be angry and more reasons to be loving. In so doing we transform ourselves into loving people and anger melts away.

Strengths and weaknesses

Often our anger is at ourselves for not managing well. When we do not deal with anger well, or with other emotions, we are made aware of our weaknesses. If we have a weakness we do not need to see it as something bad. It is simply something where we have to work a little harder and develop skills. If we are to move out of anger it is helpful to not judge ourselves or others as good or bad, rather to see ourselves as having strengths and weaknesses. If we do not judge ourselves and others so harshly there is not the same need to be angry.

Compassion, acceptance and trust in the flow of life

Three main keys help us to move away from anger: compassion, acceptance, and trust in the flow of life. We need to have compassion for other people, and for ourselves. When we accept that we are human beings, we don't expect ourselves to be perfect. The perfectionist and the critic in us do all the whipping and denigrating of ourselves and other people. Using the phrase "I am" in our language is a step in recognising and accepting ourselves, with all our imperfections. As mentioned earlier, by using this phrase "I am," we begin to own who we are and come to learn to do that without judging ourselves. As we learn to stop judging ourselves in a negative way we also begin to see how we can stop judging others in such a negative way; thereby, we develop compassion and acceptance. We begin not to expect perfection from others or ourselves, and start to be able to simply "be."

We also need to develop trust in the flow of life. When we have trust, our self-centredness decreases, as we do not have to use our energy in protecting ourselves or "getting for ourselves" because of suspicion or mistrust. When we have trust, it supports and calms us. To stand against the flow of life demands lots of energy and creates eddies and whirlpools of friction. In not trusting the flow of life we develop a certain anxiety or arrogance that makes us need to control and interfere in life's flow.

Educating ourselves toward compassion, acceptance and trust

Sometimes we are conscious of anger and sometimes we are unconscious of a lot of our anger. We are usually unaware of the fact that there is much about ourselves of which we are unconscious, and hence we think we know everything about ourselves. To change this and open to growing we need to try to bring some of the unconscious contents to our conscious mind to be dealt with. By making things conscious and exposing them they can be worked through and released. By shining the Light on something, it is no longer dark, hidden or secret.

We have to become conscious and act in ways we are not used to. We need to educate ourselves to new ways, to train our thoughts, feelings, and actions. It is not something that someone else will do for us. We can ask for help, and the Light will help in our process of transmutation. But we have to do our part by using our will, taking responsibility and by learning to be assertive. The following exercises for exploring anger may be of help in this process.

Exploring our anger - some exercises

A constructive process for exploring anger

1. Find someone with whom you would like to look at your anger. Think about a time in the past or recent past where you feel that you dealt with your anger quite well. Describe the situation and talk about what you did to successfully deal with the anger, or write it in your journal. Here you will find your strengths.

2. Now we will look at the weaknesses. Think of a time when you dealt with anger unsuccessfully, when it all went wrong. Think of an actual situation and talk about that situation, or write it in your journal. What happened? Here you will find your weaknesses.

3. Think of a present situation where you are not dealing with anger very well. Look at what you did in the previous example where you dealt with it well. If you were to begin to use some of the skills you have identified above, and some others that you could transfer to this current situation, what would you do? Here you are transposing skills.

4. Brainstorm examples of what you could do to develop strength for dealing with anger. For example, you could: be honest when you don't agree, instead of keeping it in; accept what you are feeling; act, if you see something unfair; tell people the truth, speak honestly; give time and be patient; write a letter; let go and do not say anything (the latter is sometimes a weakness and sometimes a strength).

5. Contemplate who are the people in your life with whom you are angry? One by one, visualise each person and start to express what you need to express to that person. Tell them what you feel. This is best done to light, positive music.

6. Write down all the things you are angry about and why, as if you are telling someone who knows you well and from whom you have no need to hide anything.

7. Now think about this question: "What did I learn from writing down my anger?" Write down what you learned from this process.

8. Using guided imagery or Inner Voice Dialogue, as described in the chapter Discovering our many selves, talk to the angry self or sub-personality. Find out what the anger is really about. See what can be done to embrace the anger; give it expression and see what can be done to alleviate it.

Further exercises to explore and work with anger

1. Pair work: In turn, each person in the pair completes the following sentences while the other listens. "I get angry when ..." "When I imagine being angry I think ..." "I express my anger by ... "

2. Using butcher paper and pastels, draw your anger as you feel it in the body. If done in a group, process by sharing and placing individual experiences of anger onto a body drawn on the whiteboard to find differences and similarities to how others feel anger.

3. Do a guided meditation to transmute the anger and begin to open the heart, bringing forward the notion of forgiveness.

4. Do a lying-in guided process, as detailed below, to deal with a situation of anger in everyday life, looking objectively at the situation to facilitate change.

5. Do some work with role-play exploring the varying impacts of the tone of voice, the words spoken and body language messages and how to change them. This will help you learn assertion skills. You may even wish to take a course in assertion skills.

6. In small groups, find a situation to role-play where anger is evident in your own life. Each group then role-plays situations to the group, and the group brainstorms other possible responses.

Guided process

Relax with closed eyes.
Bring to mind a person you felt anger towards at a particular time in your life.
What is happening? Explore the situation.
Be aware of how you are feeling towards him or her.
Express it to him or her.
Now become more objective and consider what is going on for him or her.
Be aware of him or her.
Become aware of how he or she is feeling.
Is there anything he or she would like to say to you?
After having looked at both sides, be aware of how you feel about the situation now.

If there is anything you need to do in the situation now, let yourself do it now mentally.
Ask, "What do I need to learn here?"
Slowly let yourself return to daily consciousness.

Anger and the family

A genogram is a visual display of the family tree. For an example see the following figure:

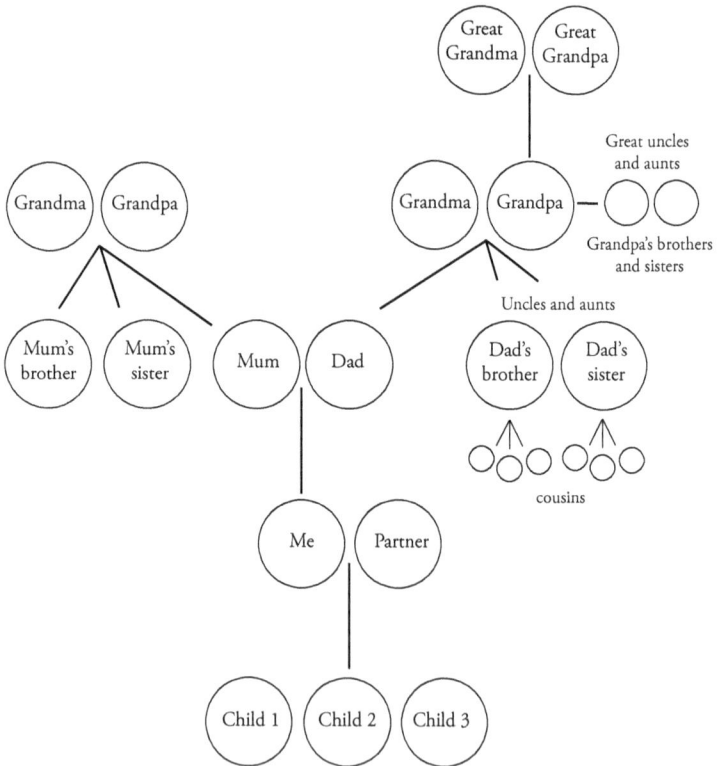

Figure 8. A genogram

Construct a genogram of your own family members. On the genogram beside each person, write how you feel each person expresses anger. Just write what you know. There may be some things you remember about the life of each person. Write that down. Share the genogram with another, looking at where anger comes from in the family and at familial patterns, or write in your journal what you have discovered. Look at how your own patterns are linked in.

Understanding the genogram

As a follow-on from your genealogical exercise on family anger patterns, you may find it interesting to complete the following.

1. On the genogram, look at others in your family whose style of expressing anger is different from yours. How is it different?

2. Think of how these others influence your anger now.

3. Answer the following: "What did I learn about anger in my family?" "Where am I now in relation to that?" "What can I do to change the expression of my anger so that it is constructive for me?"

4. Decide what patterns of anger expression you would like to change and how you will implement this.

5. Change one of the inappropriate ways you express anger this week.

How can we deal with our anger?

Using coping self-talk

How can we work to prepare ourselves for a situation where we know we may have aggressive anger? If we think of the situation, we can visualise the process. Say the situation was visiting someone with whom we are angry because they do not give us the respect we feel we deserve. We have to visit them because our livelihood depends upon it. By focusing on our inner language and making it positive, we can assist our process. Our self-talk changes according to which part of the scene we visualise. We can use self-talk before, perhaps on the way to their house; during, while we are interacting with them; and after, when it is over we may wish to tell ourselves that we did well. According to Richard Nelson-Jones (1992), in his book *Lifeskills Helping*, three different kinds of inner language can help us: language that tells us we can do it, we can cope; language that calms us, and tells us to relax or breathe; and language that educates or coaches us into learning new ways of being.

Think of a situation in your life where you know you have had to deal with your anger. Imagine yourself going into that situation again. What could you tell yourself to help you cope before the situation occurs? What can you tell yourself to help you stay calm? What could you tell yourself to coach yourself through it? Consider these questions again for what you could tell yourself during the situation and after it. You may wish to use the chart in figure 9 to record your answers. The same process can be used to deal with anticipated fearful situations.

Exploring self-talk

Figure 9 may be used to help you explore and prepare self-talk.

Situation: Describe the situation

What is your self-talk?	Before	During	After
Coping			
Calming			
Coaching			

Figure 9. Educating and preparing (Nelson-Jones, 1992)

Think of a situation in which you are normally stressed. Use the information in figure 10 (page 156) to help change your thinking from the old to the new way of talking with yourself. You may wish to replicate the chart on paper and fill in your responses.

Becoming aware of the thoughts that trigger anger, and choosing differently

Nelson-Jones (1992) suggests we look at the thoughts that trigger our emotions. To become aware of the thoughts that trigger you into anger, fill in figure 11. What are the thoughts that bring on an angry response?

Situation	Thought	Consequences

Figure 11. Situation, thought, consequences (Nelson-Jones, 1992, p.314)

Choosing differently

Use the chart in figure 12 to choose differently. Consider how you could change the thoughts and the actions that follow.

Situation	Thought	Consequences
What did I say? What did I do?	What were my thoughts?	How did that make me feel?
What could I have said? How could I have acted?	What could I change my thoughts to?	How would I then have felt?

Figure 12. Changing situation, (Nelson-Jones, 1992)

Dealing with the inner child

The inner child often has many unhealed aspects. Through guided work that allows the psyche to reveal these painful aspects, we can find where we have, for example, been abused, abandoned and rejected. We can go back to these memories through the psyche and work to transform the unhealed aspects. We can become assertive, where before we were not, and can begin to take back our own power. We can move out of victim consciousness and release the suppressed anger from deep within.

Taking responsibility

You can take responsibility for your anger by looking into the reasons behind it and dealing with them. You may also look at your own part in creating it, for example, by considering all the things you said to yourself that inflamed the anger.

To help you identify the cause of your anger, it may be of benefit to consider what is lying beneath the anger and what stresses are surrounding it. Look at the stresses that preceded the situation where you find yourself angry as well as the stresses that come directly from the anger situation. Think about what you can do that will reduce your stress. Are there more effective ways than anger to meet your needs? In order to explore other options you may like to consider the following questions:

1. Are there other ways to find support or nourishment?

2. Do you need to say no or reduce your involvement? How can you acknowledge your limits?

3. How can you negotiate without blaming the other person?

4. Can you simply let go? If other strategies fail, you either will have to let go of either the issue or the person, or find a balance or compromise. How will you go about the option you choose here?

Ways of dealing with anger constructively

Below are some suggestions about how we can deal with our anger. Some of these summarise points made throughout the chapter and some are new ideas. This list is not in any priority order and is not exhaustive. You may have additional ways of dealing with anger constructively. To deal with anger we can:

- Access and acknowledge anger within ourselves and own it.
- Take responsibility for dealing with it in appropriate ways which are not harmful to ourselves or others.

Situation	Old thinking	Consequences
Describe the situation	Write down what you are thinking about the situation that causes you stress	Describe how you end up feeling - emotionally and physically, e.g., under a lot of pressure, tense, sweating, etc.

	Negative self-talk	Coping self-talk.
	What would you normally say?	What would you say now, knowing this new skill?
Before	Write down what you say to yourself before the situation.	What would you say now, before the event?
During	Write down what you say to yourself during the event.	What would you say now, during the event?
After	Write down what you say to yourself after the event.	What would you say now, after the event?

Situation	New thinking	Consequence
Describe the situation	Write down your new thinking.	Describe how the new thinking makes you feel, i.e., the consequence of it emotionally and physically, e.g., relaxed and at peace.

Figure 10. Old and new thinking (Nelson-Jones, 1992)

- Question assumptions that assert that it is not okay to express anger.
- Explore appropriate and inappropriate expression.
- Develop the ability to discriminate what is appropriate and what is inappropriate.
- Express anger constructively.
- Explore rebellion and authority.
- Become aware of our projections.
- Take responsibility to dispel these projections and explore the truth of our anger.
- Allow inappropriate anger to dissipate so that more positive energies can manifest in its place.
- Expand awareness of options available for dealing with anger. Explore these options and learn to manage them constructively.
- Own responsibility for anger.
- Create realistic personal rules regarding its expression.
- Choose to see provocation differently.
- Use coping self-talk.
- Use visualisation.
- Understand how thinking influences feeling and action.
- Handle aggressive criticism without anger.
- Learn assertion skills.
- Develop the ability to relax.
- Meditate.
- Allow harmless balanced expression of our feelings and monitor accordingly.
- Develop self-observation and assessment skills.
- Explore where our anger comes from and what is learned from it, by looking at our family origins.
- Increase awareness of possibility for change.
- Become more aware of the effect of anger in the body.
- Move from being focused on the situation to taking responsibility for our response in a balanced way.

- Educate ourselves about voice, verbal and body messages and how to change them.
- Develop role-play skills.
- Continue to explore our strengths and weaknesses, and accept criticism as helpful feedback.
- Become aware of our choices.
- Take responsibility by transmuting negative memories of the past.

As we seek to come to know ourselves and begin to delve into our unconscious we discover that we have anger which needs to be dealt with. In this chapter we have seen the many components of anger, how it is created, why we become angry, its perpetual cycle. We have also looked at a multitude of ways to explore our anger, in order that we may come to know ourselves and disarm our anger. We have come to discover ways of asserting ourselves so that we need not get lost in anger. The choice is now ours. Will we use this information to help ourselves and to move to new and loving ways of being? Or will we let our fears prevent us? In the next chapter *Taking courage* we will explore fear, an emotion often found in the unconscious, and discover some ways we may wish to deal with it. Fear can often prevent us from expressing how we feel, and can therefore prevent us from developing true assertion.

Taking courage

In *Meeting the monster* we saw that as we delve into the unconscious we may not always like what we find there. However we also saw that there are ways to effectively deal with these aspects we find in ourselves. Exploring our monsters can sometimes bring great gifts. To be honest about ourselves takes courage. It also requires surrender, courage and a step in faith and trust to let the waters of life flow through us and lift us to a place of peace and stillness within. To do so, we must overcome our hesitation and fear. The temptation is to close our heart, often through fear that others will be hurt by our love, and sometimes through fear of the love itself. The power of love within the heart is enormous and to close down that love, not allowing it an avenue of expression, could create severe problems such as disease or even death. Love is to be given freely and unconditionally so life can flow. To hold it back causes destruction to the inner being and the life path cannot then manifest. Many are conditioned to think that their joy and love are bad but they are, in essence, pure and can do a great deal to heal all when they are allowed expression. It takes courage to not resist love because of old conditioning or fears - to allow love to come through us as a pure expression of Light and Love, to be true to our heart and allow the Love to flow through that centre to be distributed to where the need is greatest.

What am I afraid of?

We can be afraid of death, the unknown, the known, success, failure, rejection, approval, life, falling, darkness, public speaking, being alone, making decisions, beginning a relationship, ending a relationship, intimacy, asserting ourselves, helplessness, inadequacy, monsters, suffocation, heights, imprisonment, freedom, groundlessness, punishment, open spaces, ridicule, rape, violence, groups, isolation, loneliness, nuclear war, cataclysms, cold, heat, fire, torture, acceptance, conflict, meaninglessness, unworthiness, exposure, animals, insects, snakes, spiders, light, love, judgement, making mistakes, hell, invasion, responsibility, destiny, fate, karma, physical danger, future, being fat, threat to psychological space, being controlled, lack of control, power, powerlessness, vulnerability and not coping. The list goes on ... We experience fear whenever we enter into unfamiliar territory or put ourselves into the world in a new way.

Certain things that we are afraid of simply happen as part of life, such as retirement, being alone, children leaving home and getting older. Others may require action, such as public speaking, going for a job interview or making a friend. Not all fears are situation-oriented, however. Some have more to do with our inner state of mind and affect large portions of our life, for example, fear of failing, disapproval, success or rejection. According to Jefferson (1987) at the bottom of all fears is the belief that we just can't cope with or handle life.

What is fear?

Fear is sometimes used as a term to indicate the condition which contains anxiety. It is the state or feeling of being afraid, of impending danger or trouble. Fear can be a normal emotional response to something that disturbs us, and it is often felt when something is a threat to our existence. Fear may be rational or irrational, realistic or unrealistic. A certain amount of irrational and unrealistic fear is a natural part of most people's lives. It has something to do with the uncertainty of life, and sometimes the stage of life we may be in. For example, certain periods such as adolescence, the period of the mid-life crisis and even old age can be periods where a greater degree of fear is typical.

We are in a state of balance when fear is proportionate to the situation confronted. When we can come to terms with the fears we have and do not repress them, we realise that fear can be used creatively, for example, to stimulate and help identify the source and cause of the fear.

Neurotic fear is evident when the degree of fear is disproportionate to the situation that stimulates it. For example, it may be reasonable to have quite a large degree of fear if you are swimming and a large shark swims by you; whereas if you have a large degree of fear about going shopping in the middle of the day in case you meet someone you know who is friendly, this fear could be considered neurotic. Neurotic fear is destructive and paralysing to the individual and often to the structures and organisations around him or her.

Anxiety and fear are closely linked. Anxiety is distress, uneasiness or dread, caused by apprehension of danger or misfortune. Anxiety can be felt as a faster beating heart, rising blood pressure, tension in the muscles, and a painful sense of apprehension. When anxiety is successfully confronted in psychotherapy, it is often acknowledged as stemming from fear, which is then worked with to find and release the underlying causes. Fears arise from the personal need to survive, or to preserve and assert our being.

Why do we have fear?

Previous hurts and grief

Fears are often present due to previous hurts we may have encountered on our life path. Hurt in previous relationships can make us withdraw for a long time before letting another person close. It takes courage and strength to break through the barrier. It often involves re-experiencing the hurt before the person is free to open up to a close relationship again. The fear has been developed as a means of protection - to avoid having to face the pain again, but we also miss out on closeness with others.

In order to release a fear, we can look at what is and what is not appropriate about that fear. When we find there is something inappropriate about our fear, that is out of proportion to reality, we need to do some work to transmute and cleanse that fear. The fear prevents us from opening to love and relationships. Imagine that someone has been hurt emotionally, for example, in a relationship. The relationship did not end well, and one of the couple was very hurt and withdrew. It might take that person a long time before he or she will allow another person to come as close again. When that person does let others come close, a danger is felt. An alarm bell goes off. The person feels the fear of having to re-experience the hurt and quickly ends the new relationship before the feeling of hurt threatens. He or she will do anything possible to avoid that hurt being opened up again, and will probably spend a lot of time avoiding relationships, or else limiting the closeness of others. For present or future relationships to be able to embrace the degree of love felt within the first one, the person has to have the courage to allow the particular hurt to be re-experienced. It is through re-experiencing that the hurt can be released and healed. Then the person can love from a deeper place in his or her current relationships.

We may hold our hurts behind our fears and may use the fear as our protection. That is why people often don't want to let go of the fear. The fear has been developed and used as a method of protection. Fear prevents people from moving forward in their lives. We distance people because of our fears, often without realising. Sometimes the fear is the reason we don't have any friends, why there's no one around to go to in times of need. In dealing with fear we find there is often something behind it that sits in the heart waiting to be released.

162

Grief is a common example. Often grief will be experienced when, fear is being released, or very soon after. Many people have suffered the loss of friends. The grief and the fear sits in our hearts and needs to be worked through. It manifests in us through the fear of loss. Instead of working with the grief and being open to loving other people around us, we become frightened of loss. What if we were to open to the love and they die or reject or leave us? It would be very painful, so we choose not to open. We forget that it is better to have loved than not.

Even with the higher understanding of death and reincarnation, and the knowledge of the eternity of Spirit, we find it difficult when it is our husband, partner, mother, or sister who dies. In *The Healing Hands of Love* (1997) reincarnation and the eternity of Spirit are further explored. There is still grief because we knew them in the current life's personality and they will never be that again. Grief is very delicate and needs to be dealt with well. It needs to be understood through all its stages. It is quite normal to go through stages of denial, for example, where the reality of the loss is denied. It can be helpful simply to allow people to go through their denial. People need to go through their own processes. In this way they may be more in touch with who they are when they re-emerge. We can't impose wisdom or understanding on another and sometimes it's not wise or understanding to try.

Imagine a woman who was deserted by her parents when she was little. The father and mother left emotionally, because they were busy with other aspects of life and lost interest in the family. It is difficult for the woman now to open up emotionally. She also has fear of opening to what feels good. She doesn't think she is worthy of experiencing wholeness with someone and so she doesn't enter into the relationship. She chooses instead to stay alone and her actions become not so much guided by the heart but by her fears. The fear has become destructive because it stops her from loving others around her. She projects it outward onto other people because she doesn't want to acknowledge the fear. The fear is unconscious within her. She says, "Well, they were not worth being with anyway."

When we decide something about people, it gives us an excuse not to open to them. Our lack of opening our heart to them shows our choice to close down. It is up to us if we wish to overcome it. If we do wish to overcome fear, we can call on the help of the Light. The Light will stimulate the heart centre. It is up to us, however, to open our hearts and let the love and Light in - we have to decide to open and let the Light enter. When we do this, fullness is felt.

Sometimes we are very afraid of dealing with, or even acknowledging, what sits behind our fear. For example, behind the fear of opening to men a woman may find unresolved grief from her relationship with her father. We use our fear to cover up the grief and deceive ourselves about our true motives. In the example given, the woman may prefer to think that men are no good, rather than face and deal with the unresolved grief in her, as it would be too painful. Anger and guilt are also commonly held behind fear.

Fear as an excuse

Some degree of fear is quite normal given the nature of our everyday lives. However, some fears become quite deep-seated and are not appropriate for daily life. Fear can become a common defence mechanism so that we don't need to look at deeper issues. If we leave deep issues too long before we resolve or heal them, they turn into fear, and we become one step further removed from our hearts. Say, for example, we are attempting to work for a good cause. We are aware that we have fear of doing that because of the memory of previous experiences of working for a cause that led to death in other lives. We have started dealing with such experiences in therapy and we begin to experience in ourselves, behind the fear, both the desire to serve the cause as well as an unwillingness to serve the cause, irrespective of the initial fear. In this situation we are really beginning to get to the core of the issue. The point here is that sometimes we use our fear as an excuse not to face deeper issues. It is easier, for example, to see the problem as fear rather than in this case, unwillingness on our part. When we see it as fear, we feel we can blame something else rather than ourselves.

Fear can be an excuse that prevents us from moving forward, from opening to others, and from creating giving and loving relationships. Our actions become guided by our fears instead of our heart.

Think about fear and the kinds of situations you get into that you are afraid of, or probably more likely, the kinds of situations that you never get into because you are afraid of them. Sometimes we construct our lives very carefully so that we never have to face our fears. We never have to look at them because we never let ourselves go into the situation that we're afraid of. Strangely, however, when we have a fear we usually attract the situation to us. Have you ever noticed that? Why do you think this happens? What makes it happen in the first place? Attraction. Why do we attract it? We ask for it unconsciously. When we go into fear we lower our vibration. We become a little more dull and heavy and then we are more open to the negative situations that we are afraid of. Our level of vibration drops to that level and we attract that energy or situation to us. Our auras turn a grey colour when fear is present, and our normal colours and their hues are lost. Fear can feel paralysing.

Thoughts and our process

As we noted in the chapter *Empowering the higher mind*, when we think we create a thoughtform that has its own life. When we look at the thoughtforms we create and how they function, we see that when we have a particular thought, we send out an energy that eventually comes back to us, sometimes in a situation, or through experiences with people or organisations. If, for example, we put out a thought towards someone for being lazy, it may come back to us from someone else as criticism for work not done. The following is an example of what can happen from our thoughts when we choose not to acknowledge the reality of our fears.

Say I had a fear that I wasn't good enough and I didn't really want to acknowledge this fear in me. Instead, I project it onto Lisa and I start to think she doesn't like me. Whenever I'm around Lisa, I feel that she doesn't like me, so I start to become inhibited. I start not to be able to be myself around her because I want her approval. I can't really be myself because I "know" that she doesn't like me. I know she doesn't like me because I can feel the energy of it. What I forget is that I created the "knowing" from my own thoughts about myself, my own feelings of not being good enough. I put this knowing onto how I feel Lisa sees me. Whenever I meet Lisa I have to deal with the terrible energy I created. The worst part is that it won't go away until I accept that it is mine and that I put it there in the first place. If I don't want to face that, I could go for years not talking to Lisa and being very afraid of her. Think about this and about the people you are afraid of. What thoughts have you put upon them?

When I've projected this feeling of my own inadequacy onto Lisa and then become afraid of her, I will act accordingly. I might run away and tell others how dreadfully authoritarian and nasty she is. "Terrible person, beware of her!" The hypothesis that I started with, "perhaps she doesn't like me," gets further and further away from the truth, because the truth is that I have feelings of inferiority within myself. It stops and ends there. Whether Lisa likes me or not is another issue. I contaminate my relationship with Lisa, and Lisa herself, by these thoughts about myself. In order to defend them I build up strong ammunition from others to support my theory - to make it true so that I can hang on to it and be solid and safe and secure in the knowledge that she is a nasty person. I don't have to look at my own insecurities. I actually start to feel big, which is what I wanted in the first place. Then I feel powerful and I start to think, "I'm powerful. Lisa, she's got problems, she's always nasty to people." I can be near her in another way, not feeling little but feeling big and better than Lisa and I can sit in this illusion for a little while longer. Then Lisa looks at me with loving eyes and suddenly all that I built up is shattered in a minute, in a second. What is shattering it is the energy of love that comes from her pervading everything and melting all illusion, no matter how well I constructed it, and many of us do construct illusions very well. We do what we can to hold onto the illusion but sometimes love comes in anyway and takes away all of the things we've so carefully built up.

It's a bit frightening, love. We see it as something to be afraid of, because it can take away all our beliefs, securities, thoughts about life and the world and the way it is in an instant. That is a bit nerve-racking. Sometimes we simply make the walls stronger so we don't have to let the love in. But that one second of love feels good. Sometimes we feel that we'd rather have the love which then motivates us to work with and deal with our fears.

We can change those illusionary worldviews that we construct. The process will take a lot of energy and effort. We need to ask ourselves, "Why do I construct this idea that it's her doing it to me?" To feel stronger, to protect myself. "Why do I want to protect myself?" The answer lies in the unconscious. We've got things back there bubbling from the past, little hurts, little grievances, a suitcase full, all needing redemption. We are afraid to lose the love that she might give us. What are we going to do about our suitcase?

If we decide that we want to create a loving relationship with Lisa, we have to decide to look into the suitcase and deal with what comes up. If we want to do that we become motivated in another way, and we become aware of the difference between our relationship with Lisa and our relationship with other people in our past. There is a difference. We have to learn that power of discrimination. We often just decide that because of what happened in the past we are not going to relate to anyone; We are not going to trust anyone; We are not going to let any person come near us. But we do not have to decide that. The choice is ours.

Love is a very magnetic force, however, there is also the opposite effect that occurs when we go into fear. When we do that, we end up sitting alone wondering why, feeling very empty. Negative voices come up and they take over. They help us construct our negative world. They help us to keep it in place. We may have a few of these voices. They talk in both ears and they do it so we can't hear anything else, so we can't find love. These are often connected to our past and they say, "No, no, no, you can't trust. If you do, you will meet that hurt again. Don't you trust her, she's got it in for you. Can't you see it? It's in her eyes." The voices are so convincing that we just sit alone in our rooms. It may become so depressing that we start to cry, get angry at God, think that the world is a most dreadful place. Really there's nothing worth living for, we don't find any joy in anything, not anymore, and become bored by everything, "I've had enough! I don't even know why I even bother."

These are the processes we can run around in, and it's like a cycle, we go from wanting love, to doing everything to destroy the love, from being joyful, to being depressed and self-pitiful about love.

Do we want to keep doing that?

How do we overcome fear?

Choice

We have to decide to open our heart and to use our will to love. It doesn't necessarily come naturally. Once we have decided to will to love, that decision is empowered, the love comes to help us melt our fears and we can begin to learn how to act from the heart.

We can try to create a loving brother/sisterhood amongst us and not be subject to the fears that hold us back from doing that. We can do this in our relationships with our partners, with others, with organisations, and with the Divine, with whomever we have relationships. Fears get in the way of love and of opening to it. It is up to us to choose to open, to let the Light penetrate the heart. If we want to open, as a first step, we need to decide that we will begin to act with loving kindness in our lives.

What negative patterns prevent us from letting go?

Fear and blame

In choosing to hang on to our fears and not to let them go, we can become very defensive of our negative patterns. To let go of our negative patterns would mean exposing what is really beneath the fear. We may use the fear as an excuse to avoid what we don't want to do or to blame others. We may also blame others in order to justify the fear because we don't want to look at the truth and we therefore don't want to let go of the fear. For example, if I have a fear of walking in the bush, I could use it to justify not walking in the bush which is good for my health. Having the fear, I use it as an excuse. It suits the part of me that is lazy and can't be bothered going for walks. Blaming the fear and simply not going for walks in the bush means I may never address the part of me that doesn't go because I'm lazy.

Sometimes we project our fears onto others and become frightened of our own projections. For example, if we decide we are no good and project it onto others, we think they think we're no good and we become inhibited by and afraid of them. When we meet them, we have to face our own truth and deal with our own projections.

The role of desire

We fear that our desires won't be met and that we'll be left wanting and unsatisfied. Energies that are dependent on their desire being fulfilled, such as ambition, greed, jealousy, pride, possessiveness and the urge for power and control, often underlie fear. These underlying energies can be the cause of the fear. Deep-seated insecurities, inability to acknowledge our need for love, and discomfort with vulnerability accentuate our tendency to develop fear as a means of deception or protection. Sometimes we play out the fear by seeking approval from or rebelling against another. Unresolved programs of authority often surface when exploring fear. What lies below them is the need to be loved and the need to love. Somewhere in us, be it conscious or unconscious, we know that we have come to Earth to bring love. We set up the authorities to learn the lessons we need to learn to be able to love. They could be our parents, our teachers, or some of our peers who may play a particular role for us. Through them we are searching for our connection to love and our divinity. Authority figures are in our lives so that we can learn some particular lessons. Let us look at the following example:

Say I project my insecurity onto an authority figure and I think she thinks I'm insecure. I'll not do anything that she wants, not anything. I'll work against her because I decide she's a nasty person. I have the energy of rebellion. I think that I'm rebelling against her, but I'm not. I'm rebelling against my own true centre of love. The situation may unfold in another way. Say I want her love so much that I will do anything she asks. I avoid my own need for love by approval-seeking. Both of these ways prevent me from finding my own inner centre. They prevent me from finding love. Until I recognise that I have authority too, that these distortions of the authorities in me are because of my past experiences and do not relate to my current life situation, I won't be able to find love. I have to deal with my suitcase, but I don't have to carry it with me everywhere. Slowly I deal with my suitcase. It gets more manageable. I start to see that I have authority and others have authority. I start to see that I have choices. I can see "them" as nasty people or I can try to find the truth of who "they" are. I could question my perceptions and not think that I'm always right in my first evaluation of another person. I can think "Well, maybe I should re-evaluate this, maybe I should go back to the start and see what actually happened." I might find out that I put my feelings of insecurity and dislike onto the authority figure and face the reality that I dislike myself. Why, why do I dislike myself so much? I see reasons, I can see that I don't really have to keep doing that either. What would happen if I really started to like myself? It doesn't matter actually what others think or feel, I can feel all right. I choose how I'm feeling. It is my choice and my decision.

Whether we know it or not, we are choosing how we feel. It is our choice and our decision. We can take responsibility and accept that we have had some crises and we may have crises again in our lives. They are there for a purpose. If we can trust life and its flow, life gets a lot easier. The river of love can flow through us. Many of us put up the barrier of fear because we think we need to do so to survive. There comes a time when the defence of fear is no longer functional and it has to be thrown away. That time comes when we decide to love. If we decide to love, then we can no longer sit with the defence of fear. It is up to us, we can let the fear sit there if we like. That is our choice. We are given free will. But if we want to, we can melt fear by that decision to love, and another life comes forward, one we hadn't imagined.

Overcoming need

Feeling our deep and unsatiated need for love is one of the most painful feelings we can experience. We therefore either do all we can to not feel it, or acknowledge its presence - we deny its existence, or we feel it intensely, feeling always that something is missing in our lives. In the latter case we may try to have this major need met through relationships and try to derive all of our emotional satisfaction from one area. We attach ourselves to one particular area of our life and see it as our whole life. "All our eggs are in one basket" is the saying that fits most aptly here. Say, for example, we put all of our emotional energy into one relationship and that relationship either gets a bit rocky, or ends. Of course, we will feel devastated, depressed and empty. If we take another approach and derive emotional satisfaction from several areas in our lives, such as work, hobby, visiting friends, being alone, being with family, our relationship and contributing to a cause, we will be much more able to get on with life in a more balanced way if one of our relationships should end. We would still go through pain and hurt, but our "whole life" would not necessarily suffer. What is being suggested here is that our attitude to, and the way we perceive our life, determine our ability to cope with what it brings. When we experience loss, we can simply feel it and move on. Often, just through experiencing the pain, it can be released. Our next steps can then be seen. In many people this unsatiated need for love is not met until we allow love to enter our lives. Unfortunately, most people look outside for love. Instead we need to look within and allow the divine source of love to flow through us. Until we realise that the love we need is actually within us we remain unfulfilled and yearn for wholeness. We seek the Light. We seek love and it is this love and Light that essentially helps us become whole.

Why do we cling to old patterns?

Often we create unhealthy ties with loved ones based on dependency and agreements to keep ourselves stuck. To risk change is to risk uprooting the very foundations of some of our closest friendships. We can seek the approval of others over and above anything else, so it is easier not to change. To change is to challenge boundaries and relationship rules that have been long established, and it takes effort, will and persistence to do so. Perhaps we could ask ourselves, "If I can't be myself without fear in this relationship, do I really want to keep this sort of friendship?" It may be difficult to break our unhealthy ties. We must recognise that if we choose to stay bound to them, we severely limit the capacity for change and growth in our lives.

The role of the mind in creating fear

The mind can create responses in the body and increase anxiety which helps create fear. For example, you may think "I'm going to die, I can't breathe, I'm going to suffocate." Such thoughts accentuate the anxiety in the body. Many therapies designed to help us with our fears are related to the cognitive processes (the processes of our mind). They look at the linkage of our conscious beliefs and our current experiences. When we separate our experience from what is reality and see what we put onto reality with our thoughts, we see that reality might be different from what we create. We can change our thoughts by seeing the situation for what it actually is. Some fear therapy focuses on making the person aware that he or she is in the "now," and that a past situation isn't actually happening. What we think leads to the creation of our fears. We need to purify the mind.

Language

The language we use, both inner, to ourselves, and outer, to others, tells a lot about our state of consciousness. For example, when we say "I can't," we imply we have no control over our lives. When we say, "I should," we negate that we have choice. When we say, "It's awful," we invite self-pity and victim consciousness. We can employ more positive and honest language such as, "I won't," which acknowledges our "response-ability;" or "I could," which acknowledges our choice; and "It's a good opportunity for growth," which doesn't judge the events coming our way as bad. Instead, we look for the value of whatever happens to us in life.

How can we work to help release fear?

Working with feelings

When a person has a fear, there's usually a bodily response associated with the fear. The person feels it in the chest, like a tightening, or in the solar plexus, like a bubbling. There are many different ways of feeling fear. Think about how you feel fear and try to focus on where in your body it usually is. Is it in the breath? It can be different for everybody, although it is commonly held in certain places. By focusing on that body sensation we can feel the energy of fear. We can follow that feeling in our body back, back in time, and see where it takes us. When we do this we may become distressed so we have to keep very alert to this. It is better to do this work with another to help us. They can be sensitive and say at that time, "Realise that you are safe, you are here now." "Just be aware of what's happening. Where are you? What is going on around you?" Incidents from our past can affect us in many ways. Here is one example: A man who was having a lot of fear around relationships with men wanted to work more on that. He didn't really understand why. He was fine relating to women but with men there was something else happening. He got very stressed if he was alone with another man. He did everything in his life to avoid being with men. He never really associated with male friends, and he felt that this should change. He had a strong feeling in his chest which related to the issue. He was a feeling-oriented person. When he followed the feeling back, he saw himself as a child in a cot, having a great time, really happy and alive, full of life. Suddenly, in came his father, with whom he thought he had a very loving relationship. The boy was shaking the bars on the cot. He had just reached the point where he could stand. He was about two. When his father entered he became more excited. His father was really angry and he started to hit him a lot. He was sick and tired of his son shaking the cot. Quickly the boy stopped and started to cry. The father had been very angry because something had happened outside the home and all of his anger came out. The boy started to bleed. He remembers seeing the blood, feeling the blood and then he really remembers crying himself to sleep and not being the same again for a long time, not daring to venture out. He felt a sense of not trusting the male energy anymore. He learned that when men came around, if he had any fun in him he had to quickly stop it. He was much more friendly and playful around women because that seemed safe. He had never understood why.

When he saw this past experience he was distressed about it. He got angry. "Why should this happen to me and wreck my whole life, why should this occur?" The answer came. "Know that not everybody can love all the time. Do not expect that of people.

Sometimes people get angry. Understand that sometimes people are angry and sometimes people can love." He didn't expect that answer at all. He realised that in his life, in his relationships with everybody, he was expecting the people he knew to show love to him all the time. He couldn't do that himself and he knew it. Why was he expecting it of everybody else? "Let others around you be human. Recognise that sometimes they will be angry, sometimes they will be able to show love, sometimes they won't, sometimes they will be in fear, sometimes they will be in guilt. Accept this as a part of being alive on Earth. It is a natural part of being. Don't try to make everyone loving all the time." He felt a real relief. The feeling of tightness in the chest went. He realised that the pressure in his chest was the pressure he was placing upon himself to be perfect and loving. Sometimes his "lovingness" was not real. Others around him found him difficult to be with. Slowly he began to see that he didn't have to pretend any longer. He was always loving in order to hide the hurt of when his father had been not loving. He could let go. He did let go of the hurt. Now he plays tennis with some of his male friends. He joined a men's group and is really getting a lot out of doing that. Working through this fear has enabled him to do it.

By deciding to explore fear, instead of running from it, we grow to understand ourselves and even grow to make a friend of the fear. We become familiar with it and come to know what is behind it. This helps us to begin to release it. We can explore it through role-play, Inner Voice Dialogue, guided imagery and the like. When we start to open to love, we cannot expect miracles overnight in all the people around us. We all have our fears and anguish. We can help each other with them. When we have the opportunity to really feel the love come from the heart, it is beautiful. We can use it in many ways to help people. Our connection with the love might seem to disappear again. That is part of our process of development. We are like flowers. We become buds. We open. We close. Sometimes we open and the petals fall off and they go through a process where we are born again in the earth. We grow again, flower again. It is a process like night and day.

The story above teaches about acceptance of human beings and the vulnerability that we have. Sometimes we are vulnerable and not very loving. Sometimes we close for a period to understand something and then we open again. If we allow each other the space to do this, our relationships can become much more real. People who are closed will feel more free to open because they are given space to do it. We can always make the choice to open. We have to recognise it is our choice. We can take time when we need to. It allows the heart to be experienced. Sometimes we can't find silence around us, so we go inward. We have fears and guilt in order to learn. We can't just strip away someone's fear because it is there as a protection. It has to be a gentle melting of that energy. Slowly and surely it melts away until that person is ready to step forward and be something else; to be the change and be the metamorphosis that takes place as a result of the transmuting of the fear. We are always protected by the Light, and always protected by love. The energy of love is our main protection. If we will to love and to open the petals of our bud, we are protected in that process by the love. It radiates within us. If we meet an outer circumstance that isn't so pleasant, we can be aware of our separateness from that outer stimulus and we can still continue to love. If old hurts rise up, the love helps give us the courage to release them.

Sensitivity

Working with fear is an extremely sensitive area which demands compassion, patience and the ability to respond empathically on the part of a friend or a therapist. When we are sharing or working with someone and hurt starts to be re-experienced, which can happen after a time, an enormous amount of sensitivity is needed. It may help to assure the person. "Remember you are here, you are safe while you are seeing what you are seeing." It is a reminder to the person that he or she is safe and it is present time, so that the person doesn't get stuck or lost. That is how we can explore our past. If we lose that and go into the unconscious, then we can get lost. When people get very unbalanced and become lost in the unconscious, the unconscious becomes their world. We may meet people like that and say to ourselves "Where are they? What are they relating to?" Somehow they have lost touch with the outer reality.

Developing trust

Releasing fear involves developing trust in our ability to cope with, handle and deal with whatever comes our way. Often people just sit paralysed, waiting for the fear to go away of its own accord or expecting someone to come and take it away from them. "When the fear is gone, then I will ..." If we wait for this, we simply perpetuate our condition of paralysis and depression. Instead, we can release it by doing what we fear. We do it first and then the fear goes away. We need to take risks in order to have experiences that will help us develop trust in our ability to be able to handle whatever it is that we are afraid of. When we do this, we can accept that fear is a part of life and allow ourselves simply to feel it and get on with it. Fear is no longer used as an excuse to not get on with life. When we don't take risks and work through our fear by doing this, we remain in a state of helplessness. The choice to act in spite of the fear is empowering. It brings with it a sense of excitement that overcomes the paralysis and depression and creates instead positive action. The recognition that it is our choice how we react to situations in life is the key to overcoming the victim consciousness that is so much a part of the way we keep ourselves entrapped by fear. It is up to us to do what is necessary for our own growth, to create joy,. We have the power to act and the power to love. When we open to risks and challenges in life, we can expand our comfort zone and our consciousness.

Of course, we need to ensure that the expansion involved here is made of love. By that I mean that the risks taken are not in any way harmful to ourselves, or others, or the Earth, but are based on integrity and are part of a growth for the good.

Taking responsibility

When we take responsibility, we begin to let go of blame, and it becomes easier to acknowledge and release our fears. We recognise that it is us who take away our joy in life by choosing to do so. We are responsible for our reactions to everything. We can then feel the fear and do away with it. Taking responsibility includes being responsible for how we treat ourselves. We are not victim to our thoughts. We are in control of them. We do not need to punish ourselves or put ourselves down. Instead, we can recognise where we are not taking responsibility, and do something about it. We recognise the negative thoughts and feelings we create, recognise where we are stuck, and decide to change. We become aware of our choices, look at our options and choose. We take action. We practice positive thinking. We listen to inspirational tapes. We surround ourselves with inspirational books. We change our language. We live in the present, not the future or past. We place positive messages around ourselves as we go through our daily routine. We need to re-educate ourselves towards positivity. We can lead a productive and meaningful life no matter what the circumstances are. We slowly release and work through the fear. By deciding to make a choice in spite of our fears, we get our power back, we take responsibility.

Positive action

When we know we are facing a situation which creates a lot of fear in us, we can prepare ourselves beforehand. First, we need to begin to develop a more positive inner voice, to tell ourselves this situation is coming and that we can get through it. As it gets nearer and we begin to enter the situation, we need to develop inner language that supports us through it. It could be something like, "Relax, you can handle it, or "Breathe." Positive praise is also useful while we do what it is we are frightened of; "You did that well." Depending on the situation at hand, the language can be made more specific. We can prepare ourselves by going through the experience in our mind beforehand. We close our eyes and visualise ourselves going through it in a way we would like to see ourselves go through it, taking small and manageable steps one at a time. We can ask, in this situation, what can we realistically do? Often we sabotage ourselves by imagining the worst scenario and building up fear of a future that may not even happen. When we do this, we waste energy and time that could be used far more productively. We also create stress and tension that harm our health. It is our choice: will we continue to tune in to the negative part of us that predicts a disastrous future, in which we either have no control or we have negative power over others, or will we decide instead to tune in to the more loving and positive part of ourselves and develop it so that it can guide us into a better future.

Making decisions

Making decisions can bring up fear, for example, our fear of making a mistake, of judgement from others, of being in control, of not appearing stupid, and the list goes on. In *Feel the Fear and Do It Anyway*, Jeffers (1987) suggests that when we need to make a decision, after a time of processing, we generally decide upon one outcome as being the only right one. This attitude creates a lot of stress for all involved with it. It is negative perfectionism at work. It is also unrealistic. There are generally many more alternatives and possibilities, but we sometimes get too attached to one and too blinkered to see others. According to Jeffers, painstakingly we analyse options 1, 2, 3, 4 and 5. But what if there is a sixth option, which we haven't considered, which is the most appropriate action? What is important here is not that we choose the "right" one but that we are aware that each option has consequences and appropriate lessons. If we have come up with our options with the best of our understanding and knowledge, all options will provide us with something to learn. If we take option 1, we might discover it wasn't the best option to take. At least by trying it we have found that out. Then we can continue and find from what we have discovered by trying option 1, option 4 seems like the best one, and we can take that. Maybe now we know what the sixth option is and we can try that. Through trial and error we learn and grow. We can do all that is possible to give ourselves the needed information to make a decision. We need to trust ourselves and know we did the best we could at the time. When new information comes we can make adjustments to suit the situation and can know for next time. Decision-making need not be a process governed by fear; it is a natural part of life where sometimes mistakes and poor choices will be made, but when that inevitably occurs, we can simply learn from it and move on.

A bird phobia

I once travelled in Sri Lanka with a girlfriend of mine and she had a fear of birds. It was a very pronounced fear of birds and I wondered how we were going to manage because Sri Lanka was infested with black birds at the time. There were ravens everywhere, hundreds of them. We caught a train from Colombo where there were not so many birds. The train arrived at a town in the north of Sri Lanka, by the sea. We got into a truck and went to our guesthouse. It was night, when the birds were not out and flying. In the morning there were birds around everywhere. My friend refused to come out of the hotel. She sat in a corner of the room because a bird kept approaching when we were trying to have breakfast out in the sun, and it frightened her. I'd never seen such extreme reaction before and I thought, "Why can't she just let it go?" Then I realised that the cause was very deep. One day I convinced her to come on a bike ride. We started to go out into the street and the birds flew around. She screamed at the top of her voice, dived for the dirt and went into hysterical crying. Everyone in the street looked at her with big wide eyes, as if she was some strange being. I put my arm around her and took her back to the hotel. She stayed there for four days in the room not wanting to come out. She sat in the corner as far away as she could get from the door. I thought, "We are going to be in Sri Lanka a very long time if this doesn't change."

I remembered before I left that I had prepared a paper on phobias for psychology. It was just a theory to me at that time. I remembered the process of systematic desensitisation and I started to work with her in that way. I asked her some questions about birds. It was very difficult. She got very angry at me when I even mentioned them. I had to take time to come close in another way before launching straight into the bird phobia, I had to develop trust. Slowly I started to talk to her about her childhood and then she told me she had a sister. I didn't know her that well. She told me her sister had the same problem. I thought that was strange. Something must have happened to this sister and to her and I was trying to figure out what it might have been. A bird came to the window and I asked her what had been her previous experience with birds. She told me that she had been locked in a bird cage with her sister by her brother. He had a bird cage full of little finches. He would get on the top of the cage and make all the birds go crazy. The two sisters were locked in the cage. Her brother would do this quite regularly. By talking about it, visualising it, and creating calmness, peace and relaxation while talking, some of the sensitivity around it was released. The understanding that this had happened in the past and now she was somewhere else came forward. This is a very important part of the desensitising process, to make a person aware of time. There is a past and it's not here now. There is a present and we are in it. Slowly I got her through this process and got a ferry booked to take us away. Getting her on the ferry was a very slow day-by-day process. This process made me realise how extreme phobia is. It is not something where one can say to someone, "That's stupid, just get rid of it!" It doesn't work. A person has to come to it in his or her own space and time. For each of us it is different, we each have different levels of sensitivity. Our astral (emotional) bodies are different, so we have to be aware of and alert to that in each other.

Systematic desensitisation to deal with phobias

In systematic desensitisation, the events that trigger unrealistic anxiety are isolated. It is a visually-based technique in which the therapist assists the client to imagine a clear and vivid picture of the anxiety-provoking stimulus while he or she is deeply relaxed. The method of progressive relaxation training produces a peaceful response instead of an anxiety-ridden one. Wolpe (1958) adapted the progressive relaxation technique to concentrate on systematically relaxing the different muscle groups of the body to produce a state of calmness. The therapist, together with the client, constructs a hierarchy of stimuli that the client finds mildly stressful to very threatening. Beginning with mildly stressful as the first stimuli, the process of systematic desensitisation takes place; by continuing one by one. Each part of the hierarchy is worked with until the calmness is felt. Then the next stimulus is worked with.

Systematically the fears are worked with and the sensitivity around the issue is taken away. Such work is often done for children who have what is called school phobia; phobia about going to school. This is a very common phobia for children. The parents have difficulty getting the child off to school. A systematic approach can be taken by working with the child using the desensitising method. One day the child gets dressed ready to go. The next day he or she starts to walk down to the gate and the next day he or she goes to the gate, and maybe drives past the school, until eventually the child has gone to the school and has gone into the school. The mother stays with the child during the class. They stay for one class and come home. They stay for two. The time there gets longer and longer, until eventually the child can be left in the school alone and spend a whole day. It a very slow process that takes a lot of sensitivity, and a lot of working with the child to keep him or her relaxed and in the present.

Questions we can ask ourselves to help us explore our fears

The following are questions we can consider to help us to explore and understand the nature of our fear.

1. Is it appropriate fear?
2. Is it inappropriate fear?
3. What is learned from the fear?
4. What is behind the fear?
5. Where does it come from?
6. What is its purpose?
7. Does it need to be transmuted or changed?
8. Is there a need for forgiveness of self and/or others?
9. How can I release the fear and open to love?

In what other ways can we help release fear?

When we find there is something inappropriate about our fear, something that is not in proportion to the reality we are met with, we need to do some work to transmute the fear and desensitise ourselves to it.

Ways of dealing with fear include: counselling; spiritual healing; guided imagery; regression; homoeopathy; dreamwork; creative visualisation; meditation; coping, coaching and calming self-talk; psychosynthesis; alchemical work; drawing; painting; sandplay; role-play drama healing and ritual.

Therapy and counselling help us to discover, explore, release and deal constructively with our fears. Different types of therapy have different foci. For example, cognitive therapy focuses on the linkages between symptoms, conscious beliefs and current experiences; psychoanalytic therapy looks at emotions that are repressed in childhood which create anxiety and stress; psychodynamic psychotherapy suggests that thoughts contributing to distress are deeply buried in the unconscious and to release distress we need to explore the unconscious; Jungian therapy suggests we can move from distress and return to our centre by looking at the guiding messages that come from exploring the symbols that arise from the unconscious. There are many others. Some therapists work eclectically (drawing from many methods and theories), varying the emphasis for different clients. The main thing is that you work with a therapist whom you trust.

Drawing

Drawing is a very powerful way to work with energies of fear, guilt and anger, because it helps us to bring out our unconscious. When we use our mind we take control with it. When we use our hand to draw, we take the emphasis away from the mind. The symbols we draw help us contact the unconscious. It speaks to us through the colours we choose, the shapes we form, and the feelings we have around the drawing. Through drawing we can help desensitise ourselves of fear.

Exercises for discovery

The following is a list of exercises which can be used to help us explore and confront our fears. Some can be done individually; others could be better done with a therapist or healer.

1. Meditate to discover what your fear is.

2. Using large white paper and crayons, draw the fear.

3. Explore the fear by talking with a partner (who may also wish to explore his or her own fears) using the sentence "I am afraid of ..." and allowing yourself to complete the sentence, or "I get afraid when ...," "The fear I have is ...," "To overcome my fear I can ..."

4. Do guided imagery work and talk to the image that comes as a symbol of your fear.

5. Do role-play dialoguing with your fear.

6. Using Inner Voice Dialogue work with the self that is afraid, and the self that is not afraid. Work with the child.

7. Construct a timeline of your life and place above the line crisis events in your life. Under the line write the fears you have had throughout your life. Look at whether you have or haven't overcome them. How have you overcome them?

8. Think of a time in your life where you were very frightened and you dealt with the fear. What was happening? How did you deal with the fear?

9. Think of a time in your life where you were very frightened and you couldn't deal with the fear. What was happening? In retrospect what could you have done to deal with the fear? What can you do now to deal with it?

Some hints for dealing with fear

1. Accept that we are all teachers and all students.
2. Accept suffering (but don't resign yourself to it).
3. Take responsibility.
4. Purify the mind of negative self-talk or illusions.
5. Decide to love.
6. Act from the heart.

To deal with fear we need to face it, acknowledge it, make a friend of it, give ourselves time to discover and explore it. Let us take courage, use our will, be gentle, loving and patient with ourselves. Fear contains our deepest hurts. As we identify our fears and begin to work with them, we also uncover the gateway to our heart. To admit our fears takes humility. To face our fears takes courage. To release them and turn them to love takes trust, courage and surrender.

As we learn to develop compassion for ourselves and others, suffering can take its natural form in our life. We realise it is necessary for our heart to open and we no longer need to be afraid of this process. We also realise that by living with our fears and choosing not to work through them we create unneccesary suffering. If we let our lives be guided by the soul, and take responsibility for our own part in life, we come to accept the joys and the sorrows, the hills and the valleys, for they all lead us to the path of the heart. We each have our own struggle, our own mysteries. There is Light and shadow within all. When we accept this, we come to accept the pain and the joy, for it comes when we least expect it, and rightly so, to help our heart expand in consciousness and build within it love and compassion in their true forms. We may need some idea of the direction we are headed, but even that is not always necessary. If we let love and truth navigate as we drive, and always have a seat for them to sit in, we make space for love and Light in our heart and life - and the journey will be Divine.

Finding forgiveness

Another step in our process of becoming whole is finding forgiveness. Once we have taken the courage to look within, admit to our shadow nature and deal with it, we need to be able to forgive ourselves.

It's quite a step from beating ourselves or others up with our negative inner talk, to accepting and loving ourselves and others for who we and they are. Accepting ourselves with all our errors and faults is not always easy. "Why did we do that? Why can't we be perfect, like Jane or Freda?" The perfectionist, the critic and the comparer would like to know. How do we develop compassion for ourselves, and others around us, instead of being harsh and blaming? By dealing with our guilt and finding forgiveness. We come to be less hard on ourselves and find the ability to accept, trust and love ourselves again. Finding forgiveness takes practice and commitment to moving out of old patterns of shame and blame.

As we explore and work through guilt, we come to understand about the importance of having the right motive and the right conscience. Guilt is an energy which can be used for good or ill. When we feel guilty, we usually have acted from the wrong motive and are finding it difficult to forgive ourselves for what we have done. We find it very difficult to accept, trust and love ourselves. We are also put in touch with our conscience. Guilt is useful and good when it makes us find our conscience and helps us live in a way in which we take care of our speech, thoughts and actions because we realise that they have consequences for which we are responsible. Guilt is used for ill when it serves to perpetuate our low self-esteem or to denigrate ourselves or others, rendering us incapable of being ourselves. It can be used as a tool for manipulation when it leads us to try to make another person feel guilty if he or she doesn't do what we want them to. Guilt has many aspects. To understand guilt and come to know it, we must explore it and look for its teaching, being ever ready to let go of that side of guilt which works negatively against us as we try to live with a balanced and humble sense of self.

By exploring guilt and understanding its mechanisms, we can begin to release ourselves from its negative grip and learn the valuable lessons it can teach us. When we feel guilt, we have an awareness of something done incorrectly. People who are considered guilty are those who are worthy of blame. A guilt complex is evident when we have an obsessive sense of responsibility or remorse for the particular offense we have or feel we have committed, whether real or imagined.

The positive side of guilt

Guilt has a number of positive uses which are outlined below. These are:

1. To put us in touch with our conscience.
2. To help us see when we've transgressed moral, social, ethical and spiritual laws.
3. To help us see where we can improve; to help us recognise that we are capable of better.
4. To help us discover our boundaries, limits, etc.
5. To help us take responsibility for our actions, thoughts, feelings.
6. To help us learn needed lessons in life.
7. To make us aware of the need for forgiveness.

Our conscience is the faculty we have that decides upon the moral quality of our actions. It contains our internal recognition of what is right and wrong in relation to both our actions and our motives. Sometimes it is the feeling of guilt that makes us consult our conscience. Without it we may commit many errors and not care about them. Our conscience reminds us of the responsibility we have for our actions and motives and challenges us to keep them in check.

When we go beyond the limits demarcated by the laws, whether they be moral, social, ethical or Divine, the feeling of guilt acts as a warning signal to help us see that we have crossed the line. This signal is extremely valuable in helping us learn to discriminate. Sometimes the moral codes, ethics and spiritual laws are quite subtle, and yet when the guilt comes and we take a close look, we may discover that we have gone over the line. This gives us a chance to rectify the situation before it worsens and perhaps prevent something from happening karmically if we are sincere in our efforts to change.

When we feel guilt, we know (or at least believe) we have done wrong and we can look to see how we could have done it differently. We fall short of our own estimate of what we are capable of and we realise that we could have done better. We can mentally note this and come to know better for next time.

Guilt can make us aware of boundaries and limits of our own and others of which we were previously unaware. For example, if we act in a way that creates hurt for another person, perhaps without thinking, and we suddenly find ourselves feeling guilty, we may be put in touch with the awareness of that person's boundaries, as well as our own boundary of how comfortable we feel about doing something that causes pain to another. It may also make us aware that the person means something to us. We become aware that there are consequences for our behaviour and the thoughts and feelings we create. Guilt acts like a gentle or strong reminder of our responsibility. It helps us to learn a lot of valuable lessons in life, for example, about how we should treat our fellow brothers and sisters, that we should live in love, truth and honesty, and so on. It helps us to remain humble and live in right humility.

Inevitably, after the lessons have been learned we discover that we also need to forgive ourselves. This process of forgiveness can give us empathy with others who have erred, and we also need to learn to forgive them. We come to know that we are human and, as such, we are imperfect beings who make mistakes. We are forgiven through the grace of God time and time again. This does not mean we don't need to learn. It means we learn and move on, and through forgiveness, develop the quality of compassion in our hearts. When we make a mistake, we simply realise, rectify and remember, so that it need not happen again. We do not give up, we continue.

The negative side of guilt

Guilt can also be used in a negative manner. The main ways in which this takes place are:

1. When guilt is used as a reason for perpetual self-punishment.

2. When guilt is used to perpetuate negative self-blame and hatred.

When we have a low self-esteem, there is usually also within us a well-developed inner critic which spends its time damning us, criticising us, sometimes to the point where we are rendered useless by it. Guilt is just the tool this critic needs to beat up on us. It takes us with it on a negative spiral, making our inner talk quite negative and attracting negative energies and situations to us.

Sometimes we even use our memory of the past, in a negative way, to prove to ourselves that we are worthless or to prove that others are horrible people because of what they may or may not have done. In this way guilt is used to perpetuate a negative condition or pattern that is in operation.

Why do we have guilt?

We can have guilt for a lot of reasons. It can manifest if we have not aligned ourselves to the way of good, as we know we should. We know we are actually out of alignment and not living according to the higher principles. Guilt can be for crimes of principles. Guilt may also arise from our past, although this may be unconscious. We may, at this point of our development, have changed our personality to a way of being where we wouldn't consider doing any of the things we used to do. When we can't quite contact or touch the energy of what we have done in the past, the guilt becomes quite unconscious. If we contact it and see some of those past events and see what we have done in relation to them, it can be frightening to think that we may have actually felt really good about doing such things and really good about the power which went with doing them.

The process of confession

For many years, especially in Catholic Christian tradition, the process of confession has been used as a way of releasing guilt. For many, confession conjures up the memories of both positive and negative experiences in this and other lifetimes. Confession, however, is an age-old practice and can take place not only in religious settings and contexts but also within relationships, families and in therapy sessions where the client opens up and reveals all to the therapist. The same principles apply - it is seen as a way of atonement, at-one-ment, the state of becoming one with our divinity again, thus releasing the sense of separation which guilt brings. Admission is humbling and cleansing, it brings us back to ourselves in some regard, making forgiveness possible, reuniting us with our will-to-good. In confession we may also find clarification of issues, through which we can redefine our sense of self and our sense of justice. Confession is often one of the first steps to leaving behind a negative way of being. Embedded in it is a decision to be honest with ourselves and others, and an acknowledgment of where we have gone wrong. In order to come to this, there must also be a realisation that we have done wrong, and this marks the beginning of the process of inner development. It brings great release when we begin to face the truth of ourselves, for we no longer need to put all our energy into keeping alive a lie.

Confession is a process that also has some negative aspects. We may think that by confessing we are thereby absolved from our mistakes. Often more than this is required in order to truly take responsibility for our actions. We need to ask ourselves within, "what do I need to do to make this situation right again?" Otherwise, in some cases people may confess and go out and do the same thing, feeling released from guilt.

From a counsellor's point of view

When dealing with guilt in a therapeutic situation, either through our own self-help or in therapy with a counsellor, the following questions provide a useful framework for working thoroughly with guilt when it is an issue:

1. What is appropriate guilt?
2. What is inappropriate guilt?
3. What can be learned from the guilt?

4. What boundaries or laws have been transgressed?
5. Do boundaries or laws need to be shifted or reinforced in some way?
6. Is there need for forgiveness of self and/or others?
7. How can understanding of the need for forgiveness become a living reality (that is, how can it move from a knowing in the mind to an emotional understanding that releases us fully)?

These questions are valuable because inherent in them is an acknowledgment of the positive and negative aspects of guilt, as well as the recognition that guilt comes to us as a teacher. We see that appropriate guilt and inappropriate guilt need to be separated out within the overall energy of guilt. Once separated, the negative aspects can be worked with and transmuted; the positive aspects can reveal the lessons learned; new boundaries can be defined; and forgiveness of others and self can take place, making the truth of forgiveness a living reality. When we have gone through this process, we are free to move on, with the lessons now learned, with new and positive qualities discovered to make up the being that is emerging.

When we are helping someone work through guilt we need to remain neutral in terms of judgement, to create a warm unconditional atmosphere where the truth of the matter may be revealed and explored. If we do this, it assists the person because the atmosphere is made safe enough for confession. We need to be prepared to follow through with the person as is needed. People sometimes reveal things they have not ever told others in their lives, and may reveal to themselves things they have not before dared to look at. To help deal effectively with guilt, we need to assist the person to release his or her suppressed emotions and help to re-educate the mind of the person.

What is involved in guilt?

Factors often present in a guilt dynamic

In the points below I have listed some of the factors which suggest that guilt may be present and healing needed. These points come from my observations over the last fifteen years of working with people in healing. I have listed the points here on their own so that you may look through them and see if there are any you may recognise. I will discuss them generally in the text that follows.

1. the need to be right
2. the need to be in control
3. the victim/oppressor consciousness
4. the swing from victim to oppressor
5. the need to blame self and/or others (guilt projected outward)
6. low self-image
7. exaggerated self-importance
8. inability to take criticism
9. inability to discriminate between situations and self
10. strong defensiveness
11. the need for approval
12. the rescuer
13. fear of being exposed
14. fear of facing the self
15. fear of ridicule
16. fear of punishment
17. the need for punishment
18. self-pity
19. denial

The web of guilt

Guilt focuses our attention on ourselves and exaggerates our sense of self-importance, making us incapable of perceiving the needs of others. It closes off love and prevents us from being able to live selflessly. A true understanding of how our past actions influence us will assist us to take responsibility for ourselves, but when people are caught in the web of guilt, this understanding is hard to achieve.

The victim / oppressor swing

All the factors listed above in the guilt dynamic effectively block true understanding. When we feel guilty, we very often project the guilt onto a significant other, a parent figure or partner, sometimes the counsellor or healer, who we imagine is angry at us because we have committed some sort of crime. When this happens, the significant other becomes the oppressor in our eyes; we see the other as being the cause of our inner difficulties and thereby abdicate any responsibility for ourselves. This causes relationship failures which serve to strengthen the guilt and these may be used as proof that we are "no good" after all. This swing from oppressor to victim becomes cyclic. We shift from one consciousness to the other, never really finding a sense of peace and equilibrium.

When we are caught in this dynamic there is a lot of fear of exposure, especially in relation to the oppressor aspect. This leads to a strong defensiveness in the personality and can lead to a tendency to exaggerate the faults of the other in the relationship and minimise the faults of the self. It can produce the tendency to lie and can accentuate the need to control the relationship or the other. Self-deceit becomes evident as does denial of much of the truth of the self. The blame of others gives rise to self-pity and the cry of "Poor me, I am truly the victim here."

Often a person with deep-seated guilt enters a relationship with another who has deep-seated guilt, though the guilt may manifest in different ways for each person. This serves only to magnify the problem and can lead to domestic violence either emotionally, verbally and/or physically. The victim/oppressor swing can move intensely and rapidly, making both parties involved very insecure and unstable.

Blame and shame

When we have a lot of guilt we send a negative self-denigrating energy towards ourselves. When we do so, we lose our self-esteem and begin to feel a sense of shame. Guilt produces an intense level of low self-esteem and takes us on a negative spiral. We believe that we are not worthy of life, that we are really a very bad person, and that then instigates the wrong motive for many things. Sometimes when the energy of guilt is present, we don't believe that we are worthy of redemption.

We can also project a negative energy outwards towards others, and create blame. By denying the projection, we begin to create a false sense of pride, which makes our relationships with others difficult. We will feel that they are right and establish a shell or boundary around ourselves that begins to isolate ourselves or lock us in. A selfishness and self-centredness is the result. This is noticed by others as a stubbornness and blindness to reality.

Acting from the wrong motive

Guilt can make us operate from the wrong motive. A wrong motive is a motive that is not pure. While it appears as one thing, it is actually another; for example, we may find ourselves being kind to some people to make up for being not so kind to others. Sometimes people working in the field of helping people are trying to help others for the wrong motive. People also can overcommit, or "over give" from wrong motive; the motive is guilt. People in the helping professions need to look into and release excess guilt in order to be able to work from the right motives, such as genuine compassion and caring. Of course, someone who has guilt as part of the motive can have compassion and caring as part of the motive as well. What is needed is purification of the motive and release of the guilt so that the true compassion and caring can be revealed and provide the motivational basis for the work done. When this happens in a therapist, a lot fewer games are played, and the client-therapist contract becomes much clearer. Boundaries become clear. The gift that is given when we release the guilt is acceptance and self-love. We also find a clear motive, conscience and trust.

The familiarity and paranoia of guilt

Guilt is linked to shame. For example, let us look at a board meeting where an executive officer speaks to employees about what is not going well in a production line. A woman with enormous guilt may sit in the room and think that everything that is being said is being said to her, about all the things she should change. She will go away for three days and not be able to lift her head from shame, not be able to look at her friends, and not be able to move from her office. This is likely to be guilt out of relation to reality. Many people have it. After many board meetings, upon reflection, this person may slowly begin to shift and come to think, "Oh! She is not talking about me," and start to feel a freedom in herself to choose whether the executive officer is talking about her or not. People often carry guilt with them like a big sack. A guilty person therefore often has a posture that is hunched over quite noticeably and the guilt may also give that person the tendency not to look you in the face and make him or her less likely to look others in the eyes. That's often the way we can detect guilt. If we didn't have it, we could look people in the eyes. But then what? We may have to open to the love others offer. Guilt can be used to stop people opening to love, as it is more familiar than love. Guilt then links into something else - fear.

Forgiveness versus judgement

When we look into the guilt and release it, we can start to be able to accept and love ourselves. The lesson of forgiveness comes in. It is not always realistic to judge our past. It can be like judging ourselves now for something we did when we were two years old. When we reach twenty, for example, it doesn't make much sense to condemn ourselves for what we did at two because we are at a different level of consciousness. If a lesson has to be learned, we simply have to learn it. If we've done wrong in the past, and we've moved beyond it, we have to forgive ourselves and let the guilt go.

How can we release guilt?

Changing the pattern

To begin to find relief from a strong guilt or shame-blame pattern takes time and effort. One of the things needed is to start to re-educate the mind, which then in turn helps to shift our feelings. Our thoughts are responsible for our feelings. If we think, "I'm no good," we start to feel awful. If we think, "Well, I did my best," we don't feel so bad. The latter is quite a different way of being. People can often carry guilt long after it is karmically necessary. For example, people may come into this life with a lot of guilt. They can't really work out why they feel so bad about themselves. They had good parenting and so on. Nothing really so different to others. Why do they feel so inferior to everybody else? It is often guilt from our past that comes up, and it is very deep in the unconscious. Regression work can really help that. Even when the grace of God descends, it invariably still takes time and effort to forgive ourselves and to let go of the habits of guilt and self-blame.

Letting the Light in

Many people are conscious of the need for forgiveness. They mentally or intellectually understand that the way to release guilt is through forgiveness. However, many don't know how to bring that into action within their emotional self. It often remains as an intellectual concept, like "Oh yes, I know I have to forgive them," but it doesn't go further.

Finding forgiveness takes faith. It is difficult to have faith if we don't trust. We want forgiveness to happen instantly, but we have to be patient as it may take time. Eventually it will come. It is something that we can't do with our mind. We have to open in faith and trust and bring the Light into the grievance we have been holding. We bring the grievance out into the Light from the darkness where we have kept it. As the Light enters the grievance we come to see things from a new perspective, one which makes forgiveness possible. To find forgiveness a deep asking from the heart will help. Ultimately, the mind can't keep forgiveness away.

Stimuli for exploring guilt further

By exploring guilt, acknowledging it and allowing it to come to the surface we begin the process of letting it go. The following is a series of phrases designed to help you explore guilt further. Simply allow yourself to read each one and think about the words or phrases given. What might they be referring to? What do they make you think about in relation to guilt? Some may not strike a chord in you. Simply move on to the next one and just allow your thoughts to move wherever they go. You may have memories or ideas. Just go with them.

- identifying with the little self
- conditional love
- the game of who is guilty, who is innocent
- victim versus oppressor
- the inner law court
- guilt versus conscience
- guilt and the need for approval
- guilt and its effect in creating fear, depression, shame
- finding and healing the inner child
- guilt and self-esteem
- the cycle of attack and defence
- the role of beliefs
- religious guilt
- listening to the voice of love
- guilt and the Light of Christ
- surrendering beliefs
- change in perception
- forgiveness
- pride versus humility
- redemption
- healing our wounds
- moving beyond guilt, loss, rejection and deprivation of love
- re-educating the self to release us from the prison of guilt
- the prison of the mind

- being prepared to stand naked before God and to open to the higher mind
- releasing guilt and opening to conscience
- acceptance, compassion, trust
- never giving up, not being frightened to look, taking responsibility
- confessing
- looking for the good and for what to do to make amends; surrendering to God
- what have I learned?
- what can I do to make use of this learning in my life?

Locating "unhealthy guilt"

In her book *Guilt is the Teacher, Love is the Lesson*, Joan Borysenko (1990, pp. 35-43) lists the following group of phrases as indicators of unhealthy guilt to assist in tracking down where it is operating in our lives. You may find them useful. Think about whether or not they apply to you.

1. I'm over-committed
2. I really know how to worry
3. I'm a compulsive helper
4. I'm always apologising for myself
5. I often wake up feeling anxious or have periods when I'm anxious for days or weeks, about what I have done wrong
6. I'm always blaming myself
7. I worry what other people think of me
8. I hate it when people are angry with me
9. I'm not as good as people think I am, I just have everybody fooled

10. I'm a doormat
11. I never have any time for myself
12. I worry that other people are better than I am
13. "Must" and "should" are my favourite words
14. I can't stand criticism
15. I'm a perfectionist
16. I worry about being selfish
17. I hate to take any assistance or ask for help
18. I can't take compliments
19. I sometimes worry that I am being - or will be - punished for my sins
20. I worry about my body a lot
21. I can't say no

Healing guilt

Guilt can be healed by letting in the Light and being prepared to deal with the guilt rather than keeping it hidden in the dark crevices of our psyche. By shining the Light into it, we can begin to separate the negative, self-perpetuating, darker substance of guilt from the guilt that is born of conscience and is given to help us learn. By exploring guilt we help to reveal the source of the guilt and can redeem the past situation/s that have stimulated it. One can work with directed processes such as guided imagery, where dialogue can be initiated with a symbol representing the guilt, and information about the role and purpose of the guilt can be found. Questions can be asked about what the lessons are that need to be learned. Healing can also take place through other processes such as psychodrama. In this process a person may take the role of the guilt for us and dialoguing and role-play can commence, or, using Inner Voice Dialogue we may talk to the guilty self. In this way we can get a more objective understanding of the guilt. Regression may reveal the circumstances of the past that have produced the guilt and healing can then take place by sending Light into that past. Psychotherapy and counselling are also helpful. Perhaps the greatest healer of guilt is forgiveness.

Forgiveness

Forgiveness is an area which is difficult for many because people often feel unworthy of receiving help. It is difficult when in the shadow to open to the Light of forgiveness and to feel deserving of it. Our lack of self-worth acts as a barrier to our letting in the Light, however, it is in these darker moments when we need the help of the Light most. We need to remind ourselves to open for help in our times of inner crisis. Forgiveness is basically an act of grace, and it is through grace that we are forgiven. If we are ready to open to that grace, ready to let go of the guilt, we need to communicate our intent. This is best done with a heartfelt prayer. We can also call upon the Angel of Forgiveness to help us to forgive ourselves and to forgive others. When we do this, we attract grace.

When we call upon the Angel of Forgiveness we can visualise the light-violet Light coming into our heart centre and allow the Light to gently release the guilt we are holding onto about a situation or a person or ourselves. As we visualise the Light of forgiveness entering into our heart, we can see the heart of those we forgive radiating with pink Light, and allow the white Light to purify the link between us. We can see this Light help all of our relationships move into Light.

Forgiveness is also an attitude we can practice towards others in our daily lives. We can learn to bring it into our lives. To do so we can decide not to hold onto grievances and to live as Buddha taught us, in the way of loving kindness. We can develop compassion - as Jesus showed us - love others as we love Him. To do this we need to let go of our judgement of others and ourselves and begin to accept ourselves and others for who we are. We can also let go of comparison between each other. We are all unique.

The following prayer by St. Francis of Assisi shows us how we can cultivate the essential quality of compassion:

Lord make me an instrument of Thy peace.
Where there is hatred let me sow love.
Where there is injury let me sow pardon.
Where there is doubt let me spread faith.
Where there is despair let me bring hope.
Where there is darkness let me bring light.
Where there is sadness let me bring joy.
Grant that I may not so much seek to be consoled as to console.
To be understood as to understand,
To be loved as to love.
For it is in giving that we receive,
In pardoning that we are pardoned,
And in dying that we are born to eternal life.

When we really take these words into our heart, the true meaning of forgiveness is revealed. Once we have found forgiveness, we begin to be able to accept others and ourselves more easily. Our grievances before so tightly held have been let go. This helps us be ready to move on to the next phase of becoming whole, *Sharing from the heart.*

Sharing from the heart

Communication is the means by which we express ourselves to others. When we can communicate clearly, we are able to share with others from the heart. To truly share from the heart, we need to come from a place of truth and love. We also need to have developed our communication skills. Good communication often involves being honest with another about our perceptions, and taking time to listen to, and understand, the other's perceptions. Communication plays a vital part in creating the foundation of our relationships and the quality of our life experience. Communication can be learned. Good communication skills can be attained with the right attention and effort.

What is communication?

According to the Macquarie Dictionary (1982, p. 385), communication is:

> the act or fact of communicating; the imparting of or interchange of thoughts, opinions or information by speech, writing or signs. It is the means of conveying views or information.

To have truly communicated to another suggests that there has been a shared understanding and acceptance of a person's view or opinion. If the communication is two-way, both people will come to understand and accept each other's position. Perhaps one won't agree with the other; however, he or she will be aware of what the other thinks or feels and accept that is what the other thinks or feels. Communication then becomes a common ground where both people have a place, both people have respect for and honour each other's points of view.

Communication is one of our greatest problems. Many people see communication as someone saying something to the other and the other hearing it. Communication is much more than that. The following is an example that shows what happens when two people do not really understand what it is to communicate:

Sebastian and Joan are living together in a relationship. Joan is becoming exasperated at Sebastian's lack of thought for the tidiness of the house. Finally she says to Sebastian,

"Why don't you pick up your clothes from the bathroom?"

Sebastian's thoughts are concerned with the fact that he has the day off, which is a rarity in his busy schedule, and he finds Joan's statement to be an unnecessary attack. Joan would have liked Sebastian to be thinking like this: "Joan works very hard, she's trying to look after the household as well as balance our new relationship and it is very tough for her to keep the place tidy when she has so little time and energy. The least I can do is pick up my clothes." That's what Joan would like Sebastian to think.

Sebastian actually thinks: "Joan is a crazy, neurotic, nit-picking woman. If it's not one thing it's another, there is always something I'm not doing right!"

Joan wasn't aware of Sebastian's needs and Sebastian wasn't aware of Joan's. All they did in this exchange was reinforce their thoughts about each other. That he was a lazy partner and she was a nagging partner. This is one of the main problems with communication: people think that because they have said something to someone else that that person will automatically think like they do, but this doesn't happen. Conversations and especially arguments, often don't change anything. More often they simply serve to reinforce each person's initial standpoint. When people are attacked, they often simply defend themselves and find arguments for their current position. One problem with communication is that we often don't come to an interaction with an open mind. We have our own thoughts and issues going on when we come together with another person, and these thoughts and issues impact on the interaction. When communicating, we need to think of the language that we use when we're talking to people and consider whether what we are saying is relevant to the needs, interests or situation of the person we are talking to. The bathroom floor wasn't very relevant to Sebastian that day because he wanted to enjoy the freedom of his day off.

Often when people first come together, in relationship, there's a tendency for people to speak, trying to get the other to know them, and often not much time is spent in listening to who the other person is. When my partner and I first became involved, we went to Findhorn in Scotland. We found a game there called the Transformation Game. Each person finds an issue to work with and then takes turns in working with his or her issue until each one receives answers to his or her issue. We had been together for about a year at that time and we had spent a lot of time saying who we were; I was saying who I was and he was saying who he was. We weren't really hearing each other or listening to each other at a deeper level. When we played that game this state became really obvious. It became so hard for both of us to wait while the other person was having a turn. We wanted to interject, we wanted to say all these things about ourselves. It was a good experience that helped us see that we needed to re-examine our method of communication. Think about the conversation that you have with others. What is it that you tell people about? What do you tell your friends about? It is important that we look at what it is we are saying to each other, and why we are saying it. When we ask these questions, we may find we remain silent a lot more but we may also find other parts of ourselves apart from the ego that regularly pops up and wants gratification.

Say, for example, I talk to John. I have something I want to say. Is what I want to say for my benefit or for John's benefit? Should I be talking to him now? These are questions we need to ask. In this case I'm quite tired of John because he hasn't been vacuuming and I want him to start doing it, I'm living in the same house with him and it bothers me. I come up to John and I say, "You haven't been vacuuming!" John is not particularly interested because he's tired, he's been busy all day at his work. He has come home and all he wants to do is watch television. Do you think he'll hear me? Well, he might hear my words. Do you think it will mean anything to him? What he's likely to think is, "Gee, she's a nag," and that will just reinforce where he is. Saying what I have to John will just reinforce in me where John is in my mind. I'll think, "He's a nasty person." No communication has taken place; I've said something, he's heard me, but there has been no communication.

Communication is about being in community with other people. It depends upon the quality of our relationships with others. When we feel insecure and our self-concept is quite low, the quality of our communication suffers, and when we feel like that, we're not likely to be listening to other people either. We don't easily separate out communications from relationships. They are heavily interrelated. If we are going to be better at communicating, then we also have to become better at our relationships. We have to risk, trust, and self-disclose and see every encounter as a stepping stone to the next. When people refuse to reveal aspects of themselves, it is very difficult for growth to take place, and difficult for the Light to get in to help the work take place. Self-disclosure is often not well employed as part of the communication process. Communicating helps us to be more clear about who we are. It helps us to be clear about who others are and allows freedom of viewpoints, giving a sense of sharing common ground and belonging. Communicating clearly also increases our confidence, makes us feel more capable and stimulates initiative. If we wish to come together in community, we need to start to develop our capacities to communicate and realise how much value it is for us.

What are the barriers to communication?

Many people lack effective skills of communication and interpersonal awareness. Many people suffer from low self-concepts and often operate in an imbalanced way, defending and protecting their battered egos. Others stay stuck in shame and fear of self-disclosure, unable to appropriately express feelings and emotions. These negative patterns severely hamper our ability to live with awareness and our capacity to love one another in the course of our daily lives. The main barriers to communication are our lack of civility; our sense of shame; lack of self-disclosure; the tendency to blame; our tendency to evaluate another's communication; our distorted self-concept and our inability to deal with criticism and conflict. These are discussed in more detail below.

Lack of civility

On Earth today we suffer from lack of consciousness in many areas, especially in regard to that of the group. We lack civility, and many have simply lost a respect for others. The search for civility is a concept developed by M. Scott Peck in the book, *A World Waiting To Be Born* (1993). Civility has to do with the ways humans relate with each other. It is about being civil, and developing right reverence and respect towards each other. It is about giving to each other. According to Peck, in order to create a better world and improve communication and relationships, we need to search for civility. Civility can be both organisational and personal behaviour. About civility, Peck (1993, p. 33) says:

> ... civility requires consciousness of oneself, consciousness of the other person, and consciousness of the organisation or the larger system, relating the self and other.

> Civility is never painless. Civility is the path of growth and the road to personal and collective salvation or healing.

Civility is more than politeness, because one can be politely dishonest or unethical. Civility is consciously motivated behaviour which is considerate of others and follows high ethical standards (Peck, 1993).

Shame

Our sense of shame can interfere with our ability to be open in communication. Shame is a painful feeling that arises when we become conscious of something we have done or thought that is dishonourable in some way. We usually feel disgraced or have some regret in relation to what we have done. Shame comes when we are feeling an acute sense of failure. Low self-esteem comes into effect. Shame is something that is often talked about with guilt but it is not always related to guilt. For example, when people become older they could feel ashamed about their bodily functions deteriorating, but they do not feel guilty about that. When we feel shame, we start to get a sense of tension, anxiety or depression. These are symptoms that come with shame and are triggered by the autonomic nervous system. Our bodies start to respond in order to avoid that. What people then do is try to escape this suffering, for example by withdrawing, commiting suicide, blaming others, becoming busy, going into self-pity, overeating, abusing sex, daydreaming or taking drugs.

When acute shame experiences come our way we start to realise what we are not. Some of our glamours and illusions are dispelled.

We have no defence to this so it can be a very painful experience. In shame there is great potential for growth because truth can be revealed. It takes courage to acknowledge our shame. In doing so we can discover more about ourselves and more about other people.

Lack of self-disclosure

Self-disclosure is telling others about ourselves. Many people are frightened to disclose about themselves through fear of exposure and rejection. Yet self-disclosure is the most effective way to communicate to others and to deal with shame. When we can admit to our friends or our counsellor something very deep about ourselves and admit our failures it helps us to know more about ourselves and let the Light in. Self-disclosure also helps others in relating to us as we show them that we are human. The energy that we use to conceal issues creates a lot of stress. Deception and concealment can inhibit growth and create emotional problems and neurosis. There is a lot of fear about and resistance to self-disclosure. We don't like others knowing about our weaknesses. Why not? We all have them. People normally find self-disclosure too risky and painful. Lack of self-disclosure provides a barrier to good communication. We fear self-knowledge. We fear knowing about ourselves. We fear being honest even to ourselves. We fear intimacy. We fear responsibility. We fear change and we fear rejection.

Blame

Often when things go wrong, we do not like to look at ourselves to find the cause. Rather, we prefer to blame others and think negative things about them. This hampers communication. We need to be aware that communication is not only about what we say. It is also about what we think about another person, because through our thoughts we send out energy to that other person and we receive energy from him or her, and that creates communication.

Evaluating another's communication

One of the strongest barriers to communication is the tendency to evaluate another's communication. In the example with John, I was trying to say that I would like to have the house vacuumed. If I start to pick on his way of communicating because he doesn't quite respond in the way that I want him to, then we are another step removed from the real issue and it becomes more impossible to communicate. I state, "You're stupid!", and he states, "you're crazy!" We separate and it becomes harder to come back together because we've attacked each other's ability to communicate and have gone right away from the issue itself. It becomes harder to come back to the truth. If we were to listen to each other instead, I could say, "John, you know, I've noticed that the vacuuming isn't getting done and we did agree that we would share the vacuuming." John may respond, "Well, I haven't been doing it because I've been annoyed with you for some things." I could then listen to that and think what I have done to make him annoyed with me. We would have to look at our relationship. That would take courage and it would take an open mind on my part, not accusing him of purposely not wanting to do the vacuuming, or accusing him of being a particular sort of nasty, horrible person, but of finding out what's going on for him. My approach to the problem becomes: "I've noticed this. It is disturbing me. I'll find out what is going on for John. Maybe there is a good reason, maybe he is totally exhausted because of all the other things he's doing and maybe that's reasonable." If I thought about John before I was ready to blame him, he might be more inclined to say, "I know I've been really lazy. I should be doing it and yes I will." We could perhaps accept that.

The best approach is for me to try to understand the content of what John is saying and try to understand him. We have to be aware of our language, what we are saying, how clearly we are speaking. If I am angry with him I have to learn how to cope with my angry feelings. I have to learn to deal with my own anger. He is triggering that and helping me see that I need to deal with it. I can begin to find another way of looking at things. For example, before giving criticism I could ask myself: "Is it kind? Is it true? Is it necessary? Is it the right time?"

When we say something, it is best not to beat around the bush. Have you ever had someone come up to you and talk to you about some other thing first, when he or she is really trying to tell you something else? Say you want someone to vacuum. "I've noticed that there is some dust on the floor and yes, there is some in the bathroom as well and yes, perhaps I should go and clean it up." This shows an inability to actually say what you want to say. Don't beat around the bush. Criticise the action not the person. If I'm annoyed the vacuuming is not getting done I don't have to sit in the house with John and brood and send energy of hatred towards him or anger at him for the person he is. I can look at what is going on for him and see the person as separate from the actions. I can speak to him with the love I have for him, and let him know I have that love as I'm asking him about the vacuuming. That will make a positive difference to our relationship.

Our distorted self-concept

Our self-concept is how we perceive ourself. When our view of ourself is out of proportion to reality, it is distorted. A distorted self-concept will often lead to our being in a state of separatism. When we think we are greater than or lesser than others, it is difficult to find union with them. Separatism is the state of being separate or withdrawn from others. It is the state of being out of union with others. In order to move away from separatism and find union and shared meaning through good communication, we have to find a sense of equality with each other. In life we work within a particular pattern or set of karmic conditions or life circumstances that teach us particular lessons. We have often been either oppressors or victims. Some of us may have memories of being on both sides of that coin. This dynamic always creates a win/lose situation. As people awaken spiritually, they generally begin to strive to move away from a negative imbalance of oppressor and victim in their relationships in all areas, including areas such as business and organisations. It doesn't matter what profession we are in or how advanced we may be emotionally, mentally or spiritually; in every case we should aim to treat each other equally. Often people get the idea that they are more developed than others in some way. They may be more advanced in some regard but that doesn't give them the right to denigrate another. In fact, if the development is genuine, it should make a person more aware of the need to be loving and giving and to embody the higher principles in his or her daily life and actions. As we aspire to advance along the spiritual path, we need to learn to cooperate and work as one.

When we inflate our sense of self, the ego goes through an inflation and gratification process. When this happens, we might find ourselves speaking condescendingly to someone. Think about the language that you use. Think about the way you see yourself. Do you see yourself as more advanced than other people? Sometimes people see themselves as more advanced simply because they are part of a group. It brings a feeling of group elitism. Some people start to think that they are better than others. They may have knowledge others don't have and think therefore they are better than others because of this. This can create a lot of problems in relationships. It means that people don't treat each other with the right care, the right respect or speak to each other in the right language. This can create a lot of ill feeling and a lot of unnecessary pain and suffering.

Believing that we are better than others is a glamour. It is also an illusion which keeps us separate from others. Some see others as lesser than themselves, some see others as better than themselves. Some people see authority figures as the ones with the problem. This may manifest as, "I'm all right because I'm not an authority figure." On all levels no matter where we are, or what our status may be, we have these glamours and we need to work with them. It is the nature of human beings.

When we walk the spiritual path, we discover that we have glamours, illusions, tests and trials to work through. On every level there are tests and trials. At different stages of life, we are not able to fairly judge each other for what we are going through. What we need to develop instead of judgement is compassion and love for each other, and the acceptance that we all have our own particular skills, our own dharma (purpose in life) and our own abilities. We need to let go of our jealousies, our ambitions, our greed, and look at ourselves and see our own pride. We all get inflated at times and all have to be brought back to reality. That is the nature of life. It is good to be aware of our past and to be aware of our tendencies towards being the oppressor and/or towards having the cry of the victim as a way to cop out, so that we can work with and change ourselves where needed. We may not like those aspects in ourselves and yet we need to face them in order to work to redeem the shadow.

As we have mentioned, the shadow is the part of our nature that we would rather not acknowledge, as it encompasses the darker side of our being. Many people sit in denial that they have a shadow. If we wish to change for the better we have to become aware of our shadow, turn and look at it and come to know what it is and not be controlled by it, nor taken over by it, but become conscious of it. If we can begin to accept it in ourselves, we will start to understand and accept that other people aren't always loving, aren't always kind, don't always do things perfectly and sometimes make mistakes. We can love them for it instead of ridiculing them, and find compassion for them.

Inability to deal with criticism

As mentioned earlier in the book, receiving criticism is something that we are often not very good at, especially when we have done something wrong, and this tendency forms a barrier to good communication. Many people tend to want to stop the person who is critical before he or she completes the criticism so as not to be found out, or else they make excuses. It is good to say "Yes, I did do that," instead of "Yes, but ... I was trying to ..." and apologising for ourselves. State the reason, not the excuse. Being honest is important. If you do not want to do something, say so. For example, it is good to be honest and say, "I don't want to help you on the weekend because there are other things I feel I need to do," instead of, "I'd like to help you insulate your house but I'm allergic to dust and the doctor said that I shouldn't." Often we make excuses for ourselves because we fear being honest to another person. We all have other things to do and it is okay to say no, especially if that's what we mean.

Our use of criticism towards others also warrants consideration. By good use of criticism, we can create a supportive space where someone feels safe to be and to communicate with us. However, we can also create a climate which invites defensiveness. For instance, if I say, "the airline provides horrible food," this is threatening to someone connected with the airline. On the other hand, if I said something like, "on my flight all the meals had red meat in them and I'm a vegetarian," then I would be stating the truth and I wouldn't put the people involved in the airline in a state of defence. If I start to talk as if I'm the superior one, I arouse defensiveness in the other person. If I not only speak with equality but think of myself as equal to others, the respect and honour that people deserve will come out in my speech. If I don't think it, it won't come out in my speech.

I often hear people say, "I don't know how to speak with equality," "I haven't got the skills to communicate." I believe in some cases that's true. I also believe in some cases it is a cop out. If we know that about ourselves, we need to do something about it. We need to change our attitudes so that we don't continue to create relationships where we set ourselves up as the superior one, if that's not what we want to do. If our communication is working against and sabotaging the kind of relationships we would like to have, we have to do something about it. We have to start looking at the superior language and what is behind it. Usually we find thoughts of superiority, and what's usually behind thoughts of superiority is a very low self-concept built up inside to camouflage the very low sense of self-esteem and the shame that are there. We have to go into those places in our selves and heal ourselves if we are going to heal our relationships.

As mentioned earlier, if we are the one giving criticism, we need to consider:

1. Is it true?
2. Is it kind?
3. Is it necessary?
4. Is it the right time?

For example, something may be true but it may not be kind and it may not be necessary. Our speech should be able to pass all four criteria before we speak. We should perhaps also consider the distinction between criticism and feedback as we discussed in *Empowering the higher mind*, and work at giving feedback in a positive way, paying attention to our tone of voice and method of delivery.

Inability to deal with conflict

Conflict, or better, the inability to deal with conflict, is another barrier to communication. For example, conflicts may be conflicts of emotions, values or needs. When working with conflict, the dilemma can be resolved or exacerbated. Addressing conflict can also be avoided. Conflict generates many feelings in people such as excitement, a sense of importance, fear, anxiety and anger. It also can generate mistrust, blame, attachment to power and withdrawal. Conflict often produces competitiveness. We must always remember that there are two sides to every tale. If we take the time to listen to each other and clearly define our perspectives and feelings about the issues, we have made a major step towards conflict resolution.

Relationships can come into conflict when there is a high level of expectation about behaviour, when one party has the expectation and the other's behaviour does not meet it. Sometimes people move into conflict when they are competing for needs and psychological gains, rather than working cooperatively with the resources they have, for example, arguing about using the bathroom or competing for a partner. Another form of conflict is value conflict. It takes place when people's values conflict or they have different beliefs, for example, philosophies or religions. A conflict of information is also possible where people have a different view of what is relevant or true. When people try to resolve conflict, they often keep expressing their own point of view. This is not a fruitful approach. The other person remains unheard and usually just gets exasperated. To resolve conflict one needs to enter into negotiation. To do this, a person needs to decide he or she wants to resolve the conflict and needs to take the appropriate steps towards that resolution.

Dealing with conflict

There are many different ways in which we can deal with conflict. How do you deal with it? In table 1, various ways of dealing with conflict are presented. You might recognise some of the ways presented as ways you or others may use.

Some people stay away from issues and people that they are in conflict with. They have a sense of helplessness and hopelessness about conflict and their goals and relationships are somehow unimportant. The withdrawing person is not really stepping out far, not really interested in the issue, or else he or she is just withdrawing but maybe has a lot going on inside.

Another way to deal with conflict is to force the issue and try to overpower the opponent by forcing them to accept your solution to the conflict. In this case goals are important. People don't mean much and winning gives a sense of achievement.

There is also the person who likes to placate the other for the sake of peace. "It is not really a problem. Let's just be friends." The placater is avoiding conflict in favour of harmony, giving up the goals to preserve the relationship. He or she wants to be accepted and liked, that is imperative. Most issues can go by the wayside.

The compromiser is concerned about both the issue and the relationships, seeking to compromise, trying to find the middle ground. Communication is the middle ground, a common place for people to share. The compromiser is willing to sacrifice for it. However, there can be degrees of compromise and the person can go overboard. There needs to be a balance.

The confronter is one of the hardest positions to be in yet it is perhaps the best method to deal with conflict when handled well. When people confront well, they are highly valuing the goals and the relationship because they take a lot of risk in confronting the conflict. They could be confronting from a very overblown ego and doing it from the wrong motives. This needs to be considered. However, when people confront because it matters, through their perseverance it is possible for the tension and negative feelings to be resolved. It can be dangerous if the other person is not ready or prepared for the confrontation. Sensitivity and compassion become a major ingredient in good confronting.

We tend to use all these ways of relating in conflicts listed above and sometimes if we've been in one for too long we flip to its opposite; for example, if we've been placating for too long we may become angry and force.

Relationship versus issue

We place a value on relationship and we place a value on the issue at hand. In order to effectively resolve conflict, we have to walk a line somewhere between the two. If we focus all on the issue, our relationship goes out the window and then we have to run back and do a lot of work to make it right again - that is, if we are interested in the relationship, and some people aren't at all. If we focus all on the relationship but forget about the issue, a bit further down the track we start to be resentful, we start to feel something is wrong and we have to backtrack and find the issue again. So if we can stay conscious of this middle road between relationship and issue, we find the way we can work with confrontation and conflict.

Table 1. Methods of dealing with conflict and how a person behaves or reacts

Method	How a person reacts
Withdrawal	Stays away from issues and people he or she is in conflict with. Has a sense of helplessness and hopelessness. Decides that goals and relationships are not important.
Forcing the issue	Tries to overpower opponents by forcing them to accept his or her solution to the conflict. Decides goals are important, and that relationships are of minor importance. Winning gives him or her a sense of achievement.
Placating the other	Avoids conflict in favour of harmony. Gives up the goals to preserve the relationship. Wants to be accepted and liked.
Compromising	Has a more balanced concern with own goals and relationships. Seeks compromise. Seeks middle ground where both gain. Is willing to sacrifice for it.
Confronting	Highly values goals and relationship. Sees conflicts as improving relationships. Seeks solutions that satisfy both parties. Is not satisfied until tensions and negative feelings have been resolved.

Confrontation

If we wish to confront someone regarding a conflict, we need to check our motive. If our motive is "so that we may grow together," then we are probably safe and can go ahead. If that isn't our motive, maybe we shouldn't confront the issue. Being confronting can mean being direct and it can also mean being aggressive. The best way is to simply be direct and do it from a space of caring for the other person. If we have aggression in us we need to look at why and work with that in ourselves.

When we are confronting, we need to consider the quality of the relationship between us and the other person. Will the relationship take that? We also have to consider the current psychological state of the person we are confronting and the risk of disorganisation for that person. That person might be very severely affected by what we say and we need to be aware of that. What will our saying this do to him or her? Is it worth that risk? Is it the right time? Is it necessary? Is it kind? Is it true? We come back to those criteria again.

When I confronted John before, he might have very quickly confronted me back and I have to be prepared for that. We have to be aware of the limits of the other person's capacity to accept confrontation. Are we expecting too much of him or her? Is what we are actually causing a confrontation about valid, true, right? We need to create an environment of mutual trust and support and have a look at the contract that is going on between us, implicit or expressed. What is the contract that we have in our relationship? Is it one that gives me the right to confront him or her? Is it one that makes it a legitimate thing that I am doing? Is it according to the law, and which law is it? If it is the law of friendship, is that law appropriately and positively made? Is it the higher spiritual Law? Is it the moral or social law? Is that law or personal rule a valid one? These are all the questions that we need to ask before we go ahead and confront. The reason for this is that the confrontation might have quite severe effects on that other person and we need to be conscious of these.

Confront yourself and ask yourself all these questions to check it out. Especially ask, what is my motive? That will take us through the process of preparation for confronting another. With all that considered, go ahead. It is a lot to consider but certainly worth doing, because confronting is one of the most valuable tools for developing relationships. Scary though it may be, it starts a process where a lot can be exposed and brought out into the open. Sometimes if things have been concealed too long, then that is what needs to happen. Below is a checklist of what needs to be considered before confronting someone:

We need to consider:

1. Our motive.
2. The quality of relationship between us.
3. The current psychological state of the person we would confront.
4. The risk of disorganisation of the person we would confront.
5. The risk of opening ourselves to confrontation.
6. The limits of the other person's capabilities.
7. An environment of mutual trust and support.
8. The contract of our relationship, implicit or expressed.

No matter which method of conflict resolution we choose, the energy in which we do it is of vital importance. With a good energy, consensus is much more likely to be reached.

Couples in conflict - conflict resolution through active listening

Over the years, I have been working a lot in role-play and counselling with couples having difficulties. Often part of the problem is the inability to sit and hear and really know the other person's point of view. Good communication is an opportunity to:

1. Air views
2. Clear misunderstandings
3. Build trust
4. Express feelings.

There are a few ways in which we can do this. What I often do is I set up a couple of chairs. I would have two chairs seated opposite another two chairs. Marion and Ron are in relationship and they have come for help. The issue is that Marion doesn't feel heard, she doesn't feel that Ron is hearing her. To help them in this process, I would seat them opposite each other, and when we are ready to start work, move them into the chairs beside where they have originally sat. This helps to provide a new place for them to go into the issues directly with each other. I would then give them a task. The task is that Marion speaks what she actually wants Ron to hear. His task is to play it back, not to give feedback, not to interpret it, not to say what he thinks of it, whether he agrees or disagrees, but simply to say it back. In that way can show her he knows what she said and what she is feeling and that he understands where she is.

As the facilitator in this process, I'd outline to Ron what he needs to do. Marion would state what she feels is going on and I would get them to change chairs. Now Ron would act as if he were Marion, replaying what she has said. This is one of the strongest ways to get someone in touch with another person, to get them to role-play being that person. In doing that, Ron will find an empathy with Marion and she then has the opportunity to give feedback about how closely what he is doing approximates how she is actually feeling. If he has left something out that she feels is relevant she can say so. He has another go at that extra bit until she is satisfied. When she is satisfied they reverse roles. I usually move people into the chair beside the original seat. I do that to make them shift from themselves in some regard and they can return to themselves once the work is done. They shift by making an actual physical shift. Ron is going to do exactly the same reversed; Ron tells his side of the story and Marion changes over and role-plays Ron. He, then, has the opportunity if it's not right, to say what it is that's not right. She has another go until he is satisfied. Now both have heard and know where the other person is. Usually a marked shift has taken place from this exercise; suddenly they understand something about where the other person is or was that they never did before. From this point it becomes clear what needs to be worked on and what needs to be healed. Together with the couple you can work with that, and they can work together with each other. The problems are isolated and the work becomes a joint cooperative effort. The couple has gone a long way to resolving the problems and their conflict. The "you're not hearing me" barrier is removed. Together the couple work at this resolve and the whole dynamics change from then on. The relationship takes another road. Trust and security return to the relationship. These are imperative if the relationship is to go anywhere. A summary of this way of working with couples appears below:

1. Marion states her views.
2. Ron tells what he understands Marion's view to be in a replay fashion (not agreement or disagreement).

3. Marion then tells whether she is satisfied with Ron's understanding of her point of view and whether the position is correctly presented.
4. Agreement is reached about what Marion's view of the situation is.
5. Steps above are repeated with Marion and Ron's roles reversed.
6. Agreement is reached about the substance of each other's views and a great deal of intensity is released.
7. Each point of view is accepted through mutual understanding and the conflict cannot continue to take over.
8. Trust and security return.

Working with couples in this way proves very rewarding. When a person feels heard a great deal of stress and tension is released. In being heard people feel nurtured and cared for, even if disagreement still exists. It is special simply to be understood.

Overcoming separatism

All of us have our own crises, our suffering. Our soul gives us these crises and suffering to help us learn and grow. Sometimes we manufacture suffering and blame through self-pity. Manufactured suffering is something that we can do without if we start to wake up and start to learn better ways to communicate. When we realise this, we begin to stop the blame and self-pity which create separatism and begin to find union. We also begin to take responsibility for creating our own lives.

In order to communicate, we have to open up to each other. Think about how much better you feel with people who have revealed some of the most negative aspects of themselves to you, then with people who are like walls and don't say anything, never letting you know how they are feeling. As you become more real in your relationships with other people, more honest about who you are and what you are, with all your failings, with all your mistakes, you begin to see that you are still accepted and loved, and you are then able to move into union with others. You are a child of God, a spark of divinity in your own right and that is where the true power comes from. It is in love that we find true power. True power lies at the point of equality and oneness with all. It has within it humility and grace. It is through grace that we have power.

Translating knowledge into action

When you are next in a situation or a particular dynamic with someone, perhaps a loved one or a partner, perhaps a colleague in your daily business life, think about some of the points mentioned in this chapter. Think about what you are thinking about people generally. Do you think about people in a good way? Do you think about yourself in a good way? Do you see the Light and love in yourself? Are you aware of your own shadow and how it operates? Do you see the Light and love in other people? That doesn't mean you can't be aware of their darkness and of their shadow. It is important that we are. We need to find a balance. We need to make sure we don't slip into only seeing the darkness in all but to remember the Light. Remember the love. Remember that's where the power is, the power of equality, the power of oneness.

I would like to offer you two quotes to ponder on. The first comes from M. Scott Peck (1993, p. 15) in *A World Waiting To Be Born*:

... the suffering involved in hurting others may be at least as excruciating as - and sometimes inseparable from - the experience of being hurt oneself.

The next comes from Ananda Tara Shan (1993, p. 120) from *The Living Word of The Hierarchy*:

Right human relations means acting with harmlessness when associating with other people. This also means to act with honesty, integrity and natural politeness simply because you care for people ...

Do not force yourself to come across as something you are not. Politeness does not mean cloying sweetness or artificial use of superlatives in your language. Right human relations is behaving nicely to all simply because you will not hurt them unnecessarily.

If you need to state a truth, choose the right words with care, and say the truth with heart involved. When people feel heart is involved, they may not get insulted. Do not speak nastily to anyone, for that energy will return. If you are angry, show it; but do not become malicious or scream. Instead, control the anger, yet show how you feel. Do not let the anger take over and thereby say words you regret afterwards. You are not people's teacher or self imposed oracle of truth. If you are dissatisfied with something, it is not always your job to tell people off. Your truth may be your private opinion and nothing else; beware therefore, before you impose your "truth" to people as the ultimate truth. Life teaches. Sometimes it is better to let it teach unhindered by you. Think before you speak and act. That will save embarrassments and bad karma. Think this: everything I say and do is observed by God, and it all catches up with me.

Trusting in immortality

As we start to share from the heart we inevitably contact our unresolved grief. If we are to actualise ourselves as loving beings we need to work on letting our grief go. We are always at risk. What if we begin to love someone and they reject us or die? What if we decide to trust someone and they let us down? Sometimes we may think it is better not to open to love or trust in order to avoid pain. What we forget is that if we avoid pain, we do not experience the suffering that is necessary for our growth, and we stagnate. Life is full of change. If we wish to ride with the flow of life and allow these needed changes, we must open to trust and love. With change there is usually loss and gain, grief and joy. When we learn to trust in the constancy of love and the ever-present flow of Spirit in our lives, no matter what the circumstances of our lives may be, we come to know that our joy is our sorrow and our sorrow is our joy.

However, as we open to trust and love, we are often placed in the position of having to deal then with unresolved grief that has been stored in the heart until we are ready to deal with it. The grief is held in our heart - like a grievance - until, through opening to love and life again, we are stimulated to let it go. Letting the grief go and allowing love to enter and be the centre of our lives takes time. It is a process which we need to allow ourselves the space and time to work through. It is also a journey in consciousness, a journey that takes us from mistrust to trust and from fear to love.

What is grief?

Grief is the response to loss. Some insight is given into the areas affected by grief in the following definition in *Bereavement*, by Parkes (1972, p. 25):

In the ongoing flux of life, man undergoes many changes, arriving, departing, growing, evolving, achieving, failing - every change involves a loss and a gain. The old environment must be given up, the new accepted. People come and go; one job is lost, another begun; territory and possessions are acquired or sold; new skills are learnt, old abandoned; expectations are fulfilled or hopes dashed - in all these situations the individual is faced with the need to give up one mode of life and accept another. If he identifies the change as a gain, acceptance may not be so hard, but when it is a loss or a "mixed blessing" he will do his best to resist change. Resistance to change, the reluctance to give up possessions, people, status, expectation - this I believe is the basis of grief.

Many types of loss evoke the grief response, including loss of home, health, dreams/ideals, job, profession and partner through divorce or separation, abortion, miscarriage, and infertility. When we lose our job, for example, perhaps through sudden, unexpected illness, we will have a grief response. We lose one identity and gain another. Our life changes. The definition of grief is increasingly being widened to cover all areas of loss and these areas are being embraced by grief counsellors. Many people with memory of inner spiritual connection have grief simply about being here on planet Earth. They may feel the separation from the Divine and find difficulty with incarnation on Earth. There can also be grief over the loss of our gifts and skills that we may have one day, and may lose on another; for example, a good mind and memory may be lost with age, or the ability to do physical things may be lost as illness sets in.

Moving through the grieving process is not a function of time but of active decision-making as time passes. By learning about the process of mourning and grief, we can help alleviate our grief. It shows us the part we play in that process, helps us to know we are not alone, shows us that it is a road that has been walked many times before, and lets us know that we are "normal" when we have the gut-wrenching feelings, the depression and other symptoms that are common in the process. Normal grief responses may include the feeling of going crazy; hallucinations; anger; guilt; bitterness; destructibility; difficulty in remembering; confusion; anxiety; depression; loss of appetite; insomnia; withdrawal; restlessness; fear; panic; palpitations and regret.

Disease

In *Beyond Grief*, Lindemann (1979) tells us that grief and mourning can be accompanied by certain diseases. These are cardiovascular disorders, heart disease, cancer, pernicious anaemia, ulcerative colitis, leukemia, lymphoma, lupus, hyperthyroidism, pneumonia, tuberculosis, influenza, cirrhosis of the liver, glaucoma. Other illnesses that are high risks for mourners are heart attack, cancers of the gastrointestinal tract, hypertension (high blood pressure), neurodermatitis (chronic itching and eruptions of the skin, particularly in areas of heavy perspiration and in the webbing of the fingers and toes), rheumatoid arthritis, diabetes, and thyrotoxicosis (thyroid malfunction) (see also Lindemann, 1944).

Davidson, in *Understanding Mourning* (1984), adds to our list by citing chronic depression, alcoholism and other drug dependencies, malnutrition (both under- and over-nutrition) and electrolyte disorders in which the blood chemistry, particularly salts, are out of balance. Other disorders mourners often cope with include headaches (particularly the migraine variety), lower back pain, frequent bouts with colds and flu, excessive fatigue, impotence, and significant sleep disturbances.

The stages of grief

A case study

In order to understand the full implications and depth of the impact a death or loss experience can have on our lives, let us follow the process of Marie, a woman who has lost her husband through an unexpected death. Loss through death that is sudden, expected or violent often consists not only of the primary loss of the loved one, but also of the secondary loss of companionship, income, house, support, role, security and social status. Marie has three small children and has been finding her own life quite difficult, managing them and all the housework. Her husband was working late trying to make ends meet for the family and was killed in a car accident when he fell asleep at the wheel on his way home.

Stage 1

The impact on Marie is devastating, shattering, debilitating and overwhelming. Her life has been changed but without her permission. She is shocked and feels angry, guilty, resentful, fearful, regretful and experiences waves of unexpected emotion: crying, calling out, screaming and sobbing. She has feelings of blame that move to shame and back to blame. She can't eat and feels a knot in her stomach almost constantly, has bad dreams where she wakes in a sweat and with a fast-beating heart. Sometimes she forgets that her husband is gone and becomes confused when she remembers what has happened. Her sense of reality is, on occasions, quite distorted and she cannot begin to think of the long-term implications of the loss. She spends her days trying to help the children deal with and understand the loss and sometimes she loses concentration by becoming lost in memory.

Stage 2

Marie is not sure who she is anymore, the basic structure of her whole life has altered, the future she had foreseen has disappeared and she is feeling despair. Others around her avoid the subject of death or loss. She has lost faith and feels an enormous emptiness within. She still feels anger and guilt, and more and more she spends time in a state of depression. She has started to drink alcohol at night, after she has put the children to bed, to fill the emptiness she feels; her health is going downhill. Even her best friends are not there for her, there is a strain in how they relate now that her partner has gone and it is clear to her that her friends see her as acting out of character, but she can't deal with that at this time, it is all too much, and she is only able to cope day by day.

Stage 3

Marie is beginning to realise and recognise some things that help her a great deal. For instance: it is useless to stay in the energy of blame; there are some good things about being alone, even though she may be a little awkward with her new state; it is healthy to begin to rely on herself; she doesn't need to stay angry; she can change unhealthy habits, attitudes and behaviours, and she needs to make decisions herself. She is coming to terms with her guilt. She is feeling in some ways as though her husband is still present and at other times she is experiencing her loneliness. She is aware she is quite vulnerable within relationships and is in danger of repeating old errors. Movies on the television, and songs on the radio can readily trigger the grief, though it may be masked at times. She is also aware there is a lot to do, within and without.

Stage 4

Marie has made an internal decision to start living again and has decided not to be a victim anymore, realising she is responsible for her own happiness. She has survived and she can and will make decisions for herself. She is beginning to rebuild her belief system, recognising what is good for her and that she may need help to make the transition. She is finding satisfaction returning with new friends and some old ones where the strain has cleared. She is finding a continuity in her friendships and in life itself and is more open to the mystery of life and beyond. The relationship with her deceased husband is taking a new form within her that is more useful for her current circumstances, and she is able to plan ahead for the future again.

Stage 5

Marie recognises that it is time to reconstruct her life and make some changes to establish her new identity. In spite of this, she still feels a continuing loneliness and is becoming aware of the pull of her emotions, and is more able to recognise when to allow them to flow or not. Not all her difficulties have been caused by her husband's death and she is becoming aware of that. She starts to identify priorities for herself and her life, and acknowledges her fear about the future. She is making a commitment to taking on new projects even though she still has some confusion about the future.

Stage 6

Marie realises that in order to move forward now she needs to take risks and some of her fears are being re-activated in that process. She is re-examining many of her assumptions. She is beginning to reclaim from her past what gave life meaning. She is also recognising that some of the attributes she has perceived as her husbands are actually her own good points which helps her to establish her own new identity. She is no longer feeling like a failure and is finding new aspirations that create opportunities for a new life. She is inventing new ways of doing things. She can recognise that some of her problems were not caused by the loss but simply revealed by it. She is going to a therapist who is helping her, and she is also helping herself to find new solutions. She seems to have found a peaceful place for her husband in her thoughts.

Stage 7

Finally Marie is finding clarity of thinking and integrating her experience. She is finding resources deep within herself she never knew she had and she knows how to manage herself and the children in a positive way. She has decided to engage with life fully and has found contentment. Perspective has returned.

She has come to terms with the death of her former reality, while recognising that in some ways the past continues. She is finding clarity about her values and beliefs, and is asking questions about higher wisdom and understanding of the nature of the Spirit and the universe. Although she has not established a new relationship yet, she is willing and able to do so should life bring one. She feels a purpose in life and experiences compassion for the people around her.

In this case study, the far-reaching effects of the grief process and the possible phases one may go through are clearly evident. Many of the theories about grief and the corresponding research identify the phases as an integral and predictable part of the grief process. The number and names of these phases, which many theorists call stages, differ a great deal. However, on looking closely, many similarities can be found between them.

In *The Seven Choices*, Neeld (1990, p. 7) outlines seven stages which she calls seven choices. Her map of the grieving process appears in figure 13, which appears on the next page. The case study of Marie shows clearly the stages outlined in figure 13, and the seven choices listed in the map of the complete grieving process make it clear that we play a large part in resolving our grief.

The stages of dying

The grieving process often commences before the death of a loved one. This is especially so in the case of an anticipated death due to terminal illness, old age, or in some cases the sensitivity of a person who is more psychically aware that death may occur, whether that is conscious or not. Kubler-Ross, in *Death the Final Stage of Growth* (1975) suggests there are five stages of dying: denial; rage and anger; bargaining; depression and acceptance.

1. Denial - "No, not me."
2. Rage and anger -"Why me?" and Why now?"
3. Bargaining - "Yes, but ..." Truce - beginning to face it.
4. Depression - silent preparatory grief - reactive.
5. Acceptance - peace or resignation - defeat.

Kubler-Ross, like many other theorists, emphasises that stages can be skipped and a person may be in two or three stages simultaneously. It is also possible that a person may simply stay in denial. Kubler-Ross emphasises the use of symbolical and non-verbal language in the grief process. It is important that the person grieving be given space to feel and vent whatever stage he or she may be in - without judgement. Kubler-Ross' work, as well as the facilitation by self-help movements and public interest, have brought forward more eclectic, compassionate approaches where emphasis is on assisting the bereaved to release feelings, gather or relinquish defences and master the ongoing practical demands of existence.

Kubler-Ross, like others, emphasises hope, need for teamwork, and the need to consider both the dying and the family in grief counselling.

Life
Back in Balance
Freedom from the Domination of Grief

↖

Integration
To Choose to Continue to make Choices

↖

Working Through
To Choose to Engage in the Conflicts

↖

Reconstruction
To Choose to Take Action

↗

The Turn
To Choose to make an Assertion

Life
As It Was
The Event

↓

Impact
To Choose to Experience and Express Grief Fully

↓

The Second Crisis
To Choose to Suffer and to Endure

↓

Observation
To Choose to Look Honestly

↗

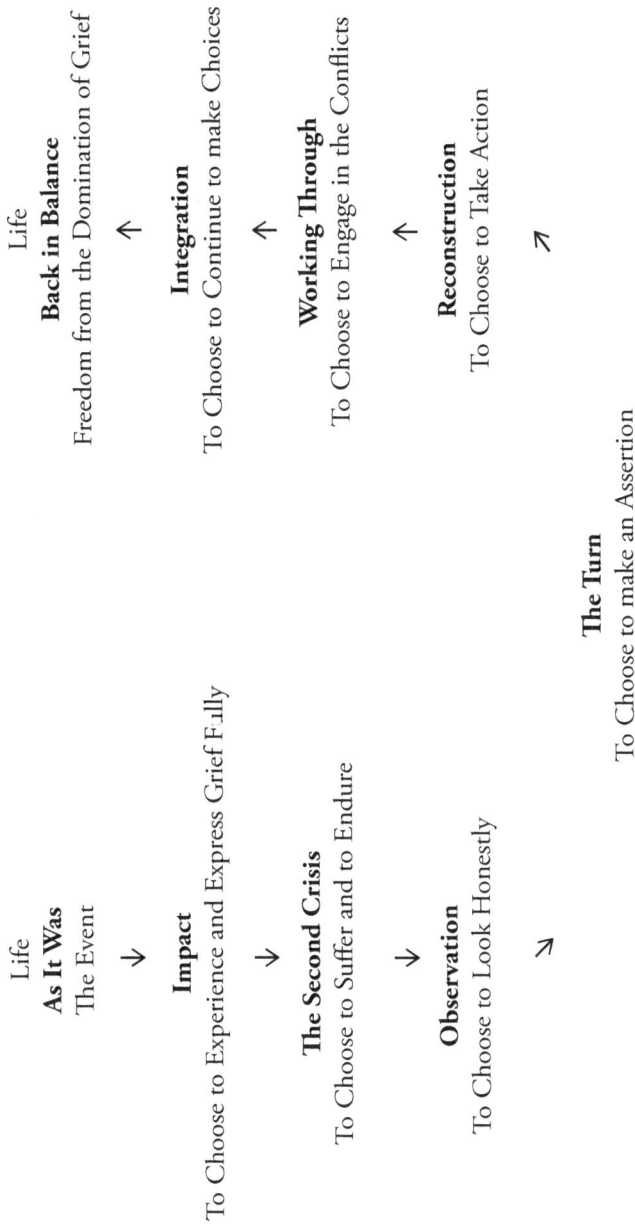

Figure 13. The map of the complete grieving process (Neeld, 1990, p. 7)

The nature of grief

Decathexis

The process of grieving involves decathexis. In other words, the person grieving is progressively withdrawing the psychic energy that connects her to the object of her love. This process requires her to move away from the earthly world and to spend time and energy in the struggle to decathect the loved one. By focusing on the lost person and bringing to consciousness each relevant memory the person grieving gradually sets him- or herself free. The choice to grieve fully is needed, as is the allowance of reminiscing and letting go. This can be stimulated by looking through the photograph album; going to familiar, shared places; listening to provocative music; and any other ritualistic and conscious efforts that are put to this task. If this phase is consciously worked through, with skilled help, the grief process can be aided considerably. Unfortunately, many turn to alcohol or drugs in order to avoid it, and sometimes, many years later, when working through the drug problem, find that grief resurfaces, hopefully this time to be felt and released. I once worked as a drug and alcohol counsellor. One of the people I was seeing at this time had commenced heavy drinking eight years prior. She had great difficulty coping with her life and was slowly distancing herself from her family. Her husband threatened to leave her if she continued drinking and at last, in a desperate attempt to save her marriage, she arrived for counselling. By working with a genogram (a chart of the family tree, a description of which can be found in the chapter *Meeting the monster*) to get some family history, I discovered that her brother had died eight years ago. Putting the two events together, and discussing it with her further, it became obvious that the drinking had begun in an attempt to suppress the grief which she felt unable to deal with at the time, due to other commitments and the need to be the strong one for the family because of other existing family dynamics. As we worked with the grief and made space for it to be experienced and dealt with, the woman's drinking problem soon halted and she lost much extra weight also.

Family

A death destroys the equilibrium of the family and its members need to reorganize the roles within their group dynamic. The person grieving not only has to grieve the loss of the loved one but also experiences the loss of the family as he or she has known it. The family dynamic makes it difficult to face the death and the reorganisation of roles is usually avoided for a time before it is confronted. The stages here are avoidance, confrontation and re-establishment. This becomes very evident at family ritual gatherings such as birthdays and Christmas. Rituals need to be re-established. The family needs to free itself as a group, as do the individual members, from the bondage to the deceased and readjustment to the new environment where the deceased is not present is necessary. New relationships need to be formed.

Grief from the past

People carry within them a lot of grief from past events that is unresolved. A current grief experience can be enough to trigger other unresolved grief that the person is now ready to deal with and let go. Often one grief experience masks other grief experiences which have been suppressed. This is why the grief reaction can sometimes be out of proportion to the current reality, bringing up with it the unresolved grief of the past. Sometimes people will become aware of this, other times not; however, either way the old grief can still be resolved and released in the healing process. Many, for example, carry with them grief that has not been worked through, but which needs to be resolved. Grief can be on a mass scale, for devastation that may have occurred, or for the loss of lives and of values, or on an individual scale for the loss of beloved ones. As we work through and redeem our past, the grief can be re-experienced and let go of, so we can then be more ready and able to trust and open to love. Grief is often found to be linked to fear, anger and/or guilt.

Fear

If grief is not released quickly enough through a balanced process of grieving, it has a tendency to turn into fear that prevents the person having to deal with the grief at that time. This defense mechanism is sometimes needed as we are not always strong enough to face deep grief. When we are able to cope and open to healing, the soul will send the Light needed to become conscious of the fear, and release the fear and the grief attached to that fear. For more understanding about the soul and the Light refer to my book, *The Healing Hands of Love* (1997).

Anger

Many people get angry when life turns out other than the way they expected it. Their anger is towards God, the person who dies or the one or ones they perceive as being responsible for changing their expected plan. Such anger shows immaturity, rebellion and resistance to the rightful flow of the universe. It can also show the desire to always be in control and reveal the selfishness of a person. When this anger is dealt with in therapy, and the outward projections are dispelled, usually a great deal of anger towards the self is found, and often low self-esteem and self-hatred need to be worked with. Facing this can be very difficult and painful; however, if it is faced, enormous release and healing can occur, changing the course of the life for the better. Anger is also used as a defense mechanism; it is often easier to get angry than to feel the pain of the loss.

Guilt

The guilt that surfaces around grief experiences is often a good indication of unfinished business that needs healing. Often the Light of forgiveness is needed. This can be forgiveness for self and others. When kept in balance, the guilt can lead us to examine our conscience and much learning can come as a result. There can also be a tendency for the bereaved person to attach too strongly to the guilt and beat him- or herself up in an unhealthy way. Again, with guilt we are looking at a defense mechanism that is perhaps easier and more familiar to the bereaved than the feeling and expression of grief. Any healing in this area needs to work with the guilt to find the gifts of learning within it and then assist the bereaved to let go of the guilt and move on to experiencing the pain of the loss, or whatever stage of the grieving process the person is in. I have had occasion to work with a number of partners of suicide victims and have noticed here the tendency to extreme guilt about matters in their daily life and conversation that occurred the preceding days and weeks before the suicide. There is a tendency to try to take on responsibility for the death. Similarly, children readily take on guilt when their parents die or divorce and concern themselves over events and circumstances that generally have no relation to the death.

Attachment

Grief can be seen as differing in intensity according to our level of attachment. In *Attachment and Loss*, Bowlby (1973) suggested that grief can be likened to separation anxiety and is a response that is gradually extinguished as the individual realises that reunion will not occur. Grief is viewed as an instinctive behavioural response where the stages evident are protest, yearning and searching, disorganisation (despair) and reorganisation (detachment). Parkes (1972) sees grief as a process of realisation in which internal awareness is adjusted to external events. This process involves the experiencing of repeated discrepancies that result from remembering the loved one in environments with which the deceased is no longer connected. The resulting frustration is eventually extinguished and the grieving process gradually ends. The stages, in this case, are seen as numbness, pining, depression and recovery.

Re-education about death and grief

People who are grieving may be conscious of the fear of the unknown, the sense of separation, the unfinished business, the pain and the suffering. There is usually also a large and very significant aspect that sits deeply in the unconscious which makes people prone to the irrational; this is the sense that death is a catastrophic and destructive force. Any re-education about death and the after-life needs to address these deep levels for people to get real help. Our understanding of death and the after-life is not much use as an intellectual concept but needs instead to be brought into realisation at all levels of our existence. The lack of education about the truth of death, the law of reincarnation, of death and rebirth makes the process of grieving more difficult than it might otherwise be. If you would like to know more about reincarnation you may wish to refer to the chapter Reincarnation in my book, *The Healing Hands of Love* (1997).

There is a cultural reluctance to experience and express grief fully in spite of the physical and psychological ailments that develop through the suppression of grief. My doctor recently told me that when he attends homes where a person has just died, in Anglo-Australian families, everyone is in the kitchen having a cup of tea, whereas in Australian-Italian families, everyone is in the room with the deceased expressing their pain and sorrow. Bowlby (1973) says that persons who will achieve a healthy outcome to their grieving are people who let themselves be swept by pangs of grief. Parkes (1972) reminds us there is an optimal level of grieving which varies from one person to another. Some will cry and sob, others will express their feelings in other ways. Many need to learn to ask for what they need from family and friends. Family and friends need to realise that the bereaved has a painful and difficult task to perform that cannot be avoided and cannot be rushed. Help can be given by freeing the bereaved, in any way, to the process of grieving.

The following quote from Ananda Tara Shan (1993, p. 99) in *The Living Word of the Hierarchy* gives a good indication of the kind of re-education needed about grief in the world today:

> We must learn to appreciate the good and loving things in life. For example, in a world that has not much love in it, it has become nearly a miracle to have loving parents, who, on behalf of Spirit, are raising and educating their children with a true purpose and true love. We must learn to appreciate the small things in life. We must learn to appreciate every day of good health with joy and laughter, and must be prepared and ready for the grief and sadness it is to "lose" a loving parent, a loving partner, a loving friend. For such is life that we must learn to take both joy and pain with a smile on our lips. We must believe in the Theosophy that has taught us that there is no death, only life to the ones who live with God. And so we as a matter of fact, as a reality, never lose love; but love is a magnet that shall attract us to embody with the same souls throughout time.

Remembrance

As mentioned earlier, C.W. Leadbeater, in Besant and Leadbeater's *Talks on the Path of Occultism* (1991, p. 150) tells us that the Lord Buddha's Noble Eightfold Path has as its last step, "Right Remembrance." The Lord Buddha said to His followers:

> You must be very careful what you allow yourselves to remember. If you say you cannot help remembering everything, then you have no control over your memory, over the mind which is part of yourself. It is as though you went along the street gathering up all the rubbish which came in your way; you are sweeping into your memory all kinds of useless and undesirable things. You should remember the right things and be particularly careful to forget the others.

Leadbeater said that the Lord Buddha stated that people should forget "all unkind words spoken to them, fancied slights and injuries" (p. 151) and remember the kind words and the kind deeds and good qualities we have seen in our neighbours. We may remember the "bad" things, but only to look at what needs to be learned and to take that learning with us. Often, however, this is not what people do. In the chapter *Finding forgiveness*, we saw how this lack of forgiveness of "bad" experiences stimulates anger and guilt; grievances are harboured and forgiveness is withheld. Another issue arises when we remember people who have died. The memory we hold can become unrealistic and out of proportion to the reality of what they were really like. The deceased person can become a fantasy hero; the lost partner is idealised to avoid dealing with needed issues. This can be quite destructive to the healthy resolution of the grieving process.

When we reincarnate, grief is part of the memory carried over. This unresolved grief can create problems for us in life. Ananda Tara Shan (1993, p. 162) states:

> Beloved ones lost is something we do not forget though we return in other lives. We bring the grief with us from deep-seated unresolved emotion.

We can make ourselves very unhappy when we get stuck in the lower nature of grief, thinking only of ourselves, how hard and sad it all is. The energy becomes that of self-pity and takes us into a negative cycle of selfishness. Leadbeater and Besant (1991) suggest that the remedy for grief and selfishness is to go and do something for someone else, work and cease to think of yourself. She suggests we learn to love, without the thick coating of selfishness that often accompanies it, without asking for anything in return.

We should also recognise the tremendous source of help from the Divine which is there for us, as is explained in the following quote by Ananda Tara Shan (1993, p. 12), from *The Living Word of The Hierarchy*:

> Lean against God. Embrace the Son, and your grief and suffering shall melt away. Give yourself up in trust and in faith to the heavenly Father-Mother, for in Them we find solace and comfort. Life on Earth is not easy for anyone. Earth is a school. Life is teaching the lessons necessary to leave school.

Another quality we should consider to help us overcome grief is that of desirelessness. By attempting to cultivate desirelessness and making that quality a part of our character, we could more easily let go and accept when things do not go our way. Part of opening to this quality involves questioning what "I" is: "I want," "I wish." Which part of us is it? The higher nature or the ego? As we come to trust the flow of life, and begin to accept the existence of karma and reincarnation, we can move through the process of grief in a more balanced way. Psychologically, as we have seen, we must go through decathexis, and we need to give ourselves the time and space to grieve fully for the person which we will no longer meet on the earthly plane. We must remind ourselves that we are still one in Spirit and that in reality there is no loss. As this understanding becomes integrated into our view of life and death, we can change the approach to death in our society. We can also help ourselves enormously to move through our grief and allow it to be the transforming and healing process that it is.

Resolution

Resolution of grief is a task that spans over a lifetime. Successful resolution helps us to grow emotionally, to understand ourselves better and to improve our life skills. Our social conditioning has an effect on our ability to deal with grief, which can also be learned by modelling. In *Coping with Separation and Loss as a Young Adult*, LaGrand (1986) suggests that the tasks of resolution are:

1. Accepting the reality of the loss
2. Confronting emotional and physical pain
3. Confronting associated losses
4. Reinvesting in life
5. Accepting recurrences and reminders
6. Exposing oneself to the risk of losing again

How grief is viewed

As mentioned, many theories that describe the grief process emphasise the grief experience as occurring in phases or stages. Youngson (1989), for example, suggests the stages of shock, searching, anger, depression, acceptance and growth. These do not necessarily occur one after the other; however, each stage people find themselves in may need some resolution before another can be fully entered into. However, it is possible that we can flip backwards and forwards between stages, for example, from anger to depression to anger - so we can enter another stage before full resolution of the previous one.

Theories that explain the processes involved in grief emphasise that depression and stress underly the grief experience. The focus is on how we respond emotionally (depression) and on the psychological and physiological responses to a stressful event and the effect these have on our ability to cope (stress).

Getting help

Counselling

The aim of counselling is to transform distorted grief reactions, into normal grief responses. Counselling aims to aid us by providing a space where our expression of grief can occur and be shared. It also aims to help us in considering the consequences grieving has on our lives. It will often emphasise reviewing the relationship with the one who has died or left, and re-assimilating it into a new form within the person concerned. In counselling a caring attitude is needed. One that assists us to release feelings, gather defenses if they are needed, or relinquish them, as the case may be, and be able to deal with the ongoing demands of everyday existence.

The complex and idiosyncratic nature of the grieving process lends itself to an approach designed to consider us in whatever stage of the grieving process we may be in.

Issues in counselling

Establishing a relationship with someone who is grieving depends on their willingness to open up and on the stage they are in. The purpose of counselling needs to be defined and the loss explored. Furthermore, the circumstances of the death, what it means to the one grieving, their personal and social responses and the associated psychological trauma also need to be looked at. Sometimes there may be stress after a trauma. Gradually the bonds to the lost person are let go of in such a way as to work towards the future life with the living. Current life experiences and the relevant past need to be explored by looking into areas such as practical issues, finances, housekeeping and emotional support. Supportive counselling should facilitate and complement social processes that will encourage natural grief and mourning processes.

Areas that often become relevant in grief work are drug and alcohol problems, work and social impairment, relationship failures or family disintegration. The use of medication may inhibit the grieving process and careful monitoring is needed. The person in grief may give up hope. This is especially likely with the elderly. Where a grieving person may transfer his or her need for love to the person helping them, transference may become an issue which needs to be carefully worked with. Referral to self-help groups can help. The counselling work is designed to help people accept the reality of the loss and experience and live through the emotional, physical, and behavioural pain. When death is anticipated, counselling can be offered in advance. Loss is not necessarily totally resolved by counselling, but the process enables the person grieving to function in their life and maintain their life, adapting to the change in circumstances without being dominated by the ties and memories. Positive outcomes can be achieved in one session, but generally several are needed. Kubler-Ross (1975) suggests that if the person grieving has access to support around the clock in the initial stages, the denial stage can be worked through more quickly. It is often in the early morning hours or late at night when people need help. For this reason telephone counselling can be very beneficial, and a number of community services are offered for that purpose.

How are those grieving at risk?

When one partner dies there is a high risk that the partner who is left may commit suicide. When people experience the intensity of the grief response, they are at risk of developing deeper problems with their personality through despair, depression, hopelessness and even delusional guilt. Raphael and Nunn (1988) suggest issues which we can consider in determining whether the person grieving may be in danger of developing ongoing problems:

1. The nature of the relationship - level of dependency, sense of abandonment, ambivalence.

2. The circumstances of the death or loss - sudden, violent, suicide, stigmatised, death of children.

3. The social support - reflects society's interactional patterns and themes of a particular culture as well as the surroundings of an individual.

4. Multiple stresses - if several losses at once, and/ or experience injury themselves: the grief can be overwhelming.

5. Background variables - previous losses, socio-economic disadvantage, housing difficulties. lacking access to systems.

6. Bereavement in the family - the functioning of the family system, its openness and flexibility for effective sharing and support.

Ways of working with grief

In grief work, emotional release and general upliftment may be brought about through the use of music, art, dance, yoga and play therapy. Meditation may be used to help contact intuition. Massage and Rolfing may be used to assist grief release on the physical level. People may be able to express what they need to the deceased on the inner, giving them comfort and a sense of completion they may not have had, depending on the circumstances of the death. Empathic listening can help to facilitate the expression of feelings of grief and generate insight into the grief experience. Guided imagery work can be extremely valuable as can work that focuses on the feeling of grief manifesting in the body and discovering the connection to the underlying emotions. Visualising the person and speaking to them on the inner, as well as role-play work helps with good-bye rituals. It also helps with the withdrawal of projection onto the deceased so that the person grieving can feel the full realisation of the loss. Sometimes people think quite irrationally about death. For example:

"I am bad because I was not there when she died."
"I loved her too much to be able to be happy again."

Counselling needs to be done very sensitively and can be used to explore destructive thought patterns which may be interfering with adjustment. It can be useful with clients who have low self-esteem or dependency issues with the deceased.

Some therapies focus on behaviour, working with relaxation and even exercise. Others take a skills-based approach, working with self-talk and visualisation to practice new behaviours that are more appropriate. Group therapy work and family systems therapy may also be useful. Rituals serve a therapeutic function by providing a setting for expression and completion. Our awareness of our ability to make choices about how we approach grief becomes paramount in our ability to readapt to the new life. Helping people through the stages and helping them slowly back into their usual activities can help bring release and readjustment, as can making use of available social support and control of drug and alcohol use.

Working with grief in healing

Spiritual healing can be of great benefit to a person in the grieving process. It may facilitate release on many levels. Contact is made with Spirit through this process which often helps the person grieving regain the sense of immortality and find peace again. Care, sensitivity and compassion are needed. It is important to allow people to be where they are and express what they need to express. The healing given can heighten the grieving person's awareness of the naturalness of life and death (as natural as night and day) and connect them to the inner world where many insights can be gained and healing can be given on all levels of consciousness. Shock, stress and tension can be released, depression lifted, emotional and heartfelt expression enabled and help given in understanding and accepting what has happened. Sometimes the communion with Spirit that can take place assists the grieving person to let go and complete unfinished business with their loved one. Perhaps they never managed to tell the person they loved them. Doing that can give great release. Sometimes forgiveness is needed for unresolved issues. The sensitivity and alertness of the healer can help a great deal in this process.

Be cautious of techniques that "cut the ties" between people without proper psychological assistance to work through what that might mean and what the ties are. Generally, the pain needs to be felt, and there are no short cuts. However, spiritual healing can assist in helping the grieving person in letting go of and in releasing the ties and attachments to the loved one so that both parties may be set free. It brings a sense of comfort and mercy to this natural process.

Some stories

In the story following we see grief being explored in a session of guided imagery. Previous guided imageries had pointed to a number of issues that needed to be explored in order to decrease the occurrence of illness in Jocelyn's life. Grief was one of them. On this occasion it was time to explore the grief trapped within her. By going into the grief and exploring it, understanding and release could occur.

The grief bubble

Today it was time to explore more of the grief bubble. Jocelyn tuned in to the feeling of grief within the chest. It had a sense of numbness about it.

"Imagine it like a flower opening," she was told, "and go to the very centre of it." The response within was immediate. A golden flower with soft yellow petals opened out and in the centre was a radiant nucleus. As she focused on its centre, the orange colour took the form of a tiny Buddhist monk. She could see that he was grieving.

"Why are you grieving?" she asked. "What is your pain?"

"I wonder" the monk said, "what has happened to the simplicity of life. It has become so complex in the western world."

The more Jocelyn looked into the monk the more she could sense an energy of frustration and pain. It was as though he wanted to scream, "No, stop!"

"What has happened to you to make you feel like this?" she asked.

"I used to live in a monastery," he replied, "but aristocracy came and turned it into a school."

She could sense his pain and wondered if it wasn't personal, so she asked:

"What's wrong with that?"

"They didn't honour the wisdom and they stopped teaching it. That is where my pain lies."

At this point she could feel the pain within her.

"Why are you in me?" she asked.

"We share the same pain," he replied and Jocelyn could feel that it was true.

"That is why you become tense and sometimes ill shortly after you return home from the university, because you intuitively know that the wisdom is not being honoured in much of what you are taught and your body closes down because of the disappointment you experience, even though to a large degree it is unconscious."

"How can I release this expectation and not respond in such a way with my body?"

"Live with right effort."

"How do I do that?"

"Live a balanced life, do work for others as well as your own inner work. Honour the wisdom yourself and have no expectation that others should do that also. Look for the Light in their hearts as I am in yours. It is there in everyone, the potential for simply being. Take time to do simple things. Paint the golden flower and me within it. Allow your heart to express and write about me so that the wisdom may be honoured."

"But when will I find time?" she replied, aware of the many tasks on her plate.

"You need not see it as a task, simply follow your inspiration when it comes. Doing this will free you of stress which builds up when you resist doing this. It takes a lot of energy to stop the Divine flow. Many human beings end up sick when they do so. Much illness could be averted if people would listen more to the inner call from the heart. It is in the balance of listening on the inner and acting on the outer that true health resides. Since we share the same pain, we can work together to make sure we honour the wisdom and it is within oneself that one must start."

Jocelyn was amazed. She thought that in entering her grief bubble she would find some traumatic event that would be difficult to face. Instead, she found great wisdom and a friend for life and beyond.

The next story is about learning to trust the power of love and the importance of trusting in immortality.

Camilla

It took a long time to decide whether I should take her. The story behind her was not one of good fortune but then if I allowed myself to act on every story I heard that spoke of tragic circumstances I imagine I would be a very long way from where I was meant to be. It had been six months and I was still contemplating it. That in itself said something. Perhaps she was to be mine. She was a saluki dog by the name of Camilla, whose grace and presence I had no idea about and of whose ability to teach me I had not yet conceived. She was one year old and had had a number of homes before mine; a number of owners who, I'm sure, all did their best to accommodate her but who, for various reasons could not keep her. I decided to take the plunge and enter into relationship with this dog, to be her owner and to care for her in what way I could. The day came when she was to arrive. The people were late in bringing her. I had planned an outing that afternoon. It was half an hour before I had to go when they arrived. "Make sure you give her a place in the house that is hers. Salukis like that. Then she'll settle in." I scanned the room quickly but it seemed she'd already found the place she liked and I placed a blanket beneath it. She preferred the lounge chairs, it seemed. There was an air of royalty in her presence. But this did not bode well with me and I attempted to get her to resume position upon the blanket.

The people left. What had I done? Wherever I walked, she followed - in a somewhat nervous fashion. I'd think about it later, I thought, but I had to go out. I knew I would be back in a couple of hours. That shouldn't be too long.

The look in her eyes made me feel as if I had abandoned her and I imagined what it would be like for a mother to leave her child for the first time. I became immediately aware of how much I would learn from this experience. It broke my heart to leave and all sorts of emotions and feelings came up within me. I felt guilt, fear, love. This was something to really set my programs in motion. One thing was clear. I would need to learn to be more detached. About 2 hours later I returned to the house and I went from room to room looking for Camilla. I liked the name so I kept it. It seemed to suit her. She was nowhere to be found and I went into the bedroom. I could see that the wire on the window had been eaten through and she was gone. I couldn't believe it. I had left the window only a couple of inches open. Somehow she must have pushed it up higher in order to escape. The people who sold her to me had told me that if a saluki gets free it will just run and run and not return. The memory of their words came back. I felt pain, grief and concern over what would happen to her now. A short-lived union, yet the feelings were quite strong. No sooner did I begin to experience this than she appeared by my side, having come through the front door. She looked up at me and communicated telepathically. "If you give me trust I will be trustworthy and I will never run away." I bent down and hugged her; our relationship had begun.

For the weeks that followed I showered her with attention and affection - not once did she respond. She seemed to hold her nose in the air and act as if she were "holier than thou." "Trust me to get a dog like this," I thought, "one who would expect me to do all the giving." It seemed in keeping with my relationships at the time, or at least my attitude towards them. Eventually I gave up wanting her to respond. I began to see the need to simply give my affection unconditionally and provide for her as I had undertaken to do, without expecting her to do anything, to give anything other than what she was. It was a beautiful realisation to come to and it freed me of the frustration of insatiable want that had been affecting my life for some years. One evening soon after this realisation, Camilla came to me when I was reading. She put her paw on my arm and licked it. She nudged my elbow with her snout and simply sat and looked at me. I looked back for a time and patted her ears. She nuzzled my arm and I became aware that balance could enter my life, there could be give and take. There were many ways to express love, to give and receive love. I was just beginning to discover them.

Love was the only way. The moment I attributed more power to myself because I was a human being was the moment I lost her. Not only could

I not communicate, I also couldn't discipline or maintain any element of control over her actions. It seemed that love was the key to help create the link to the animal kingdom. When there was love coming from my heart towards her, I could feel a link to the spiritual worlds where we were both beings on earth, moving towards our own evolution.

October 21, 1991

Camilla had been agitated for some hours. I sat down to try and formulate the names of the puppies. The names I chose were Sanskrit ones. I selected nine names in all. I could choose from these.

5.00 a.m. I felt Camilla's paw on my arm. I opened my eyes from sleep and peered directly into hers which were wide and looking a little fearful. A deep groan came from her being and I knew it was time. A room had been organised for her to whelp in, but it was clear there was no time to get to it. I reached for newspaper and plastic to put under her and the birthing began. One by one they came, their little heads making bumps under her skin as they moved along the birthing canal. The first three were blonde and male. "Four, five, six," they kept coming." "Seven, eight, nine." A variety of colours and sexes. Camilla knew exactly what to do. One by one she ate away the tissue from the sacs. No sooner did she lick clean one, than another arrived. Nine little beings, all ready to find a place in the world. The months that followed had me busy, looking after these little creatures, who grew up, each with their own markings and personality. It brought out the mother in me and helped me understand more of the Divine Mother as I had put my trust in her.

I found myself seeing beauty in the form. I noticed that when I'd think one was beautiful the others would pale into insignificance in my mind. When I did this I would lose touch with love and feel a sense of possession. The moment I decided one was to be mine I was unable to see the beauty in the others. I realised I had to let them all go and know that what was mine would come to me. When people came to look I

259

decided to let them choose and I felt they would leave me with the ones I was meant to have. Be it one or two or none.

The saluki has the quality of grace. They are regal creatures. They also, it seems, teach people about love. Their heritage goes back to ancient Egypt, having spent much time in the temples of kings. I contemplated the link between the human and the animal kingdom. Some people cannot open to other people but can open to animals. For such people it is through this link that love can be learned and sometimes it is their only access to love.

I pondered whether I would keep any of this litter. I felt I could provide a good home, but I decided it was not for me to control the outcome of this. I took it as a step in trusting the Universe, and decided to be open to what happened. I began to let go.

I took the puppies to the vet for their shots. Everything had gone fine. It was the first time the vet had met Camilla and he commented,

"Do you know what Camilla means?"

"Yes," I replied, "it means 'freeborn servant of the temple'!" I replied, well aware of the truth of this meaning and I pondered upon the extent to which Camilla seemed to provide a protective shield against certain psychic energies. Salukis have some connection to the Egyptian annubis.

"No, it doesn't," he replied, bringing me back with a thud. It means 'attendant at a funeral.'"
With my mind set I found it difficult to relate to this comment. I guess it depends on what book you look in. I gathered Camilla and the nine pups and left, aware of the ironies and the separate realities within which we exist in life. It was later that evening the learning began.

The pups were out feeding and I did my usual head-count - eight! I found him, number nine, lying in the shed. As I approached I could tell there was something wrong and I instinctively picked him up, drawing him close to my heart. As I did this, his insides - a combination of blood and mucous - fell onto my foot from his anal passage. As I looked into his eyes, I realised that he was not in his body. There was half a glimmer of light and I could feel the mortality of his form. I rang the vet, aware there was no time to lose and drove him several kilometres. I took Camilla with me. I could tell by the look in the vet's eyes that there was little hope and I also felt the commitment of the vet to do his best. Leaving him there for proper attention, I journeyed home with Camilla by my side. As I drove I began to feel the grief. I could feel it within me like an enormous pit in my stomach that contained deep pain. I remembered the vet's comments from earlier that day - "attendant at a funeral"- the words echoed and the grief became overwhelming. My stomach convulsed and I was swamped by tears from within. I was so overcome by the emotions that I could hardly keep my eyes on the road, and I prayed that the puppy, Sai Ram, be let live.

All of a sudden the grief stopped, as Camilla put her paw on my heart centre. For a moment I looked into her eyes and could see the senselessness of human emotions. She could see my pain and lifted her head high as if to say, "This is how you do it - be strong and continue." She turned her head back towards the road with eyes fixed upon it. It was her pup who was dying and her response was so accepting of life that it provided a lesson for me. I could see my attachment and the pain it caused. I could see her detachment and the flow it gave her life. In the hours that followed I found myself oscillating between the strength Camilla had mirrored and the despair for my own loss.

Fortunately that day I had a therapy scheduled. In it I did some inner guided work. As the session began I felt a weightiness on my chest and felt and saw the image of jewellery, golden and laden with stones upon me. The deeper I went the stranger the feeling became until I felt trapped and suffocated in the human form. I felt entombed. I pondered upon beliefs held in ancient Egypt. People were playing with life and death, coming from wrong motives. Some were attached to the form, *wanting to preserve their bodies, their possessions, believing they could return to them in time to come. Others were attached to Spirit, wishing to speed up the process of initiation. Both were in the wrong. I could feel the overwhelming panic of suffocation. The realisation had been deep within me. It was as though I was in Egypt those thousands of years ago, encased in the tomb, approaching my death. As I went through the suffering, I could feel the enlightenment approaching and I vowed from deep within that I would never play with Spirit in such a way again. Never try to contain it, to force it or to speed up the process of my evolution or that of others. I would leave that to God and allow the Plan to unfold as it should. I immediately prayed to God that Sai Ram be set free. That his spirit be able to live or die, whatever was right in God's Plan and I felt shame for the part of me that had been so self-centred as to demand he remain on Earth. I thought of all the people I try to possess in whatever form through relationships and family and I prayed that I in no way interfere with their path. I could feel the responsibility I have for my own spiritual destiny and the importance of using my energies correctly; of surrendering everything to God. And I thought of the puppies, the beauty of all of them and the different lives they would live. I could see the need for balance in life. Looking within I could see many threads of dark entanglement turning to Light and every cell filled with the fullness and warmth of golden white Light. I could see the form of Sai Ram empty and the Light particles of the soul ascending. He had been set free.*

The healing had taken an hour and a half. It commenced at 2.30 p.m. I rang the vet afterwards. Sai Ram had died at 3.00 p.m.

One by one, the pups found their homes. I was very glad it wasn't all at once. The grief would have been overwhelming but I was spared that by the perfect timing of the Universe.

Embracing the Grail

If there can be a final step in the process of becoming whole, it would be that of embracing the Grail. Essentially this means that we must embrace the notion of soul and Spirit. For many years psychology has addressed human nature in terms of people's personality, considering the way that we as humans, think, feel and act. Our behaviour and the reasons for it have been studied and analysed. However, the notion of soul and the acknowledgment of the Spirit of a human being have not been adequately addressed. As we approach the second millennium it is becoming obvious that if psychology is to remain a contributing field, it will need to begin to address soul and Spirit. Many are awakening to the Light within. This Light is the fulfilment for which many yearn. It activates healing and transformation for all who seek it, and provides the key to becoming whole. This Light is not new. It has been experienced within people's hearts, written of for centuries, and spoken of perennially by philosophers and religious scholars of the east and west.

The Holy Grail

The Light of Spirit is evident in the story of the Holy Grail, an event which occurred about 500 AD and has been revived in myth and legend since, especially during the fifth and sixth centuries and the twelfth and thirteenth centuries, and it is again alive and current in the twentieth and soon twenty-first centuries.

On the physical level the Grail is the cup used by Jesus at the Last Supper. The Grail contains the seven drops of Christ's blood, thus giving it a power beyond the physical, transcending the ego to the Spirit or the Divine. Symbolically, the Grail is the vessel through which the Light of Spirit pours.

The Grail radiates a supernatural Light that brings enlightenment, and can be found within the heart of all. It not only enlightens but renews and gives us the power of victory over the darkness within and around. The Grail gives spiritual nourishment and life. This nourishment eventually destroys every material craving and helps us find the vision of angels. It has the power to heal our wounds, it vivifies and brings life to the pure of heart. The Grail gives to each of us precisely what we need. It is universal and contains the potential to provide anything and everything that is necessary for our growth. It is the key to accessing our divinity.

To those not pure of heart, it can blind, and can act as a vortex for the abyss. The Grail has great power. It is the power of pure Spirit, so when someone not pure of heart approaches, the glamours are stimulated, the ambition rises and the negative self is seen. The person wants union, but feels separated, and he or she is separated by his or her own darkness, and the power and strength of that darkness make it impossible for that person to come closer to the Grail, as it highlights the darkness and shows where he or she must work to become whole. The Grail, corresponds to the feminine, vivifying and enlightening aspect in both men and women. The phoenix is another symbol which represents the Grail and it hints to the alchemical virtues of the Grail Light. It is sometimes called the Stone of Light and has been seen as the philosophers' stone.

The quest for wholeness

The quest for the Grail symbolises the quest for wholeness, the union of soul and personality. The quest is essentially an inner event - the objective being a spiritual goal representing inner wholeness, union with the Divine and self-fulfilment. In the Grail legend, the scene is usually set in a far-off country or paradise, where the Grail is found in a temple on top of a mountain, surrounded by water and protected by obstacles which only the chosen few can overcome. Its guardian is both a priest and king, and the rewards of the hero, successful in the quest, are good fortune, blessings and sometimes the hand of the king's daughter.

The key to finding the Grail is to be pure of heart, and if a man or woman can become pure of heart, he or she can be given the power to become the Grail in action, which in essence is love in action. The energy of Spirit can freely flow through them. Many have not understood the Mystery of the Grail, for the Grail is pure Spirit, which is given to empower those pure of heart. People often look from the earthly perspective and see it as a treasure to be possessed. Yet it cannot be possessed for the wrong reasons - it can be sought after for the wrong reasons, but in that case it won't be found. It symbolises the spiritual quest, and the need to bring Spirit into matter and spiritualise life. As one passes each test associated with the attainment of the Grail, one's own particular learning is revealed. Each approaches the Grail in his or her own unique way and the Grail gives the tests and trials accordingly. It may be difficult but it is a necessary process to wake us up, and to help us come to greater consciousness.

The path to the Grail is accomplished "degree by degree" (Ravenscroft, 1995, p. 15). For example, Parcival, one of the main legendary protagonists who goes in search for the Grail, grows "from naive dullness, through the torment of doubt ..." to having connection with his soul, which gives "the attainment of blessedness ..."(p. 15). In the outer events and the inner development of Parcival's life the factors of fate, freedom and grace are in operation. These factors play a major part in all of our lives as we seek the fulfilment of the Grail. As we watch those seeking the Grail, we become aware of their strengths and weaknesses which aid or hinder their cause; for example, by craving enjoyment beyond what the world is currently offering us, we create a sense of separation. Because we try to cling, pain, suffering and death arise. The Lord Buddha showed us how to accept the existence of pain and suffering. The prophet Zarathustra sought to transform the experience of pain and suffering into a positive way of life through spiritualising ourselves (Ravenscroft, 1995). In the chapter *Creating alchemy*, and throughout this book generally, we have seen ways to move through our darkness and become Light. We have been given many of the steps we need to walk if we are to become whole and find the Grail within us. On the quest for the Grail we discover and come to know that as we awaken our God-self, the human soul can become a living vessel of the Spirit, and we can move to higher and higher levels of consciousness until we rebuild the temple of God within us.

Through the Grail legends, we learn that it is possible to redeem the negative self within us. We also see the effects of the negative within us through certain characters. In looking at the idea behind the symbol of the holy vessel, we seem to catch a glimpse of a dual-natured Grail figure representing God as male and female contained within a single image of wholeness, the Grail. The men and women who seek the Grail vary in their approach to its attainment.

The best psychological interpretation of the Grail legend I have found is the one given by Jean Shinoda Bolen (1982, pp. 99-101) in her book, *The Tao of Psychology*. As you read her initial description, think of the country as being the self and the king as ruler of the country, as the ego. Also think of the Grail in the king's castle as the Spirit or the spark of divinity within us. Jean Shinoda Bolen tells us:

> The country's problems are related to the wounded Fisher King who suffers continuously because his wound will not heal. The Grail is in his castle but the King cannot touch or be healed by it until, as prophesied, an innocent young man comes to the court to ask the question "Whom does the Grail serve?"

... If the ruler of the country, the ego, could be touched by the Grail and experience the spirituality of the Self or the inner Christ, it would have the power to heal him. Synchronistically, when his wound was healed the country would recover. Joy and growth would return. The wound may symbolise the situation of ego being cut off from the Self, where the separation is a wound that never heals and causes continuous pain in the form of a persistent, chronic anxiety and depression.

... For many individuals, and certainly for our culture as a whole rationalism or scientific thinking is the ruling principle. In the Grail legend it is cut off from the spiritual communion vessel, through which healing and return of vitality would flow. The wound that will not heal is the result of the severing of a connection crucial to well being. The King cut off from the Grail is the rationalist ego cut off from spirituality, thinking separated from feeling ...

This analysis forms an analogy to life today. When we do not acknowledge Spirit, our life loses meaning and we feel somehow that something is missing. Jean Shinoda Bolen goes on to tell us that this missing aspect becomes the wound which we experience as a "gnawing, pervasive, persisting insecurity" (1982, p. 100), and it affects our capacity to open to love and let it flow through us. Instead, we seek money, power or sex to compensate, and probably also enter a state where the world ceases to have meaning for us, where depression, anger, fear and resentment take hold. It is not until we open to the inner child, which contains the needed purity of heart and innocence that we can be healed; when we open to the innocence of our heart.

... then the internal landscape which has been a wasteland or dry desert, may bloom and be green again, as emotion

and spiritual feeling, in touch with the symbolic layer
of the unconscious, are brought into the personality.
(Bolen, 1982, p. 101)

If we cast our minds back to the case study of Jim, in the chapter
Looking for meaning, we may begin to see ways in which he can
become whole.

Parcival

Let us consider our quest for the Grail through the protagonist
Parcival. His name is Parc-i-val - he must "pierce-the-veil"
(Ravenscroft, 1995, p. 77) so that the Light that has the power to
penetrate and shine in the shadows can illuminate the darkness
within. Parcival provides us with many keys as to the quest for
wholeness; for example, according to Ravenscroft (1995) in *The
Cup of Destiny*, Parcival can see inner pictures but he cannot hear
spiritually what they mean. He needs to activate both sides of
the brain further in order to master the intuition. It is in the
intuitive faculty that we find the transcendent kingdom of the
Grail. Ravenscroft also tells us that one cannot approach the
Grail through earthly understanding, or through intellectualism.
Parcival is not ready - he does not have the correct garments.
We must pass through the denseness of our matter into the
Spirit which lives within us. When we do this we open to the
perception of the archetypes. Unless a man activates his anima,
his feminine self, and works to develop that, he cannot become
whole and will forever feel disconnected and separated from God
the Father-Mother. The Grail mysteries are feminine mysteries
and they give the key to the knights and Kings like Arthur. For a
woman, the Grail becomes an inner reality when she frees herself
from the bondage to the patriarchal conditioning, which tells her
that she is somehow "less than", and activates her animus, or the
inner masculine. When a woman realises herself, she becomes the

Grail. Men and women each have their own journey. We must walk it ourselves, none can really come with us as each journey is unique. As we focus on the inner vision, the rest will follow, as night follows day.

Parcival also goes through a process of self-reflection, with the purpose of finding self-awareness. This is a process we all must go through when we make errors. Through self awareness comes awareness of social responsibility, a renewed sense of purpose and strength of willpower. The process demands that shame, guilt, fear and anger must fall away and that dogmatic beliefs, moral attitudes and preconceived ideas must be surrendered when they are having an adverse effect. Serious Grail searchers scrutinise themselves psychologically, and look at the patterns and programs evident throughout their whole life, contemplate objectively and search for truth. We must look at how much our ego is involved, how much it is inflated, and what the true motivations are. False pride and arrogance need to be revealed. The Grail seeker must recognise the meaning of his or her personal destiny pattern, and stage by stage make atonement. This process is often painful. The vital energy it releases, however, helps us to be able to distinguish reality from illusion. Through the search, as we persevere, we work through our issues and release them, until we reach a moment where we unite with Spirit. From that expansion of consciousness look down upon our ego self. This is how we transcend the personality self and find the consciousness of unity, and how we touch the truth of immortality. Parcival did not recognise the activity of the soul; it is only when he opens to God and acknowledges the soul that the Mystery is revealed to him. At the very moment that Parcival calls out to God from the loneliness of being separated from his soul, he is guided to a place where he can learn the secrets of the Grail and receive initiation (Ravenscroft, 1995).

The Grail messenger attempts to alert Parcival to the fact that he cannot come to the Grail castle alone but must bring his brother or sister (Ravenscroft, (1995). This gives us the key that we can come closer to the Grail within by developing the quality of selflessness, not seeking our own development but rather, seeking development so that we can help others. We must move beyond attachment to the ego. The Grail messenger also informed Parcival that he must also not only come with those who can see the Grail and wear a white robe, but must also lead to the Grail those who appear black and white. This person may not see the Grail but will see the Grail bearer and how he or she behaves in practical life (Ravenscroft, 1995). This message lets us know that we must acknowledge the "blackness" in ourselves, bring it into the Light and educate it by being a living example of the radiant Light of the Grail. The black in us may then be enlightened by the Light of the Grail. Eventually, Parcival learns, and through his adventures we come to find faith that when we make errors we can make good again. Parcival eventually connects with his heart. Through him and the presence of Galahad, the Grail seeker, the knight who is able to embrace the Grail, we see how the quality of purity of heart leads us to the Grail. Parcival becomes the Grail King. When he takes the Grail "the Spirit passes from the sun and pierces the veil of the crescent moon." (Ravenscroft, 1995, p. 191) The sun represents the masculine principle and the cresent moon, the feminine. The masculine and feminine principle are united. The Trinity is acknowledged and Parcival's love is now free from egoism; it becomes a healing love of free and radiant blessing streaming out to the world.

At the moment where the Grail is found, a rebirth is experienced where one experiences oneself as soul and Spirit, and perceives the birth of the Light within. The path to the Grail is the path to true identity, and the Grail is the cup of destiny (Ravenscroft, 1995). In the presence of the Grail, all must be as sister and brother. One cannot hold grievances towards another, but must look for the Light within others. People must recognise each other on even ground and acknowledge that we are all children of Spirit.

We all have our processes and unique learning in the quest for the Grail, yet this learning is often mirrored in the collective. Hence we can associate with the pain, trials and tribulations of others, and we can have empathy. Take Gawain, for example, who is constantly asked to learn to live with the fact that others' deeds are laid upon him to carry as a burden, for Gawain takes the path of the heart. He is not a doubter, as Parcival once was; however, he is the object of doubt and is slandered, he is constantly exposed to false accusations (Ravenscroft, 1995). Gawain must pass through this test and constantly purify his heart - though the accusations are not true, something in his pattern is connected with it and his process is to work with that.

The feminine principle

Throughout the stories and legends of the Grail, women play important roles. For Parcival, his sister Sigune - sometimes seen as his cousin Dindraine - is also on the quest for the Grail and holds the office of the Lady of the Lake. The Lady of the Lake holds the secret and power of the mysteries. Similarly, Morgan La Fay is one of the Ladies of the Lake. She is Arthur's sister, holds the secrets of healing and in her higher aspects is able to work with the power of the Grail very well. Guinevere in her higher aspects embodies courtly love. Many of the women know the path to Avalon, the isle of the wise women and the highest aspect of the feminine, and know the secrets of its healing powers. The women, like the men, go through shifts in consciousness as they grow through their experiences, and as they reach initiation, more understanding of the Grail is received. The roles of the women are brought to light through their representation in courtly love and priestess work as well as through the roles in the Grail legends as mothers, sisters and mentors.

To explore our search for the Grail further, let us look at the role of the feminine in the myth of the Holy Grail, and specifically at the lives of two of the chief female characters within the Grail legend. Both women, Morgan La Fay and Guinevere, represent aspects of the Goddess, the feminine principle, in action. Exploring myth gives insight and provides learning for ways to cope with psychological elements of the time. It helps us open to the winds of change. Myth is a living entity and exists within every person. As Johnson (1989a), in *He: Understanding Masculine Psychology*, tells us, the most rewarding mythological experience is to see how myth lives in our own psychological structure. To explore myth we can look at everything that happens as part of ourselves. As we explore the feminine archetypes represented by Morgan La Fay and Guinevere, we will consider the role of these archetypes within us, as part of the Goddess, the feminine aspect.

Morgan La Fay as archetype

Morgan La Fay was a Celtic priestess who ruled the isle of Avalon, the isle of wise women. She is closely associated with the Earth and was a shapeshifter able to perform magic, much of which she learned from Merlin and earlier Ladies of the Lake. She contains the Kali or destroyer aspect of the Goddess with the power to destroy that which is outmoded. She also contains the Tara aspect, which brings forth compassion and healing. She represents the Goddess, as enchantress and political woman. She was also King Arthur's sister, and throughout the Grail legend she moves through many transitions and much transformation. As with myth generally, there are many different versions which cast light or shadow upon Morgan La Fay's character according to the slant the writer wishes to take. Each version paints a different picture. This is one of the beauties of myth, for it enables us to see the many aspects from different viewpoints which helps reveal the values and judgements of the time. As the high priestess, Morgan La Fay represented the matriarchy at a time when the stronghold of the patriarchy was taking a new stand, as Christianity was renouncing the way of the Goddess. She stood for the spiritual wisdom, the planting in cycles and the attention to the inner world of intuition. Morgan La Fay also represents the Mother Goddess; however, she is often not seen in that light, as the enchantress aspect is the aspect that most who look upon her accentuate. Through time, her Mother Goddess aspect has been taken from her in the harsh light of patriarchal criticism, and she is presented in the form of a vain, power seeking, hateful, mortal woman who wishes only to cast evil spells upon others for her own gain. Morgan La Fay is misrepresented in this way throughout some of the literature and films. In the film *Merlin*, Morgan La Fay is portrayed in a shallow, narrow role as a selfish and vain sorcerer, dying young. This to me was an extreme example of a common misrepresentation of her status. It splits off one of the negative characteristics of her archetype and reduces her to that. This is not to say that she did not have negative attributes, as we all as humans have, but this is far from being representative of her as a whole and valid being. Imagine some of your worst aspects. Can you imagine being reduced to those negative characteristics? Morgan La Fay's archetype has much in common with the Persephone archetype. Persephone was queen of the underworld, twin goddess of love and death, containing the Kali aspect, and the wise old woman, witch or crone. Morgan La Fay, like Persephone, was abducted early in life to the underworld, taken from her mother Igraine.

Morgan La Fay's embodiment in Arthur's time represents and is symbolic of the degradation and the betrayal of the feminine. She was ridiculed, minimised and cast out, because to be a woman of power in a world where this was not acceptable meant that she had to be eradicated, stopped, thwarted at every turn. It is no wonder that she resorted to manipulation. Manipulation, as such, is not negative as we are always manipulating forces and sometimes this is done for the purpose of goodness. Magic is not negative when it is used for goodness. However, she was not without her failings and her magic was not always for the purpose of good - this was one of her lessons. She went through many lessons during her lifetime. Early in her life she was caught in darkness, as when she slept with her brother Arthur to create Mordred, who perpetuated this darkness. But like many of us, she learned from it and came to understand how the darkness within her worked. This lesson became part of the learning she needed to help her become whole. It is difficult to judge another, as often we do not see the whole perspective. It is difficult to have the dual nature of a strong and rich inner life and yet live on a planet where this flow is not possible. Despite Morgan's shadow, she was also a healer. She knew of herbs and the powers needed to heal even Arthur. Without her help he would not have come as far as he did. She helped heal him when he was dying, tended him in Avalon, and though she had parts of her which wanted Arthur's power, she loved him nonetheless. The part of Arthur's power which she wanted was that of being respected and honoured and cherished for what she was, and also the ability to act in the physical world as only men were able to do in that era. But the world in which she lived did not give her that. She was not given credence, and so her power which could have helped the synthesis of humanity, the synthesis of religion and spirituality, was denied expression. Humanity said no and Arthur's kingdom collapsed, and Morgan went to Avalon to teach the priestesses who would be reborn in lifetimes to come to try yet again to bring forth the power and the wisdom of the feminine.

If the feminine principle is unable to manifest, we cannot function as whole human beings, and the kingdom collapses. When men cut off their feminine aspect and live only in the masculine they become aggressive and stubborn and resistant to the flow of life. Of course, women also may become aggressive and stubborn if they do not allow their feminine self expression. The feminine is the flow of life that nurtures and makes whole. Men and women alike must awaken to the power of the feminine to heal the Earth and all life upon it. The anima and the feminine principle is the receptivity to Spirit. Through it we have the bridge to the inner worlds - one which we walk to connect with the intuition of the soul.

Caitlin and John Mathews (1992) in *Ladies of the Lake* tells us that in the mainstream Arthurian tradition Morgan La Fay makes her first appearance as Arthur's chief physician. After all her attempts to deprive Arthur of kingship she is mostly concerned with healing his wounds. Like Merlin, she was able to appear at will under most shapes and guises. She, along with other priestesses, gives the knights their weapon training. We see from these extremes of character that she has the potential within her of compassion as well as power mongering. If we look at this as aspects of her archetype, we see that there is potential for positive or negative manifestation of the various qualities associated with the archetype. In western society we often label or judge different aspects of the archetypes as good or bad so when we come across an archetype that has divergent aspects within it we do not know what to make of it. Morgan has the power to heal or harm, this is her learning. Morgan's archetype vacillates from Goddess to healing sister, to enchantress, to bitter woman. As Morgan the Raven Queen she represents the functions of victory, battle and prophecy. Yet her name, Morgan La Fay, means a "sea-born fairy," and she heals using the waters of the Lake. These are the possibilities open to such a being, and to us all, depending on our choices. We also make choices about how we manifest aspects of the many archetypes we embody.

Morgan also comes to test others in the story: Arthur, Guinevere, Gawain, Lancelot and others. In the story there is an essential tension between them, a tension designed to test them and help them learn.

> To transform opposition into paradox is to allow both sides of an issue, both pairs of opposites to exist in equal dignity and worth. Opposing forces will teach each other something and produce an insight that serves them both. This is not compromise but a depth of understanding that puts life in perspective and lets us know with certainty what we should do. (Johnson, 1993, p. 86)

Guinevere as archetype

Guinevere in her highest aspect represents the Empress - she stands for the Venus aspect of love, also for sexuality and nurturing. While Morgan is the Fairy Queen, Guinevere is the May Queen, the mortal representative of the other world. She is the fairy maiden. She is also a representative of the Aphrodite archetype, as she is Queen to King Arthur. Yet she is in love with Lancelot, thus creating a romantic triangle. There is one woman, Elaine, who likewise is in love with Lancelot, but he is in love with Guinevere. Tennyson's famous poem *The Lady of Shalot* is the story of the tragedy of the Elaine-Lancelot-Guinevere triangle. It shows the shadow of romantic love. The pain of love unrequited drives Elaine to take her life.

Just as a man may wield the power that Lancelot does, so is the feminine nature armed with the capacity to "take the knight to fairyland." The feminine charm can capture the fantasies of a young knight, causing him to be caught in a web of infatuation, rendering him useless for his knightly work. Likewise, the charms of a woman can, when used with purity and right motive rather than selfish or manipulative purpose, inspire the knight to his higher calling, and help him fulfil the duties of his knighthood. This is the test of Guinevere and the potential of her archetype.

In the film *Merlin*, the Lady of the Lake gave Merlin some words of wisdom to ponder upon. She told him that "when you forget us, we cease to exist." This goes for Light as well as darkness. If we focus on Light, we nurture the burning flame within and it exists in our life - and if we cease to think of darkness, it loses its power over us. Merlin rises above the struggle with darkness when, instead of battling with darkness, he chooses not to engage with it.

This provides the key to Guinevere. Her myth and archetype can be for us whatever we like. If we think of her positively, she will be that. If we think of her negatively, she will be that. Often we judge people according to where we are standing. We either look at others and think the grass is greener on their side of the fence, or we judge and degrade them for not living up to the standards we aspire to, whether we are living according to them or not. When we do this, life often takes mysterious turns and, lo and behold, we find ourselves in the position of someone we have judged and we are challenged to find compassion and empathy, so we can then learn and grow. Guinevere may incite jealousy and envy for her position and envy or admiration for her ability to indulge her passions or follow her heart. At the same time, she may inspire admiration for being a symbol of courtly romantic love, especially amongst the chivalrous knights who appear to need her to find their own power. All these aspects of Guinevere are given as examples from which we can learn. She contains the potential for succeeding or failing within her archetype, depending on what viewpoint one is coming from.

Like Morgan La Fay, she has been reduced to a whore in the eyes of some critics, who would see that by her acts of adultery with Lancelot she has brought this degradation upon herself. Yet others would admire her still, having compassion and understanding of the love and passion she chose to fulfil. But this choosing did lead to her downfall and Arthur's, and indeed that of the entire kingdom.

What are the lessons this myth reveals, what can we learn from the Guinevere archetype? Guinevere is a symbol of the conflict of office and personality (Knight, 1983). She had a task in admitting knights to the Round Table which was esoteric in nature, yet her love for Lancelot became an obsession and blinded her, preventing her from fulfilling her dharma (the life aligned to her soul's purpose). Here we see the shadow of romantic love where, though we are taken to the Divine through love, we project the Divine onto the human partner and hence lose touch with the true path to the Divine. Guinevere is a great beauty, full of grace. Arthur and Guinevere were unable to have a child, yet she is able to bring the motherly quality to the court. But as the saga continues, Guinevere's jealousy of Lancelot's association with Elaine arises and the social court and the Round Table split in battle over her. When she sleeps with Lancelot, Arthur authorises a public punishment of Guinevere through being burnt at the stake, a fate from which Lancelot saves her. Guinevere and Lancelot could have been examples of a new liberated form of relationship, which could have been representative of the right balance between a man and a woman in platonic relationship. But they did not manage to do that very well. I ask you to suspend your judgement for a moment.

Guinevere, as I mentioned earlier, was in a conflict between her office and role as Queen to Arthur. She was contracted into marriage to Arthur and was seen to exemplify the virtues of courtly love. She is Goddess, the Divine feminine shining forth in human female reflection in pure way. She meets her dual soul Lancelot and there is a strong attraction between them. Her downfall came when she took it to the physical level. The failure was that she lost herself in the emotional realm because her obsession blinded her to her true purpose and she forgot about her dharma. She did not lift the energy up into the spiritual. This was part of her learning, how she ultimately became the Empress. But at that time she failed - her spiritual development was insufficient. The suffering of not being able to have Lancelot as her King was what was required to help her learn, develop and grow. Through her tragedy, she learned the importance of queenly life and the power of higher love. Because she loved Arthur as well, when he was destroyed, she was also destroyed.

Like Morgan La Fay, many aspects of Guinevere which we represented through the interpretations of myth are split off from her wholeness. Guinevere's archetype shows three aspects of the wifely role: the wife who was faithful, the loyal wife who remained in her position; the disloyal wife who could not love Arthur as he wanted to be loved, but who loved Lancelot; and the wife who was the Queen (a role model for women of that era), the May Queen (a role model of courtly love for men), Fairy maiden and Flower Bride.

Yet the fact that the fairies love Guinevere tells of her purity on many levels. Her errors with Lancelot were human and part of her earthly learning. Had she loved Lancelot, loved Arthur and stayed in her role, remained loyal to both by not bringing the love for Lancelot down to the physical plane and allowed it to stay on the inner and to flourish as a platonic love, the kingdom could have flourished. However, this is not to say it was Guinevere's fault the kingdom fell; she was a reflection of her flock. Her failures echoed and mirrored those of that time. Values were out of alignment with the spiritual, people were becoming materialistic, wanting land, wanting power, and Guinevere wanted the physical, wanted

Lancelot - and the people judged her. Yet she was a reflection of them. It is difficult to know what lies behind the action of a person, what inner tests and trials they are enduring. What is apparent is not always reflecting the reality. Yet it is precisely these tests we find ourselves in, where there is seemingly no way out, which challenge us to grow, suffer, learn our lessons and become whole.

Lancelot and Guinevere were dual souls who had come to teach each other. Through her actions, Guinevere showed that she was not quite ready for her dharma and that she had more to learn. She would also have acquired a certain karma for her actions. Yet, in the higher levels of her being, Guinevere remains the Empress, and like all archetypes, contains strengths and weaknesses from which we can aspire to learn without placing judgement. We can put ourselves in her shoes and come to learn through the tragedy that she experienced which will ultimately have helped her develop strength.

Misuse of energies between men and women have taken us off the spiritual path. Much healing and redemption need to be done. What is needed is devotion and cooperation with Spirit so this straying from the path can be turned around. Many of us have experienced the misuse and abuse of the masculine and feminine energies. Much redemption is needed in an effort to bring the polarities back into balance. Now we have the opportunity to come to new awareness and set it right, through each of us making the decision to become the Grail - and radiate Light. Those further ahead in their development toward being whole can bring others to the Grail and live by setting an example, manifesting the higher aspects of the archetypes, so we can all come to know the Grail.

In our life, to follow our spiritual destiny, to allow our personal selves to flourish and to manifest our greatest potential, we must walk towards the Grail and allow ourselves to become it. Each of us must walk on the journey allowing the Grail to be at the centre. Only then can we become whole.

The journey towards wholeness can be a rich one. It involves accepting ourselves and allowing ourselves to be. It also demands a certain diligence and desire to better ourselves, not in terms of outer success, though that may come, rather, in terms of aspiration to live in Light, integration of our shadow and the manifestation of an inner peace which comes through living in truth and love.

Let there be peace on Earth and let it begin with me

The Heart of Love

Feel the love of Mother Earth
travel on a sunbeam
to the Heart of Love
that is Father Sun

Walkk with a loving heart
make no distinction
open your heart to all
love all as one

Open to Father Sky
become the bridge
between Him and Mother Earth
surrender to Great Spirit

Let harmony and balance
flood the Earth
with the
joy of peace

Make your journey pure
open to your knowing
let go of pain and fear
be aware of what you are sowing

Return to Mother Earth
feel her wings of fire
come forth and nurture you
let go your desire

Open to Love and Light
open to Spirit
day and night
let the owl speak to you
awaken in your dreams

You have a medicine path to walk
one that your soul wishes
let the Sun guide your way
you'll find it in your heart.

Bibliography

Towards a lightness of being

Beck, A.T., Rush, B.F., & Emery, G. (1979). <u>Cognitive Therapy of Depression</u>. New York: John Wiley.

Carkhuff, R.R. & Anthony, W. A. (1979). <u>The Skills of Helping: an introduction to helping</u>. Amherst, MA: Human Resource Development Press.

Egan, G. (1990). <u>The Skilled Helper: a systematic approach to effective helping</u> (4th edn). Belmont, California: Brooks/Cole.

Ellis, A. & Harper, R.A. (1975). <u>A New Guide to Rational Living</u>. North Hollywood, C.A: Wilshire Books.

Fromm, E. (1962). <u>Beyond the Chains of Illusion</u>. London: Abacus.

Jung, C.G. (1964). <u>Man and His Symbols</u>. London: Pan.

Jung, C. G. (1976). <u>The Portable Jung</u>. Edited by Joseph Campbell. New York: Penguin.

Macris, P. (1994). <u>Transformational Depression</u>. Lecture at Jung workshops. Monash University: Caulfield.

May, R. (1961). <u>Existential Psychology</u>. New York: Random House.

Meichenbaum, D. (1977). <u>Cognitive-Behaviour Modification</u>. New York: Plenum.

Meichenbaum, D. (1983). <u>Coping With Stress</u>. London: Century Publishing.

Meichenbaum, D. (1986). Cognitive-Behaviour Modification. In F.H. Kanfer & A.P. Goldstein (Eds.). <u>Helping People Change:a textbook of methods</u>. New York: Pergamon.

Moreno, Z.T. (1987). Psychodrama, role theory, and the concept of the social atom. In J. Zweig (Ed.). <u>The Evolution of Psychotherapy</u>. New York: Brunner/Mazel.

Nelson-Jones, R. (1984). Personal Responsibility Counselling and Therapy. Milton Keynes: Open University Press.

Nelson-Jones, R. (1988). Practical Counselling and Helping Skills (2nd edn). Sydney, Australia: Holt, Rinehart and Winston.

O'Connor, P. (1992). Understanding Jung. Melbourne: Octopus Publishing Group.

Peck, M.S. (1978). The Road Less Travelled. Melbourne: Rider.

Perls, F.S. (1873). The Gesalt Approach and Eyewitness to Therapy. New York: Bantam Books.

Rogers, C.R. (1951). Client-Centred Therapy. Boston: Houghton Milflin.

Rogers, C.R. (1957). The necessary and sufficient conditions of therapeutic personality change. Journal of Consulting Psychology, 21, 95-103.

Singer, J. (1994). Boundaries of the Soul: the practice of Jung's psychology. New York: Bantam Doubleday Dell Publishing Group.

Yablonsky, L. (1975). Psychodrama: resolving emotional problems through role-playing. New York: Basic Books.

Yontef, G. (1969). A Review of the Practice of Gesalt Therapy. Los Angeles, C.A: Trident Books.

Walsh, R. (1989). Asian psychotherapies. In R.J., Corsini, & D. Wedding, Current Psychotherapies. Illinois: Peacock.

Creating alchemy

Assagioli, R.(1980). Psychosynthesis: a manual of principles and techniques. Northamptonshire: Turnstone books.

Johnson, R. A. (1993). Owning Your Own Shadow. San Francisco: Harper.

Jung, C. G. (1976). The Portable Jung. J. Campbell (Ed). New York: Penguin.

Moreno, Z. T. (1987). Psychodrama, Role Theory and the Concept of the Social Atom. In J. Zweig (Ed.). <u>The Evolution of Psychotherapy</u>. New York: Brunner/Mazel.

Peck, M. S. (1993). <u>A World Waiting to be Born: the search for civility</u>. London: Arrow.

Sharp, D. (1988). <u>The Survival Papers: anatomy of a mid-life crisis</u>. Toronto: Inner City Books.

Stone, H. & Stone, S. (1997). <u>Embracing Ourselves: the voice dialogue manual</u>. California: Nataraj Publishing.

Discovering our many selves

Assagioli, R.(1980). <u>Psychosynthesis: a manual of principles and techniques</u>. Northamptonshire: Turnstone books.

Hardy, J. (1987). <u>A Psychology with a Soul: psychosynthesis in evolutionary context</u>. Ringwood, Victoria: Penguin.

Jung, C. G. (1935). The Tavistock Lectures. In <u>The Collected Works of C.G. Jung </u>(Bolligen series 1953-1979.Princeton: Princeton University Press.

Sharp, D. (1988). <u>The Survival Papers: anatomy of a mid-life crisis</u>. Toronto: Inner City Books.

Stone, H. & Stone, S. (1997). <u>Embracing Ourselves: the voice dialogue manual</u>. California: Nataraj Publishing.

von Franz, M. L. (1990). <u>The Way of the Dream</u>. Ontario: Windrose Films Ltd.

Empowering the higher mind

Bailey, A.A. (1979). <u>Letters on Occult Meditation</u>. New York: Lucis Publishing Company.

Bailey, A.A. (1987). <u>Ponder on This</u>. New York: Lucis Publishing Company.

Beck, A.T., Rush, B.F., & Emery, G. (1979). <u>Cognitive Therapy of Depression</u>. New York: John Wiley.

Borysenko, J. (1990). <u>Guilt is the Teacher, Love is the Lesson</u>. New York: Bantam.

Dhammananda, K. Sri. (1994). <u>Treasure of the Dhamma</u>. Kuala Lumpur: Buddhist Missionary Society.

Dryden, W. (1984). <u>Rational Emotive Therapy: fundamentals and innovations</u>. Beckenham, Kent: Groom-Helm Ltd.

Ellis, A. (1962). <u>Reason and Emotion in Psychotherapy</u>. New York: Lyle Stuart.

Ellis, A. (1975). <u>A New Guide to Rational Living</u>. North Hollywood, California: Institute for Rational Living Inc.

Ellis, A. (1977). <u>Rational Emotive Psychotherapy</u>. (Cassette recording). New York: Psychology Today, Ziff-Davis.

Ellis, A. (1980). Overview of the clinical theory of rational-emotive therapy. In Grieger & Boyd, <u>Rational-Emotive Therapy: a skills based approach</u>. New York: Litton Educational Publishing Inc.

Ellis, A. (1985). <u>Overcoming Resistance: rational-emotive therapy with difficult clients</u>. New York: Institute for Rational Emotive Therapy.

Leadbeater, C. W. (1986). <u>Thoughtforms</u>. Wheaton, Illinois: Quest.

Meichenbaum, D. (1977). <u>Cognitive-Behaviour Modification</u>. New York: Plenum.

Meichenbaum, D. (1983). <u>Coping With Stress</u>. London: Century Publishing.

Meichenbaum, D. (1986). Cognitive-behaviour modification. In F.H. Kanfer & A.P.Goldstein (Eds.). <u>Helping People Change: a textbook of methods</u>. New York: Pergamon.

Nelson-Jones, R. (1990). <u>Thinking Skills: managing and preventing personal problems</u>. Melbourne: Thomas Nelson Australia.

Sheinman, N. (1987). <u>The Medicine of the Mind: guided imagery workshop for personal and professional growth</u>. Class handout. Melbourne, Australia: Paramartha School of Spiritual Education and Development.

Van der Leeuw. (1987). <u>The Fire of Creation</u>. Wheaton, Illinois: The Theosophical Publishing House.

Walen, S., DiGuiseppe, R. & Wessler, R. (1980). <u>A Practitioner's Guide to Rational-Emotive Therapy</u>. New York: Litton Educational Publishing Inc.

Walsh, R. (1989). Asian psychotherapies. In R.J. Corsini & D. Wedding. <u>Current Psychotherapies</u>. Illinois: Peacock.

Looking for meaning

Ananda Tara Shan, (1991). <u>The Living Word of the Hierarchy</u>. Daylesford: Maitreya Surya Publishing House.

American Psychiatric Association (1987). <u>Diagnostic and Statistical Manual of Mental Disorders</u> (3rd ed.). Washington, D.C: American Psychiatric Association.

American Psychiatric Association (1987). <u>Diagnostic and Statistical Manual of Mental Disorders</u> (3rd ed. Rev.). Washington, D.C: American Psychiatric Association.

Barnon, I. (1990). <u>Fifteen Steps to Overcome Anxiety and Depression</u>. Auckland: Octopus.

Beck, A. T. (1967). <u>Depression: clinical, experimental and therapeutic aspects</u>. New York: Harper & Row.

Beck, A.T., Rush, A.J., Shaw, B.F. & Emery, G. (1979). <u>Cognitive Therapy of Depression</u>. New York: Guilford Press.

Berke, J. H. (1979). <u>I Haven't Had to go Mad Here</u>. Ringwood: Penguin.

Besant, A. (1978). <u>A Study in Consciousness</u>. Adyar: Vasanta Press.

Besant, A. & Leadbeater, C. W. (1991). Talks on the Path of Occultism: at the feet of the Master, vol. 1. Madras: The Theosophical Publishing House.

Carpenter, W. T & Stephen, J. H. (1980). The Diagnostics of Mania. In R. H. Belmaker & M. D. van Pragg. Mania: an enduring concept. New York: MTP Press.

Cochran, S.D. (1984). Preventing medical noncompliance in the outpatient treatment of bipolar affective disorders. Journal of Consulting and Clinical Psychology, 52, 873-878.

Crowcroft, A. (1975). The Psychotic: understanding madness. Ringwood: Penguin.

DeRubeis, R.J., Evans, M. D., Hollon, S. D., Garvey, M. J., Grove, W. M., & Tuason, V. B. (1990). How does cognitive therapy work? Cognitive change and symptom change in cognitive therapy and pharmacotherapy for depression. Journal of Consulting and Clinical Psychology, 6, 862-869.

Fennell, M. J. (1991). Depression. In K. Hawton, P. Sallkovskis, J. Kirk, & D. Clark (1991). Cognitive Behaviour Therapy for Psychiatric Problems: a practical guide. New York:Oxford University Press.

Goldman, H. Gomer, F. & Templer, D. (1972). Long term effects of electro- convulsive therapy on memory and perceptual motor performance. Journal of Clinical Psychology, 28, 32-34.

Govinda-Rose, T. (1992). The Language of the Heart: is spoken all over the world. Melbourne: Lotus House.

Jung, C. G. (1987). Modern Man in Search of a Soul. London: Routledge.

Jung, C. G. (1973). Psychology and Religion - West and East, Collected Works of Jung. New Jersey: Princeton.

Kraeplin, E. (1913). Psychiatry. Liepzig.

Macris, P. (1994). Transformational Depression. Lecture at Jung workshops. Monash University: Caulfield.

Murray, J.B. (1989). New applications of lithium therapy. The Journal of Psychology, 124, 55-73.

Peck, M. S. (1986). The Road Less Travelled. London: Ride & Co.

Peck, M. S. (1993). A World Waiting to Be Born: the search for civility. London: Arrow

Robinson, L.A. Berman, J. S. & Neimeyer, R.A. (1990). Psychotherapy for the treatment of depression: a comprehensive review of controlled outcome research. Psychological Bulletin, 108, 30-49.

Sanchez, V.C., Lewinsohn, P.M., & Larson, D.W. (1980). Assertion training: effectiveness in the treatment of depression. Journal of Clinical Psychogy, 36, 526-529.

Shaw, B.F. (1977). Comparison of cognitive therapy and behaviour therapy in the treatment of depression. Journal of Consulting and Clinical Psychology, 45, 543-551.

Shaw, E.D. Stokes, P.E. Mahn, J. & Manevitz, A. Z. A. (1987). Effects of lithium carbonate on the memory and motor speed of bipolar outpatients. Journal of Abnormal Psychology, 96, 64-69.

Shopsin, M. D. (1979). Manic Illness. New York: Raven.

Simons, A. D., Lustman, P. J., Wetzel, R. D., & Murphy, G. E. (1985). Predicting response to cognitive therapy for depression: the role of learned resourcefulness. Cognitive Therapy and Research, 9, 79-89.

Storr, A. (1991). Jung. New York: Routledge.

Stafford-Clark, D. & Smith, A. (1978). Psychiatry for students. London: George Allen & Unwin.

Winters, K. C. & Neale, J, M. (1985). Mania and low self esteem. Journal of Abnormal Psychology, 94, 282-290.

Embodying the dream

Ananda Tara Shan. (1993). The Living Word of the Hierarchy. Daylesford: Maitreya Surya Publishing House.

Hillman, J. (1975). Re-Visioning Psychology. America: Harper and Row.

Jung, C. G. The Collected Works. Translated by RFC Hull. Bollingen Series. Princeton: Princeton University Press. (1933). Meaning of Psychology for Modern Man. (1934). Practical Use of Dream Analysis. (1945). On the Nature of Dreams.

Jung, C. G. (1963). Memories, Dreams and Reflections. London: Fontana Paperbacks.

Jung, C. G. (1964). Man and His Symbols. New York: Doubleday Windfall.

Jung, C. G. (1971). Individual dream symbolism in relation to alchemy. In Campbell, J., The Portable Jung. America: Viking Penguin.

Leadbeater, C.W. (1984). Dreams. Adyar: Vasantu Press.

O'Connor, P. (1988). Understanding Jung. Port Melbourne: Mandarin Australia.

O'Connor, P. (1986). Dreams and the Search for Meaning. Ryde: Methuen Haynes.

Roberts, R. (1983). Tales for Jung Folk. California: Vernal Equinox Press.

von Franz, M.L. (1987). The Way of the Dream. Canada: Windrose Films Ltd.

Meeting the monster

Ananda Tara Shan. (1989). Eight Fundamental Steps Towards Right Human Relations. Paper on Right Human Relations. Daylesford: Maitreya Surya Publishing House.

Alberti, R.E. & Emmons, M.L. (1986). <u>Your Perfect Right: a guide to assertive living</u>. California: Impact Publishers.

Australian Psychological Society. (1986). <u>Code of Professional Conduct</u>. Melbourne: Australian Psychological Society.

Corey, G. & Corey, M.S. (1982). <u>Groups: process and practice</u>. CA: Brooks/Cole Publishing Co.

Corey, G., Corey, M.S. & Callanan, P. (1988). <u>Issues and Ethics in the Helping Profession</u>. CA: Brookes/Cole Publishing Co.

Dryden, W. (1990). <u>Dealing With Anger Problems: rational-emotive therapeutic interventions</u>. Sara Sota: Professional Research Exchange Inc.

Fennell, M.J. (1991). Depression. In K. Hawton, P. M. Salkovskis, J. Kirk, & D. Clark, (Eds.). <u>Cognitive Behaviour Therapy for Psychiatric Problems: a practical guide</u>. New York: Oxford University Press.

Fuller, M. (1993). <u>Contemplate Your Genogram</u>. Class handout. Melbourne: R.M.I.T.

Gawain, S. (1985). <u>Creative Visualisation</u>. New York: Bantam.

Hawton, K., Salkovskis, P.M., Kirk, J. & Clark, D. (1991). The development and principals of cognitive-behavioural treatments. In K. Hawton, P. M. Salkovskis, J. Kirk, & D. Clark, (Eds.) (1991). <u>Cognitive Behaviour Therapy for Psychiatric Problems: a practical guide</u>. New York: Oxford University Press.

Lerner, H.S. (1985). <u>The Dance Of Anger</u>. New York: Harper & Row.

Lushkins, A.S. (1964). <u>Group Therapy: a guide</u>. New York: Random House Inc.

<u>Macquarie Dictionary</u>. (1981). McMahons Point, Australia: Macquarie Library.

Meichenbaum, D.H. (1977). <u>Cognitive-Behavior Modification: an integrative approach</u>. New York: Plenum.

Meichenbaum, D.H. (1985). <u>Stess Inoculation Training</u>. New York: Pergamon.

Nelson-Jones, R. (1991). <u>Leading Training Groups: a manual of practical group skills for trainers</u>. Sydney: Holt, Rinehart & Winston.

Nelson-Jones, R. (1990). <u>Thinking Skills: managing and preventing personal problems</u>. Melbourne: Thomas Nelson Australia.

Nelson-Jones, R. (1992). <u>Lifeskills Helping: a textbook of practical counselling and helping skills</u>. Marrickville: Holt, Rinehart & Winston.

Novaco, R.W. (1975). <u>Anger Control</u>. New York: D.C Heath.

Rakos, R.F. (1991). <u>Assertive Behaviour: theory, research and training</u>. London: Routledge.

Sainsbury, R. & Westhorpe, M, (1993). <u>Understanding and Debunking Some Familiar Patterns of Anger</u>. Class handout. Melbourne: RMIT.

Sheinman, N.D. (1987). Guided Imagery for clinicians. Reprinted from M. Rossman, <u>Imagine Health</u>. Privately published.

Tavris, C. (1989). <u>Anger: the misunderstood emotion</u>. Sydney: Simon & Schuster Inc.

Wiemers Okiishi, R. (1987). In the field: the genogram as a tool in career counselling. <u>Journal of Counselling and Development</u>, 66, 139-143.

Taking courage

Ananda Tara Shan. (1993). <u>The Living Word of the Hierarchy</u>. Daylesford: Maitreya Surya Publishing House.

Assagioli, R. (1980). <u>Psychosynthesis</u>. U.S.A: Psychosynthesis Research Assoc.

Beck, A.T. & Emery, G. (1985). <u>Anxiety Disorders and Phobias: a cognitive perspective</u>. New York: Basic Books.

Jeffers, S. (1987). <u>Feel the Fear and Do It Anyway</u>. London: Arrow Books.

Jung, C.G. (1989). <u>Psychology and Alchemy</u>. London: Routledge.

May, R. (1961). <u>Existential Psychology</u>. New York: Random House.

Miller, B.F. & Keane, R.N. (1983). <u>Encyclopedia and Dictionary of Medicine, Nursing and Allied Health</u>. Philadelphia: W. B. Saunders Company.

Moore, T. (1992). <u>Care of the Soul</u>. New York: Harper & Collins.

Wolpe, J. (1958). <u>Psychotherapy By Reciprocal Inhibition</u>. Stanford: Stanford University Press.

Yalom, I. (1981). <u>Existential Psychotherapy</u>. New York: Basic Books.

Finding Forgiveness

Ananda Tara Shan. (1993). <u>The Living Word of the Hierarchy</u>. Daylesford: Maitreya Surya Publishing Company.

Borysenko, J. (1990). <u>Guilt is the Teacher, Love is the Lesson</u>. USA: Warner Books.

Di Caprio, N.S. (1976). <u>The Good Life: models for a healthy personality</u>. New Jersey: Prentice Hall.

Jampolsky, G.G. (1985). <u>Good-bye to Guilt</u>. USA: Bantam.

Lerner, H.G. (1993). <u>The Dance of Deception</u>. New York: Harper & Row.

<u>Macquarie Dictionary</u>. (1981). McMahons Point, Australia: Macquarie Library.

Rosetti, F. (1992). <u>Psycho Regression: a new system for healing and personal growth</u>. London: Judy Piatkis Publishing.

Sharing from the Heart

Ananda Tara Shan. (1993). The Living Word of the Hierarchy. Daylesford, Maitreya Surya Publishing House.

Bales, R. F. (1970). Personality and Interpersonal Behaviour. New York: Holt, Rinehart & Wilson.

Besant, A. (1978). A Study in Consciousness. Adyar: Vasanta Press.

Burns, T. & Buckley, W. (1976). Power and Control: social structures and their transformation. London: Sage Publications.

Champion D. (1975). The Sociology of Organisations. New York: McGraw-Hill.

Egan, G. (1973). Face to Face. California: Brooks Cole.

Green, P. (1981). The Pursuit of Inequality. Oxford: Martin Robinson.

Hinton, B., & Reitz H. (1971). Groups and Organisations. California: Wadsworth Pub.

Huse, E., & Bowditch, J. (1973). Behaviour in Organisations. Sydney: Addison-Wesley.

Jung, C. G. (1987). Modern Man in Search of a Soul. London: Routledge.

Jung, C. G. (1973). Psychology and Religion - West and East, Collected Works of Jung. New Jersey: Princeton.

Katz, D., & Kahn, R. (1978). The Social Psychology of Organisations. New York: Wiley.

Macquarie Dictionary. (1982). McMahons Point, Australia: Macquarie Library.

McKay, H. (1995). Why Don't People Listen? Sydney: Pan McMillan.

Peck, M. S. (1993). A World Waiting to Be Born: the search for civility. London: Arrow.

Ollman, B. (1973). <u>Alienation: Marx's conception of man in capitalist society</u>.

Salaman, G. & Thompson, K. (1973). <u>People and Organisations.</u> London: Longman.

Storr, A. (1991). <u>Jung</u>. New York: Routledge.

Wilson, J. (1966). <u>Equality.</u> London: Hutchinson.

Trusting in immortality

Ananda Tara Shan. (1993). <u>The Living Word of the Hierarchy</u>. Daylesford: Maitreya Surya Publishing House.

Barbato, A. & Irwin, H. J. (1992). Major therapeutic systems and the bereaved client. <u>Australian Psychologist</u>, 27, 22-27.

Besant, A. & Leadbeater, C.W. (1991). <u>Talks on the Path of Occultism: at the feet of the Master, vol. 1</u>. Madras: The Theosophical Publishing House.

Bowlby, J. (1973). <u>Attachment and Loss: separation, anxiety and anger, vol.2</u>. New York: Basic Books.

Bowlby, J. (1980). <u>Attachment and Loss: sadness and depression, vol 3</u>. New York: Basic Books.

Bowlby, J. & West, L. (1983). The impact of death on the family system. <u>Journal of Family Therapy</u>, 5, 279-294.

Davidson, Dr. G. (1984). Understanding Mourning: a guide for those who grieve. In E. H. Neeld, (1990). <u>Seven Choices: taking the steps to new life after losing someone you love</u>. U.S.A.: Delta.

Ellard, J., Volkan, V., & Elspeth, W. (1974). <u>Normal and Pathological Responses to Grief</u>. New York: MFS Information Corp.

Freeman, S. J. (1991). Group facilitation of the grieving process with those bereaved by suicide. <u>Journal of Counselling and Development</u>, 69, 328-331.

Gendlin, E. T. (1978). <u>Focusing</u>. New York: Everest House.

Govinda, T. (1997). <u>The Healing Hands of Love: a guide to spiritual healing</u>. Daylesford, Victoria: Deva Wings Publications.

Kavanagh, D. J. (1990). Towards a cognitive-behavioural intervention for adult grief reactions. <u>British Journal of Psychiatry</u>, 157, 373-383.

Kubler-Ross, E. (1973). <u>Coping with Death and Dying</u>. Psychology Today Cassettes. New York: Ziff Davis Publishing Company.

Kubler-Ross, E. (1975). <u>Death: the final stage of growth</u>. Englewood Cliffs, NJ: Prentice-Hall.

LaGrand, L. E. (1986). <u>Coping With Separation And Loss As A Young Adult: theoretical and practical realities</u>. U.S.A.: Charles. C. Thomas.

Lifton, R. J. (1979). <u>The Broken Connection: on death and the continuity of life</u>. New York: Simon & Schuster.

Lindemann, E. (1944). Symptomology and management of acute grief. <u>American Journal of Psychiatry</u>, 101, 141-148.

Lindemann, E. (1979). <u>Beyond Grief: studies in crisis intervention</u>. New York: Jason Aronson.

Melges, F.T., & DeMaso, D. R. (1980). Grief-resolution therapy: reliving, revising and revisiting. <u>American Journal of Psychotherapy</u>, 34, 51-61.

Neeld, E. H. (1990). <u>Seven Choices: taking the steps to new life after losing someone you love</u>. U.S.A.: Delta.

Parkes, C. M. (1972). <u>Bereavement</u>. England: Penguin Books.

Rando, T. A. (1988). <u>Grieving: how to go on living when someone you love dies</u>. U.S.A.: Lexington Books.

Raphael, B. & Nunn, K. (1988). Counselling the bereaved. <u>Journal of Social Issues</u>, 44, 191-206.

Yongson, R. M. (1989). <u>Grief: rebuilding your life after berevement</u>. London: David & Charles.

Embracing the Grail

Bolen, J. S. (1982). <u>The Tao of Psychology: synchronicity and the self</u>. New York: Harper & Row.

Bradley, M. (1984). <u>The Mists of Avalon</u>. London: Sphere Books.

Conway, D.J. (1994). <u>Maiden, Mother, Crone: the myth and reality of the triple goddess</u>. St. Paul, Minnesota: Llewellyn Publications.

Evola, J. (1997). <u>The Mystery of the Grail: initiation and magic in the quest for the spirit</u>. Vermont: Inner Traditions.

Govinda-Rose, T. (1991). <u>The Language of the Heart: is spoken all over the world</u>. Daylesford, Australia: Lotus House.

Heline. C. (1986). <u>Mysteries of the Holy Grail</u>. Santa Monica California: New Age Bible and Philosophy Centre.

Knight. G. (1983). <u>The Secret Tradition in Arthurian Legend</u>. Northamptonshire: Aquarian Press

Johnson, R. A. (1989a). <u>He: understanding masculine Psychology</u>. New York: Harper & Rowe.

Johnson, R. A. (1989). <u>She: understanding feminine Psychology</u>. California: Harper Perenniel.

Johnson, R. A. (1993). <u>Owning your Own Shadow: understanding the dark side of the psyche</u>. San Francisco, USA: Harper.

Jung, E. (1957). <u>Animus and Anima: two essays</u>. Dallas: Spring Publications.

Mathews, C. & Mathews, J. (1992). <u>Ladies of the Lake</u>. London: Aquarian Press.

Mathews, J. (1997). <u>The Grail: quest for the eternal</u>. London: Thames & Hudson.

Ravenscroft, T. (1995). <u>The Cup of Destiny: the quest for the Grail</u>. New York: Samuel Weiser Inc.

Walker, B. G. (1985). <u>The Crone: woman of age, wisdom, and power</u>. San Francisco, New York: Harper.

Woolger, J. B. & Woolger, R. J. (1990). <u>The Goddess Within: a guide to the eternal myths that shape women's lives</u>. London: Rider.

Glossary

Actualisation

A basic human drive toward growth, completeness and fulfilment.

Alchemy

The process of developing from the denseness of lead into pure gold; that is, being infused with soul. It is the process of bringing Spirit into matter.

Anima

The female archetype in a man; a man's feminine self.

Animus

The male archetype in a woman; a woman's masculine self.

Annubis

A temple dog from Egypt which had the role of protector of the temples.

Archetypes

A pre-existing form from the collective unconscious which can emerge as psychological themes which become activated and influence us. They have their own agenda and energy.

Aspiration

To long for and aim towards union with Spirit.

Assertion

The ability to openly express both positive and negative feelings.

Astral body

Our emotional body

Bodhisattva

The World Teacher, the Christ or Lord Maitreya, the Eastern name for the Christ, meaning compassion. In this context The Christ Buddha. An Enlightened Being.

Collective unconscious aspect

Symbols collective in nature and origin, purely unconscious. Shared by others. Set of memories from human and prehuman ancestors not consciously recalled. It is the basis for archetypes universally experienced.

Birth, death, power, magic, unity, God and the self. Part of human experience.

Desire

To want or crave for that which is material or of form.

Dual soul

A soul who comes from the same soul group, who embodies with another soul, life after life.

Etheric matter

Magnetic energy which is finer than gaseous matter which gives us our health and vitality.

Glamour

A strong attachment to a desire; being emotionally attached.

God

The Divine Source of all things which is greater than ourselves but within which we utimately live and have our being.

Higher mind

Part of us that is one with the Divine Mind. A higher intelligence which relates to higher aspects of our being, functioning where there is no form. Higher qualities such as compassion and love are part of its nature.

Illusion

A strong attachment to a thought which is not true; being attached to what we think.

Individuation

The process of becoming whole.

Inner bodies

The form of our physical health and vitality, our emotions, our mind and our soul.

Karma

"As you sow, so shall you reap." The Divine Law of Cause and Effect.

Kundalini

The creative power within us which has a masculine and feminine component, as well as that of pure Spirit.

Legitimate suffering

A necessary suffering that is given by the soul for our growth.

Persona

A mask used to help us interact with our environment which is often at odds with who we really are.

light

That which makes things visible.

Light

The Light of Divinity. Spirit in manifestation through soul. The major characteristic of the soul. It illuminates. (see soul and Spirit)

Lower mind

The mind we usually refer to. Our intellect and vehicle for thought.

Master

One who has become Enlightened. A very spiritually advanced Being who no longer needs to incarnate and who helps others on the Path to Enlightenment.

Personal unconscious aspect

Components once conscious, becoming unconscious through forgetting or repression. Relating to the individual.

Redeem

The act of infusing Spirit into matter in a away that makes amends for our past and helps us develop better character; salvation; a way in which we pay back karmic debts.

Reincarnation

The cyclic process of returning again and again from the inner worlds into physical embodiments.

Self-disclosure

Revealing or telling another about aspects of yourself.

Shadow

Contains the hidden, repressed and often unfavourable aspects of the personality which are the opposite of what we consider ourselves to be.

Split-off

A situation in which a person splits off part of self as a polar opposite, for example, competent and incompetent.

Soul

The basis of and source of awareness which is produced through the union of spirit and matter.

Spirit

The principle of life - a pure formless body of consciousness that is the Essence of God.

Symbols

Repressed contents of the psyche appearing in the conscious mind in the form of a symbol which have deeper meaning.

Theosophy

The Divine Wisdom, the understanding of Spirit and all that pertains to it.

Thoughtforms

Forms created by our thoughts.

Transmute

The process of changing from one nature or substance into another through alchemy. The change is from a denser matter to a lighter one.

Transference

The therapy situation where a person responds to the helper as though he or she were a significant figure in his or her past, usually a parent.

Transform

The change in form from one substance into another; metamorphose. By the process of transmutation we are transformed.

Transformation

A change in composition and character.

Unconditional positive regard

Non-possessive caring and acceptance of a person as a human being irrespective of one's own values. (Rogers, 1951)

My heartfelt thanks to all who contributed
to creating this publication, especially

Gregory Govindamurti,
Mary Faeth Chenery,
Joana McCutcheon,
Almut Beringer,
Jenny Raynor,
Rai Faith,
Joav DeMurashkin,
and Henning Klibo

Deva Wings Publications

Deva Wings Publications was formed on Right Human Relations Day in 1994. Its purpose and objectives are:

1. to spread the Light by creating literature and other materials that help us to understand Spirit and make the teachings of Theosophy (Divine Wisdom) comprehensible to all.

2. to educate people in the theosophical principles.

3. to educate people in spiritual psychology so that we may come to understand ourselves and become that which we truly are.

Deva is a Sanskrit word meaning shining one or angel. The concept is such that the Light and teachings of Spirit will spread over the Earth on the devas' wings.

TARAJYOTI GOVINDA
(1958-1999)

B.A. Dip. Ed. Grad Dip. Psych. Couns. MAPS

After a spiritual awakening and death experience in 1983, Tara followed an inner calling to establish herself as a professional healer, counsellor, teacher and group facilitator. She became a psychologist whose major focus was the synthesis of spiritual and psychological transformation. Tarajyoti was the founder and director of The Transformational College of Education and co-founder and director of The Theosophical School of Healing.

Her main interests were Theosophy (the study of Divine Wisdom); Jungian psychology; music; native spirituality; being in nature; painting and other creative endeavours.

Tara is also the author of *The Language of the Heart: is spoken all over the world* (1991); *The Healing Hands of Love: a guide to spiritual healing* (1997); *The Archangels and the Angels* (1998) and *The Joy of Enlightenment* (1999).

Tarajyoti ascended 5 April 1999 after many years of devoted efforts for the Cause of Love in this world.